Phantom Ladies

Phantom Ladies

Hollywood Horror and the Home Front

TIM SNELSON

RUTGERS UNIVERSITY PRESS
NEW BRUNSWICK, NEW JERSEY, AND LONDON

LIBRARY OF CONGRESS CATALOGING-IN-PUBLICATION DATA

Snelson, Tim, 1973–
Phantom ladies : Hollywood horror and the home front / Tim Snelson.
Pages cm.
Includes bibliographical references and index.
ISBN 978–0–8135–7043–3 (hardcover : alk. paper) — ISBN 978–0–8135–7042–6 (pbk. : alk. paper) — ISBN 978–0–8135–7044–0 (e-book)
1. Horror films—United States—History and criticism. 2. Sex role in motion pictures. 3. Motion pictures and women. 4. Women in motion pictures. I. Title.

PN1995.9.H6S6185 2014
791.43'61640820973—dc23 2014000069

A British Cataloging-in-Publication record for this book is available from the British Library.

Visit our website: http://rutgerspress.rutgers.edu

Manufactured in the United States of America

For Lucy, Butch, and Wilson
(collectively, The Snacksons)

CONTENTS

ACKNOWLEDGMENTS

This research was made possible by funding from the Arts and Humanities Research Council. First, I'd like to thank Mark Jancovich, who has been a part of this project from its inception and has provided invaluable guidance, motivation, and support. Yvonne Tasker, Peter Stanfield, and Peter Kramer have also provided indispensable advice and encouragement. In addition, portions of this book have been read by Christine Cornea, Lawrence Napper, Diane Negra, Frank Krutnik, Richard Nowell, Jim Whalley, Daniel Martin, Pietari Kääpä, Earl Gammon, and Nick Anstead. I thank them all for their friendship and advice. Thanks also to my current and previous colleagues at UEA, particularly Sanna Inthorn, Brett Mills, and John Street for their assistance and support as equally brilliant (but unique) Heads of School.

I would like to thank the staff at the Margaret Herrick Library in Los Angeles, the USC Cinema-Television Library, the USC Warner Bros. Archive, the UCLA Performing Arts Special Collections Departments, and the BFI National Library in London. I'm particularly grateful for the help and expertise of Barbara Hall and Jenny Romero at the Margaret Herrick Library, Ned Comstock at the USC Cinema-Television Library, and Lauren Buisson at UCLA. A massive thanks to everyone at Rutgers too, especially Leslie Mitchner for her excellent advice, ongoing support, and, most vitally, patience in waiting for this book. And a huge thanks to India Cooper for her amazing copyediting.

Finally, my deepest thanks go to my family for their unfaltering love and support, which in the case of my parents has often been financial as well as emotional. Thanks, Diddy and Jan, you're the best. Most of all I would like to thank my soon-to-be wife, Lucy Jackson, who has provided me with confidence, motivation, proofreading, love, and Prosecco at all the right times. Love always.

Phantom Ladies

Introduction

Horror on the Home Front

We begin with a warning. The unholy sights and bloodcurdling chills you will encounter in *Phantom Ladies* are neither pleasurable nor suitable for refined, feminine tastes. Any unescorted women should turn back now before it is too late. Those who believe they can take it are advised to bring along a group of like-minded female friends or, preferably, a male escort. If you choose to proceed alone, however, you do so at your own peril and against the advice of the house. You have been warned!

Despite, or perhaps in part because of, such promotional hyperbole, American women flocked to see Hollywood horror films during the war. Often alone, sometimes in groups, wartime women defied both the sexist provocations of these "can she take it" exploitation stunts and a whole body of scholarship in not only watching such films but also actively taking pleasure in them. Newspapers reported in 1943 that "according to movie surveys, women are more enchanted by horror films than men."[1] This concurs with previous research conducted by Mark Jancovich and me into the infamous grind-house cinema the Rialto in Times Square, New York, which almost exclusively programmed horror and gangster films through most of the 1930s and 1940s.[2] While in the 1930s the Rialto was promoted as a masculine space where the discomforting sights and uncomfortable seats were set up in opposition to a feminized, mainstream cinema culture, there was a significant shift in the gendering of its audience during the war. Its manager, Arthur Mayer, reported that, much to his surprise, "feminine attendance started to zoom" in the early forties. He noted not only a shift in women's attendance and tastes but also a change in their behavior. He explained that in wartime, during the prizefight newsreels, "there could be heard more feminine than masculine voices in the darkness yelling 'hit him with the right,' 'kill the bum' and other such expressions of maidenly advice."[3] This shift in downtown theater audiences from masculine to feminine voices had its equivalency onscreen, as women took up monstrous roles "once . . . considered exclusively a male province."[4] To me, these corresponding shifts in consumption and production of horror seem more than mere coincidence. But what came first? The female horror fan or the female monster film?

The phantom ladies of this book's title, therefore, are both the female horror audiences and the coterie of ape-women, she-wolves, and lady-vampires that Hollywood created to feed these "strange" wartime demands.[5] A cycle of female monster films emerged in the early war years targeted explicitly at this burgeoning female market for horror. The unprecedented success of RKO's low-budget female Gothic and monster movie amalgam *Cat People* (1942)—reported to have taken a domestic gross of $4 million in 1943, putting it up there with the year's top earners—inspired a Hollywood-wide production cycle.[6] Character types and themes from the female monster films were resultantly incorporated into popular film franchises and overlapping cycles, such as the "female mystery drama" and "psychiatric pictures"—critical categories that have now been subsumed into overarching categories of film noir and the women's film in feminist film scholarship and genre histories. By reintroducing and mapping these films, cycles, and "local genres" into their contexts of production, mediation, and consumption, I will provide a much richer understanding of film production trends in this largely misunderstood era, while challenging existing scholarship on gender, genre, and the politics of taste.[7] Women could not only take these new horrors but created them by overturning the expectations of producers, critics, and exhibitors.

Film scholars continue to struggle in explaining the relationship between women and horror. Following a tradition of psychoanalytically informed feminist film theory, most accounts rely on the assertion that the horror spectator is typically positioned as male and that the genre is founded upon the subjugation of women; female horror spectatorship is at best a displeasurable and at worst an untenable textual position. Feminist critics argue that women are attacked in the horror film not just because they embody a sexual power that is threatening to men but also because they represent "monster mass culture."[8] The female spectator is not only denied pleasure, therefore, but also made the scapegoat for representing it. Where is the fun in this? Even when women are allowed to step into the role of monster, Barbara Creed explains, this "reveals a great deal about male desire and fears but tells us nothing about feminine desire in relation to the horrific."[9] So why wouldn't women "refuse to look" at their victimization and destruction onscreen, as Linda Williams suggests?[10]

But real women pose a problem. Brigid Cherry's audience research with contemporary female horror fans shows that most of her respondents not only take pleasure in viewing horror but actively "refuse to refuse to look."[11] She also reveals that women and men consume horror differently and have different tastes and preferences. This is significant, as the forties horror films that I focus upon contain the types of strong heroines, sympathetic monsters, quality production values, complex character development, and tragic romance themes favored by Cherry's female fans. The throngs of women who filled the auditoriums of the Rialto in Times Square and the Hawaii in Los Angeles when *Cat People* was playing around the clock in December 1942 cannot be so easily accessed, however. They exist now only as textual traces in exhibitors' records, trade press reports, industry memos, and suggested promotional stunts. A high-profile example of one such textual trace is an extraordinary *Photoplay* article penned by Lana Turner's newborn baby, Cheryl. It reported that Turner, a horror fan, was a regular at the Hawaii's monster movie bills in 1943—though, significantly, not attending unaccompanied. Baby Cheryl explained, "Every night when Daddy was up from Fort MacArthur (he was a Private in the Army until just recently, when he got an honorable discharge for medical reasons), he had to take Mother to the Hawaiian Theater to see *The Wolf Man* or *Frankenstein's Sister*, or some other horror picture. Mother was crazy for them. They went so much (and loaded down with popcorn, too!) that the ushers began to say, 'Hello, Lana and Steve,' just the way they said hello to each other every night."[12] We might want to question the legitimacy of this account, as much as that of its authorship, but this studio-sanctioned fan magazine article is a useful primary source. Lana Turner's penchant for horror is marshaled as part of a wider strategy to position her as the resourceful and capable feminine ideal of wartime. As embodied by Turner, however, this new type of femininity must be a supplement to rather than replacement for more traditional modes of womanhood. She is celebrated, like other working women in the media, for balancing and synthesizing the multiple demands of career, motherhood, sexuality, and leisure, in a way that the female monsters in the films I discuss in *Phantom Ladies* cannot.[13]

I need to be clear here, though. My purpose is not to uncover the inherent meaning of these films or the dominant understandings of their contemporary audiences, nor indeed to decide whether their politics are progressive or conservative—such a task would be impossible and futile. Instead, by adopting a historical reception studies approach, I will situate this cycle of films in relation to the diverse cultural concerns and ideological interests that intersected with them during their "public circulation and . . . engage as fully as possible the range of [their] social meanings within [their] historical moment[s]."[14] It is crucial to historically situate these film cycles within their discursive contexts (economic, political, social, and cultural) rather than simply read these discourses from the films themselves.[15] Using comparable methodological approaches that situate film cycles in relation to their production histories and promotional strategies before moving on to analyze the film texts themselves, Rhona Berenstein and Richard Nowell have challenged assumptions about the gendered address of classic horror movies of the 1930s and slasher films of the late 1970s and early 1980s.[16] Even more than Berenstein's and Nowell's examples, the 1940s horror cycles I am focusing upon were produced and received during a period of complex and conflicting cultural negotiation around the meaning of femininity and the female body.

These cycles of media production and their reception must be situated within wider discursive struggles around American women resulting from the "radical transformations" in their work and leisure practices due to the war.[17] Although it is obviously of great importance, the extent to which these changes endured is of less significance for me here than the perception of change within the wartime period. Reflecting on home-front life in 1943, the liberal journalist and academic Max Lerner asserted that "when the classic work on the history of women comes to be written, the biggest force for change in their lives will turn out to have been war, [which] curiously produces more dislocations in the lives of women who stay at home than of men of who go off to fight."[18] Although Lerner was optimistic about this palpable change in gender roles, he also showed some concerns about the "new type of tough girl emerging, although still a minority; she can out-drink, out-swear, out-swagger the men. . . . There are signs that the medieval court-of-love women, whose type still is dominant in our day, is doomed."[19] Lerner's conflicted opinion regarding the transformations in women's roles and, importantly, bodies in wartime provides a distillation of the complex ideological negotiation going on in media, government, and scientific discourse in the war years. As Lerner's contradictory discourses indicate, the celebration of the newly realized capabilities of women's bodies was accompanied by an increasing fear of their possible culpabilities.

A complex bifurcation was imposed on the image of woman, with the female body specifically positioned as the home-front battleground where the war would be won or lost. Although women were celebrated in some newspaper columns for overturning myths about the inferior female body by taking male jobs, they were scolded in others for shunning their biological role of motherhood; while they were encouraged to imitate provocative pinups plastered on soldiers' walls, they were attacked for engaging in promiscuous behavior that was guided by misplaced patriotism.[20] The ideal of patriotic womanhood was embodied in Norman Rockwell's blue-collar heroine Rosie the Riveter, introduced on a 1943 *Saturday Evening Post* cover. Strong, competent, resilient, and practically dressed, she came to symbolize the reality of millions of American working women's lives and, albeit perhaps temporarily, challenged the feminine ideal of domesticity and fragile glamour. In actuality many women were resistant to the idea of war work, thinking it boring and unglamorous. The iconic Rosie had her opposite number in the wartime "slacker," whose unproductive body was attacked as a direct threat to the war effort.[21] The government and media had to implement a barrage of propaganda in order to attract "Mrs. Stay-at-Home" to war work; in fact, these campaigns had to reassure many resistant women that their services were only required for the duration in order to persuade them to enter the workforce.[22] These campaigns warned that "a soldier may die if you don't do your part," insisting that it was irresponsible as well as "old fashioned" to be merely a good wife and mother.[23]

Those women who did overturn the myth of the inferior female body by taking war jobs were still prompted to balance the dual demands of productivity and desirability. The war worker was expected to be "still feminine but not fluttering or 'vampy'; she wore simple clothes and sensible shoes, used lipstick, powder and rouge, fixed her hair in a short, smooth, neat style, and did not indulge as much as she had before the war in coffee drinking, smoking or gossiping."[24] Women were told that they were irresponsible and selfish for prioritizing glamour over practicality but were simultaneously "obliged to fashion themselves into pinup girls worth fighting for."[25] The cheesecake images popularized by stars such as Betty Grable and Rita Hayworth are often attacked by critics for objectifying women and telling them that it was their patriotic duty to be sexually attractive and available to men. As cultural historians such as Robert Westbrook and Maria Elena Buszek demonstrate, however, "the pin-up girl also addressed herself to American women" and "helped popularize a remarkably self-aware and aggressive female sexuality."[26]

Likewise, although often represented as antithetical in wartime media, the phenomena of the "victory girls" and "patriotutes" were the logical extension of the idealized pinups. These women in their late teens and early twenties were attacked in the media for seeking "sexual adventure in . . . dingy amusement sections of the community" such as Times Square.[27] While government and military discourse proclaimed that the wartime promiscuity among young women and teenage girls was guided by "misplaced patriotism," it concluded that their sexual availability was ultimately counterproductive to the war effort, particularly in terms of spreading venereal disease to soldiers.[28] John Costello explains that the victory girl's claim that she was doing her "patriotic duty to comfort the poor boys who may go overseas and get killed" was often used as an alibi for indulging in the greater sexual freedoms that arose out of wartime conditions.[29] Like the contradictory figure of the pinup, the real-life victory girl was probably as much about self-fulfillment as self-sacrifice. Correspondingly, even though mothers were encouraged into defense work through public childcare programs, some newspaper reports blamed their "maternal neglect" and "bad example" for the sexual promiscuity of their daughters.[30] Women were told it was not enough to be a good wife and mother, but those who did work were at risk of being attacked for neglecting their "latchkey kids" if they got involved in the social aspects of home-front life.

As the discussion above reveals, the experiences of wartime women were fraught with more complexity, contradiction, and consciousness than the individual institutional and media discourses of the time and many of the recent historical studies of home-front life suggest. This was a period of complex ideological struggle in which multiple voices vied for control in defining the meaning of female identity and the meaning of women's bodies specifically. While much of this discourse is clearly disciplinary and constraining, this contingent and transitory moment opened up possibilities for contestation whereby women could redefine their own identities, even if the hegemony unequally favored certain parties. It is within such a discursive context that the female monster films and their reception and exhibition must be understood. Film critics and social commentators debated women's wartime occupation of previously male roles of horror monsters and mystery detectives; at the same time, studio publicity celebrated this as indicative of wider shifts in women's work and leisure. Newspaper articles made explicit links between the conflicted experiences of wartime women and those of the classic horror monster. For example, aping the promotion for many of the female monster films, one 1943 newspaper report characterized young women as "Jekyll and Hydes, shop and office workers by day and sexual adventurers by night."[31] The female monster cycle can be seen, therefore, as both mediation upon and response to women's shifting wartime roles and experiences. The strategies were far from stable or coherent in either case, however, so it is necessary to chart and map the cycle's historical development.

Phantom Ladies is structured around the female monster cycle's emergence, evolution, consolidation, diffusion, and decline over a five-year period, spanning America's entry into World War II at the end of 1941 and the immediate postwar landscape up to the end of 1946; this allows some films produced in the run-up to and just after the war to have been released and received. I adopt Rick Altman's simple model of how individual production cycles worked in the classical period. He argues that once a new cycle has been initiated by a studio successfully bringing a "new type of material or approach [to an] already existing genre," then, assuming these new features can be imitated by other studios and that "conditions are favorable," other studios will adopt the model for development of their own projects, including their prestige productions. When this previously successful model "reaches saturation point, studios must abandon it, restrict it to 'B' productions, or handle it in a new way," thus instigating "a new round of genrification."[32] A more complex consideration of factors external to the industry—such as the function of critical reception and role of audiences—and a charting of overlapping and adjacent cycles are equally significant, however. So I supplement Altman's model with the theoretical frameworks developed in Peter Stanfield's empirically grounded research of Hollywood film cycles.[33] In applying them, I test Stanfield's assertion that "tracking the dialectic between repetition and innovation across runs of films can make legible not only changes in their cinematic environments but also, to some degree, in the public sphere within which they were produced and consumed."[34]

Chapter 1 charts the emergence and evolution of the female monster cycle. It explains how the financially struggling RKO Radio Pictures helped to revive its fortunes by fusing Universal monster movie and female literary Gothic traditions, to produce *Cat People* (1942), *I Walked with a Zombie* (1943), and *The Seventh Victim* (1943). While most genre histories claim that these films had little or no influence on wider trends in forties horror, I detail how Val Lewton's RKO production unit evolved a new type of female-centered horror film that would become the model for an industry-wide cycle.[35] Drawing upon RKO production records and scripts, promotional materials, Production Code correspondence, Gallup research, critical reception, and textual analysis, I demonstrate how these texts and their intertexts tapped into both debates about and desires of wartime women. Analysis of critical reception, promotional discourse, and shooting scripts shows how these films were understood in relation to women's shifting work and leisure practices and the resultant reorientation of the topography of the female body.

Chapter 2 confirms the assertion regarding the influence of Lewton's RKO films by demonstrating how Universal and Columbia adapted or changed current production schedules in order to follow the female monster film model—even incorporating female characters into successful franchises such as Sherlock Holmes and the Mummy. Focusing particularly upon Universal's *Captive Wild Woman* (1943) and *Son of Dracula* (1943) and

Columbia's *Cry of the Werewolf* (1944) and *Soul of a Monster* (1944), I demonstrate how the cycle was consolidated through strategies of sequelization, adaptation of current series and franchises, and investment in "queens of horror" double bills. Drawing upon studio production and promotional materials, Production Code correspondence, critical reception, social scientific discourse, and textual analysis, I illustrate how critics identified these films as part of a distinct cycle of female monster films instigated by the box-office success of *Cat People* and *I Walked with a Zombie*. These films were explicitly marketed to wartime women by associating the shifts in women's roles onscreen to those in the auditorium. Such strategies, however, also evoked critical distain and a gendered politics of taste that questioned both the artistic merits and moral influences of these films.

Chapter 3 stresses the diffusion of the female monster film tropes into prestige productions and adjacent production cycles such as the "female mystery drama." I begin by challenging dominant genre histories, demonstrating the more expansive use of the term "horror" in industry and critical discourses in the forties. Focusing on two class-A horror productions, Paramount's *The Uninvited* (1944) and Universal's *Phantom Lady* (1944), I explain how studios employed major stars, escalated budgets, and brought in female executives in order to tap into the market for female monster films. These generic innovations then fed back into the female monster films produced by Lewton at RKO, particularly through bigger stars, larger budgets, and secularizing narrative impulses. Drawing upon studio correspondence, Production Code files, exhibition materials, critical reception, and textual analysis, I explain how escalated budgets also intensified media fears about what wartime women were getting up to in cinemas and other leisure sites.

Chapter 4 charts the decline of the female monster, or more accurately her transformation—not into the film noir femme fatale but into the schizophrenic of the postwar "psychiatric picture" cycle. Focusing upon the shift from Universal's final female monster films of late 1945 and early 1946 to the newly formed Universal-International's *The Dark Mirror* (1946), I demonstrate how the irresolvable corporeal confusion of the female monster became the curable, or at least confinable, psychosis of the psychoneurotic. Drawing upon studio and Production Code correspondence, critical reception, a range of media and academic reports, contemporaneous pop-psychology literature, and textual analysis, I argue that wartime horror cycles were brought to an end not due to lack of interest or quality, as often reported, but due to interventions from the psychiatric profession.

This was good news for the high-minded critics, who had been calling for psychologists and psychiatrists to study, explain, and curtail the demand for this "unprecedented crop of monstrosities" throughout the war. The *Baltimore Sun*'s Donald Kirkley was clear in apportioning agency and blame, if not in providing an explanation. He protested, "The Hollywood people didn't plan or provoke this weird cycle; it is strictly a matter of popular demand. . . . The public can't seem to get enough vicarious killing, as if the newspapers aren't enough to satisfy this curious crush of death in violent forms. . . . The phenomenon can be laughed off, as being merely a quirk in the mass mind; or it can be thought of as a really serious symptom of an alarming sickness of mind." Although my approach is historical rather than psychological, I have had, as Kirkley proposes, "a lot of fun in the process of dissecting and analyzing the theatergoing habits of this nation in wartime," even if, for the melodramatic *Baltimore Sun* reporter, this investigation has come seventy years too late.[36] But Kirkley, like many contemporary scholars, has missed a trick in interpreting women's "mania" for horror as reflecting only the psychological sickness and emotional tragedy of wartime. As one woman living in North Hollywood during the war explained, "While my conscience told me the war was a terrible thing, bloodshed and misery, there was an excitement in the air."[37] In focusing upon the bloodshed and misery, film scholarship has missed the excitement, adventure, and fun that wartime cinemagoing provided for women. These female-centered horror movies and the downtown exhibition experiences they afforded tapped into the limitations and liberations of wartime women's lives in ways that home-front films like *Since You Went Away* (1944) did not. The emotional complexities and contradictions of wartime were embodied in this book's phantom ladies, who occupied previously exclusively male cinematic spaces, both on screen and off, but only for the duration of the war. I hope you have as much fun revisiting the unholy sights and bloodcurdling chills they enjoyed as I did.

1

Rebecca Meets *The Wolf Man* at RKO

The Emergence of the Female Monster Cycle, 1942–1943

There's a new kind of horror picture nowadays–snappy little spook shows full of beautiful girls and sharp dialogue, good food and French lullabies. . . . They show us pretty girls changing into man-killing cats, registered nurses who believe in zombies, and gorgeous lady executives joining screwball societies dedicated to satanic pursuits.

–Barbara Berch, *Collier's* (January 29, 1944)

In her article "Gold in Them Chills," Barbara Berch identifies an emergent cycle of horror films placing women in their central roles. She proposes that the novel characterization and stylistic traits of RKO's *Cat People* (1942), *I Walked with a Zombie* (1943), and *The Seventh Victim* (1943) have opened up a new market for horror—beyond traditionally male-orientated grind-houses like the Rialto—in neighborhood theaters associated traditionally with more refined, feminine tastes.[1] She explains that these films had generated a "gold rush at the box office—not only in theaters specializing in 'triple Horror Show Tonight' but in neighborhood houses where the whole family gathers."[2] In this article, Berch identifies the creation of a cycle, in Rick Altman's terms, with RKO bringing "a new type of material or approach to an existing genre" to produce a "successful, easily exploitable model" that is, at least initially, associated with a single studio.[3]

Focusing on the three films Berch identifies here, this chapter explains how the RKO production unit led by Val Lewton developed a new formula for horror through its innovative female Gothic and monster movie amalgam *Cat People.* The unprecedented box-office success of this film and its follow-up *I Walked with a Zombie*—conceived by Lewton as a "West Indian version of *Jane Eyre*" and received by RKO test audiences as "*Rebecca* in the West Indies"—confirmed a burgeoning wartime market for female-centered horror texts.[4] This chapter will analyze the production, mediation, and reception of these films. It will detail the industrial contexts and hybrid generic traditions from which these films arose, the topical narrative and marketing strategies they used to broaden horror's appeals to wartime audiences, and the mediation over the appropriateness of their generic and gendered appeals in newspapers and trade presses. The box-office and critical success of these films would resultantly inspire studios spanning PRC to MGM to invest in their winning formula. But the story begins at RKO, with Orson Welles's magnificent flop and belief in a lurid, audience-tested title.

"Showmanship, Not Genius": *Cat People* and the Lewton Horror Unit at RKO

A 1942 review in the New York newspaper *PM* noted that *Cat People* "indicates that RKO-Radio, which booted Orson Welles downstairs with the fine philistine trade slogan 'showmanship in place of genius,' hasn't yet decided which is which, and which pays."[5] Like this critic, subsequent scholars have stressed the paradox in Val Lewton's innovative and intelligent B pictures being the cornerstone of RKO's "showmanship, not genius" policy—the result of the studio's near bankruptcy, which was unfairly blamed upon Orson Welles's box-office failure *The Magnificent Ambersons* (1942).[6] The contradictory aesthetic and generic impulses of RKO's wartime horror films are typically attributed to the creative tensions between Lewton as auteur-producer and RKO's production chief, Charles Koerner. It is perceived, therefore, that Lewton and his creative collaborators—particularly the directors Jacques Tourneur, Robert Wise, and Mark Robson—succeeded in spite of rather than with the help and support of their boss. In fact, Koerner provided the initial inspiration for the production unit and a number of its films, including *Cat People.* Furthermore, his widely reported clashes with Letwon seem to be somewhat exaggerated.[7] From the outset Koerner, or certainly his marketing department, was alive to the promotional possibilities of accentuating the creative tensions and resultant hybrid appeals of *Cat People*.

An article printed in a number of regional papers—taken directly from an RKO press release—stressed that "Mr. Koerner, a showman with an eye for a showman's dollar," chose "Val Lewton, who used to be story editor for David O. Selznick, to make some quick money via the horrors." It stressed, however, that Lewton "too, seriously, is sold on horror" and had "concocted" *Cat People* following a "picnic of research" into "hundreds of books on the occult."[8] The film was presold, therefore, as an amalgam of serious research and quality filmmaking, savvy exploitation and populist appeal. Coming from the exhibition side of the business, Koerner had a talent for exploitation and promotion. By channeling this into a superior product that would sustain business through positive reception and word of mouth, Koerner and Lewton devised a winning formula.[9] The lurid titles for the first six of the RKO horror films were audience-tested and mandated by Koerner. RKO was the first studio to commit to George Gallup's Audience Research Institute (ARI), signing a contract in March 1940 that would furnish sustained research regarding various audience groups' preferences in story types, stars, and specific title choices. An initial survey for RKO revealed that a quarter of audiences bought tickets on the basis of the film's title alone, thus explaining Koerner's commitment to his audience-tested titles.[10]

Despite its low budget and, arguably, low subject matter, *Cat People* has a prestige feel about it, one imbued by its expert team experienced in high-profile productions. Previous to his appointment at RKO, Val Lewton was script editor and production assistant for David O. Selznick, most famously helping to package *Rebecca* (1940) and *Jane Eyre* (1944), writing sections of *Gone with the Wind* (1939), and acting as second-unit producer on *A Tale of Two Cities* (1935). In this capacity he oversaw the second-unit director, Jacques Tourneur (son of the celebrated silent filmmaker Maurice Tourneur), for the storming-of-the-Bastille scene, thus striking up the partnership that would produce *Cat People, I Walked with a Zombie*, and *The Leopard Man* (1943). Lewton also met *Cat People*'s main scriptwriter, DeWitt Bodeen, whose play on the Brontës, *Embers at Haworth*, he had seen and admired while working on the preproduction of *Jane Eyre* for Selznick. Therefore, Selznick was one of the key influences on the RKO unit, not only in terms of introducing its literate team but in nurturing their prestige aesthetic and thematic concerns. As the example of *Rebecca* suggests, these strategies were geared more toward female audiences. In an interview with François Truffaut, Alfred Hitchcock bemoaned *Rebecca* as a "novelette [typical of] a whole school of feminine literature at that period, and though I'm not against it, the fact is that the story is lacking in humor."[11] To the outrage of Selznick, his producer, the director attempted to inject "humor" into the film by inserting scenes of onboard vomiting, which the producer saw as epitomic of Hitchcock's attempted script changes, ones that he insisted "removed all the subtleties and replaced them with broad strokes." Selznick stressed that the film's success relied on engaging the female audience's empathy with the subtleties of Joan Fontaine's character, thus capturing the spirit of the novel; he stated that "every woman who has read it has adored the girl and has understood her psychology."[12]

Although prestige films of this era such as Selznick's literary adaptations are often associated with female audiences, *Rebecca* perhaps more than any other resonated with imagined female spectators as Selznick had hoped. According to Gallup research on the sex composition of 114 pictures released in 1941, while the split between male and female tastes for more recognizable horror tales such as *Dr. Jekyll and Mr. Hyde* (1941) and *The Hunchback of Notre Dame* (1939) was fairly equal, the composition of the audience for *Rebecca* was 71 percent female; it was the film of all 114 that had the largest split favoring one sex.[13] A subsequent report revealed that *Rebecca* was the reissue most demanded by women of any film title in mid-1942, only two years after its initial release.[14] This implies an ongoing female demand not just for *Rebecca* but for other female Gothics, a cycle that would not really be consolidated until after *Jane Eyre* and *Gaslight* were released in 1944, but one that was arguably bridged by Lewton's female Gothic and horror amalgams. These included *I Walked with a Zombie*, which self-consciously references *Rebecca* in its dreamlike opening voice-over, as this chapter will move on to explain.[15] Despite its less obvious feminine literary intertexts, *Cat People* replicates many of the thematic and aesthetic subtleties of the prestige female Gothics that bracket its release, particularly the intimations of sexual tension and gender distress experienced by a sympathetic female protagonist.

Even Selznick was alive to the potential exploitation angles of *Rebecca* and other prestige productions. Following Orson Welles's controversial

Halloween broadcast of *War of the Worlds* (1938), Selznick sold him the radio rights to *Rebecca* and instructed Lewton to investigate the resultant *Mercury on the Air* adaptation for potential inspiration for his screen version.[16] Selznick, like Lewton, acknowledged that showmanship and genius were not mutually exclusive. In a memo dated December 14, 1942, Selznick, who had just seen *Cat People*, explained that he was very proud of his protégé Lewton, particularly for his overturning of generic and aesthetic expectations. He commended Lewton on "an altogether superb production job [that] is in every way better than ninety percent of the 'A' products I have seen in recent months. . . . Indeed I think it is one of the most skillfully worked out horror pieces in many years."[17] The film's ambiguous status, between high and low cultural forms, is mirrored in Val Lewton's eclectic personal history.

Before *Cat People*'s success Lewton was most widely recognized as the author of a series of pulp novels dealing with the seamy underbelly of New York life. The best-known of these was *No Bed of Her Own* (1932), a socially conscious tale of a girl's struggles during the Depression that was bought by Paramount but transformed into a romantic comedy for Clark Gable and Carole Lombard, *No Man of Her Own* (1932), following objections from the censors.[18] Much of the inspiration for Lewton's books came from his work as a journalist and pornographer in Manhattan. Therefore his literariness was complemented by a less readily acknowledged propensity for low genres and sensational subject matters, a dialogism that would inform his best work. In fact, Lewton's twin inspirations for *Cat People* were his own short story "The Baghetta" (1930) for *Weird Tales* magazine, which details the hunt for a mythical shape-shifting cat woman, and "a series of French fashion designs . . . drawings of gowns worn by models with the heads of cats."[19]

Although later accounts by critics and some of Lewton's colleagues have pointed out the producer's dissatisfaction at some of the audience-tested titles, it is unlikely that he would have left his mutually beneficial association with Selznick if he had been as perturbed by the prospect of producing horror films. RKO made it clear following the success of Universal's new horror cycle—one instigated by the re-release of *Dracula* (1931) and *Frankenstein* (1931) on a 1938 double bill—that the studio wanted only horror movies, with budgets limited to $150,000 for placement on double bills in lesser theaters.[20] The film that sealed RKO's decision to start its own horror unit was *The Wolf Man* (1941), which proved very popular with audiences, returning over a million dollars, despite being considered "a dubious booking under present war strain" by *Variety*, because it was released only four days after the bombing of Pearl Harbor.[21] *Cat People*'s subtle approach certainly provides a corrective to some of *The Wolf Man*'s more lurid details, but the films also have a great deal in common. Both narratives revolve around a doomed romance focusing on a troubled yet sympathetic outsider who cannot escape a hereditary fate, and formally they share a number of stylistic features and set pieces. Lewton assimilated the motif of footprints changing from animal to human, the nightmare montage, and animals' fear of the shape-shifter, as well as the reversed human-to-animal transformation at death.[22] As Kim Newman and Rick Altman respectively suggest, Lewton was seemingly "less concerned with finding original material than he was with tackling it in an original manner" or bringing "a new type of material or approach to an existing genre."[23]

Despite these parallels with *The Wolf Man* and other Universal precursors, *Cat People* marks the realization of the shift of horror narratives to the reality of the American present, which would become the dominant setting of the horror genre during the war. *The Wolf Man* occupies a liminal positioning between old-world mythology and the modern world; it is set in an unspecified time, with a mise-en-scène combining modern cars with horses and carts, and an eclectic set of architectural referents intimating a more general historic Europeanness than modern-day Wales, where the film is supposedly set. Part of *Cat People*'s resonance with audiences, according to critics, was due to this decision to bring the horror closer to home, both geographically and epistemologically. The trade press pinpointed the film's originality in being set "in New York of today," focusing upon "a group of normal, rather common place people," and confining its horror to "psychology and mental reactions, rather than transformations to grotesque and marauding characters for visual impact on audiences."[24] *PM* went further, centering its innovation in its sympathetic female protagonist—"a very real, up-to-date character who even goes to a psychiatrist."[25] The reviewers saw the film's distinctiveness as stemming from its engagement with the reality of home-front audiences, allowing them to engage with its central panther woman character, Irena.

Significantly, "early studies for RKO led the Audience Research Institute to formulate a theory of viewer identification that strangely echoes [Jacques] Lacan's concept of the mirror stage."[26] They concluded that audiences tended to prefer actors who mirrored themselves in terms of age, gender, and background. Congruent with these findings, another survey revealed that contrary to popular belief "the best way to attract women is to have women in the advertisements. The best way to attract men is by having men."[27] It is understandable that the most audience-aware and therefore market-led studio of the era should be the initiator of a popular production cycle, instigated through faith in easily exploitable, Gallup-tested titles. It is perhaps more surprising that RKO should focus much of its energies on a series of horror films that centered women as the subjects of their promotional and narrative address, in light of ARI's findings in regard to the importance of same-sex identification.

Cat People's targeting of female audience through its promotional and narrative strategies can be understood, to a large extent, as a result of wartime contingency rather than auteurial vision. As *Cat People* was being filmed in August 1942, a survey by the Women's Bureau of the Department of Labor was released confirming that the war industries' expansion was permitting women to work alongside men in roles as diverse as lathe operators, ground mechanics, stock exchange floor employees, and flying instructors. In the same month Detroit reported that female employment had increased from 44,000 to 107,000, an indicator of a nationally experienced trend.[28] Therefore, certainly by the time *Cat People* was released in December 1942 the mobilization of women into wartime employment had made significant changes to many women's lives, in terms of their accepted roles within the workforce as well as more concretely in terms of their financial, social, and geographical positioning in relation to urban leisure activities.

Variety had advised as early as March 1942 that studios should gear their advertising toward women, because of "a phenomenon that never happened before. In the evening, half of the girls are attending pix unescorted, sometimes coming in little crowds of five and six." As the war progressed and women increasingly relocated to major cities or traveled in from the suburbs for shift work in factories, the "unescorted femme" became an increasingly common feature in the downtown theaters where most of these horror films had their first runs. Women thus emerged as an expanding market for theaters that specialized in horror and crime films, such as Times Square's Rialto, by mid- to late 1942.[29] At this time exhibitors were also taking note of shifts in women's tastes in film types. A cover story from the same issue of *Variety* in which *Cat People* was reviewed revealed "Femmes Shying Away from War Pictures." It explained that women were staying away from war pictures and that romances were also faring badly at the box office, perhaps "because romance in the case of couples separated by the war etc. made such picture-goers unhappy." Escapist titles were most popular with women, the report continued. Although it did not elaborate on specific popular escapist genres, an article in the *Hollywood Reporter* correspondingly revealed that "all manner of the eerie" was finding great popularity with female patrons because it "takes them far away from the realities of war during the hours of relaxation from the defense plants and war industries."[30]

These well-publicized shifts in women's cinemagoing habits might go some way to explaining *Cat People*'s targeting of female spectators in its promotions and tie-ins. The *Cat People* campaign addresses women far more purposefully than those for earlier horror titles such as *The Wolf Man*, whose proposed tie-ins are in the traditionally masculine spaces of hardware, electrical, and hunting goods stores.[31] In the "Exploitation" section of the *Cat People* pressbook, a drawing of a woman in a cat mask with a sign reading "Miau! I'm bound to see Simone Simon in *Cat People*" is accompanied by the suggestion that exhibitors should "dress a woman wearing a formal evening gown and a cat head mask and have her walk down the streets of your town carrying a large shopping bag with copy as suggested in the illustration. Have her visit food stores, department stores and others of a similar nature during shopping hours."[32] This stunt is explicitly aimed at attracting the interest of women, significantly linking their desire to consume *Cat People* to their desire for other products.

This targeting of female consumers was expanded following the film's box-office success. In congruence with the Gallup findings, promotional tie-ins were used to encourage women to see and then imitate Simone Simon's style. In March 1943, for example, *Boxoffice* magazine encouraged exhibitors to extend *Cat People*'s runs even further by arranging tie-ins with downtown florist shops (who should display "orchid corsages like Simone

Simon wears in *Cat People*") and cosmetics retailers (with the tagline "Hollywood beauties like Simone Simon use Correct Cosmetics").[33] RKO's publicity also emphasized female war workers as a key and appreciative audience for this new kind of horror film. In a March 1943 advertisement in the *Hollywood Reporter*, RKO "salutes" the Hawaii Theater in Los Angeles for its exceptional campaign and *Cat People*'s resultant thirteen-week run, a record for the cinema. In the accompanying image of the theater's cat-head ticket booth, six of the seven customers "still feeding the kitty at Hollywood's Hawaii" are women, and all are wearing the typical war worker clothing of trousers or overalls. Though this is not verification of the typical audience makeup, it indicates that the RKO publicity department wished to stress this demographic as an important market for the film.[34] The film's promotion sought, therefore, to interpellate women as simultaneously war workers seeking escape and consumers seeking active engagement with leisure. The impulse to engage with the conflicting demands and desires of wartime women is also at the heart of the characterization and narrative strategies that differentiate *Cat People* from its monster movie precursors.

The narrative of *Cat People*, like the promotional campaign, focuses on the tragic central female character. Following a chance meeting in Central Park, Irena (Simone Simon)—a Serbian immigrant who is working as a fashion designer in New York—falls for and promptly marries Oliver Reed (Kent Smith), a shipbuilder and self-appointed "good old Americano." Irena refuses to consummate the marriage, though, due to the fear of a Balkan family curse that says she will transform into a panther and kill her partner in the throes of passion. Irena believes that her matriarchal lineage ties her to a group of predatory cat women who were eventually driven out of her village by King John of Serbia. (Irena keeps a statue in her flat of King John impaling a cat, as a reminder and a warning of her ancient ancestry.) Oliver confides in, and consequently switches his romantic interest toward, his co-worker Alice (Jane Randolph), whom Irena resultantly stalks in a jealous rage. This scene is credited with introducing the technique that has been dubbed a "bus" in film scholarship; crosscut close-up shots of the legs of stalker (Irena) and prey (Alice) are suddenly interrupted by the sound of a bus's air brakes that is initially inferred—both diegetically and extradiegetically—as a panther's growl. Alice ultimately escapes on the bus. In fact, a sleazy psychiatrist, Dr. Judd (Tom Conway)—recommended somewhat suspiciously by her rival, Alice—is Irena's only human victim. When he forces himself upon her in a questionable attempt to disprove the curse, she transforms into a panther and kills him. Back in human form, she then flees to the zoo, where she lets a panther escape so it will take her life. When Oliver and Alice arrive they discover Irena's body reverted to panther form, confirming, as they had begun to suspect, that "she never lied to us."

Through its narrative strategies and thematic concerns, *Cat People* brings a new thematic and stylistic approach to the horror genre, thus creating the potential for a new cycle. The key features of *Cat People* would provide a structural and representational formula for the resultant female monster cycle. First, and most fundamentally, the film transformed the sexual dynamic of the classic Hollywood horror film. In the classic 1930s horror film—perhaps best represented by *Dracula* (1931)—two men usually fight for possession of one woman, but *Cat People* adopts the woman's film dynamic of two (typically doubled) women competing for the same man. The pressbook explains that this "new kind of thriller" blending "fear and romance" was structured around a "strange love triangle . . . laid in modern New York City."[35] This new kind of "thrill-picture," therefore, is differentiated in its triangular structure, focus on romance, and contemporary American setting.

Second, in contrast to the 1930s classic horror scream queen—according to Gérard Lenne, "an exquisite and pathetic figure, endlessly shrieking either from fear or from pain and torture"—Irena is "both torturer and tortured, sadist and masochist, monster and victim." This bifurcated model of women in the genre of the fantastic, as seen in Fritz Lang's *Metropolis* (1927), is an unrealized potentiality in Hollywood horror, according to Lenne.[36] This short-circuiting of classificatory systems is integral to the moral ambiguity surrounding *Cat People*'s female shape-shifter, however, a trope that would become central to the female monster cycle. This is reflected in much of the marketing for *Cat People* that positions Irena as simultaneously monster, victim, object of desire, and desiring subject; for example, in the pressbook, stills of Simon from the film feature the captions "dangerous," "cuddly," "alluring," and "afraid to love."[37]

Likewise the film's taglines mostly focus upon the tragedy of "a woman soft and lovely . . . cursed with the awful dread of changing into a fang and claw killer." Many address the spectator in the first person with taglines such as "I am a fugitive from evil things! I must keep myself from love—lest I turn and claw my lover to shreds!" This predominant strategy, in which Irena is subject rather than object, and figure of tragedy as much as threat, intimates this is a film about female suffering and sacrifice. This further evokes its generic linkage to more feminine genres such as the literary Gothic and the woman's film, which are typically differentiated from horror in scholarship due to their female address. Diane Waldman makes a clear distinction between the male address of horror and female address of the Gothic romance or paranoid woman's films of the 1940s. She stresses that "the central feature of the Gothics is ambiguity. . . . This it shares with other filmic and literary genres, for example, the horror film and the fantastic. Yet in the Gothic, this hesitation is experienced by a character (and presumably a spectator) who is female."[38] Likewise, through recourse to Williams's aforementioned theory, Mary Ann Doane distinguishes the paranoid woman's film from horror through its privileging of romance. She suggests that "while the horror film, as Linda Williams points out, prompts the little girl (or grown woman) to cover her eyes, the sign of masculinity in the little boy, when confronted by the 'love story,' is the fact that he looks away." Doane does acknowledge that the paranoid woman's film is infiltrated by the conventions of film noir and the horror film, but she maintains that that it cannot belong to these male genres because of its female address and the thematic centrality of romance.[39]

Romance, particularly a doomed or tragic love triangle, is central to the textual and extratextual strategies of *Cat People* and the subsequent female monster films, however, certainly far more than it is to the "anti-romance" narratives of many of the films Doane discusses. *Cat People*'s promotion mostly discusses the narrative in relation to romance, even while stressing its "eerie" and "doomed" nature, and its posters present it as a love story—albeit "the strangest love story you ever tried to get out of your dreams." It is this crossover or, in Doane's terms, "generic miscegenation" with more typical woman's films that marks this cycle of horror as distinct in narrative and thematic terms. The film's ambiguity is also extended to Irena's double, Alice, who herself alternates between vulnerability and "predatory instincts"; she tells Oliver, "I'm the new type of other woman. That's what makes me so dangerous." This subversion of expectations was purposefully instilled through casting decisions. In a preproduction memo, Lewton insisted on casting against type, choosing Simon as Irena because she was "cute and soft and cuddly and seemingly not at all dangerous" and "tall and efficient looking" Jane Randolph to play Alice because "she was not the ingénue type usually favored for such roles," namely the classic horror scream queen role.[40] The mainstream press was mostly confused by this purposeful ambiguity, proposing that the film's failings were due to the "tameness" of Simon's female monster, a "cuddly little tabby [who] would barely frighten a mouse under a chair."[41]

This confusion of classificatory systems is also extended to the film's posters, particularly through the bifurcation and paradoxical conflation of Irena's conflicted selves. This is encapsulated in the pressbook cover tagline "Lovely Woman . . . Giant Killer-Cat . . . The Same 'Person'!" The accompanying picture of Irena/Simon in a traditional pinup pose, wearing a slinky black dress that further emphasizes her doubling with the panther above, is a key motif of *Cat People*'s campaign (see figure 1). Irena's desiring gaze, provocative pose, and low-cut dress are totally incongruent with her characterization and costuming in the film. Although these pinup images might appear to be aimed at a male audience, critics assert that the pinup girl also addressed herself to American women who embraced this more aggressive mode of female sexuality.[42] What's more, Irena's conjunction of tragedy and sexual allure is ideally suited to the pinup mode, which implied a "reciprocity of obligation" between the sexes that was "felt as well as prescribed": as soldiers were expected to fight for their pinup girls and all they represented, women were urged "to be pin-ups men would die for."[43]

Jeanine Basinger proposes that the device of bifurcation in the genre of the woman's film reflected the contradictory experience of being female in American wartime society; it told a woman "that she ought to conform to the roles society approved for her at the same time as it allowed her the freedom to see and possibly identify, however temporarily, however tangentially, with a female character who did not conform or follow the rules."[44] The double-bodied discourse of *Cat People* necessitated a simultaneous textual positioning that pushed this ideological ambiguity even further. Traditional gender binaries are blurred or even reversed. It is panther woman Irena who wishes to subsume her own identity into that of a nurturing wife and domestic goddess; she tells her husband, "I want

FIGURE 1 *Cat People*'s poster campaign bifurcates Irena as simultaneously monster and victim.

to be Mrs. Oliver Reed and be everything that name means," although as it turns out her containment to the domestic sphere is due more to her internalization of patriarchal expectations than to the influence of Oliver or Dr. Judd. Conversely, the more traditional heroine figure, Alice, is a resourceful career woman who has mastered the public sphere; she tells Irena, "Anything you want to know about the city, ask me."

In *Cat People*, the nonsynthesizable body of the tragic heroine is juxtaposed to the bodily mastery of the working woman—one able to incorporate conflicted senses of self, synthesizing the demands of productivity and desirability. Monstrosity in these films is marked by an overattachment to the domestic and the traditionally feminine. The female shape-shifters in these films are marked by a mode of excessive femininity that is counterproductive to the war effort. The promotion for the New York premiere of *Cat People* at the Rialto tellingly conflates Irena's threat with that of Japanese and Nazi invasion, as the nonsynthesizable female body is evoked as a metaphor for penetration by a foreign threat (see figure 2). The storefront display features the giant claws and the typically bifurcated tagline

FIGURE 2 The Rialto storefront for *Cat People* conflates Irena's threat with that of Axis invasion.

"Beautiful Woman or Razor-Clawed Killer," but also the warning "Keep Axis claws from our shores / Buy War Bonds and Stamps."[45] The transposition or, in fact, internalization of the old-world threat into the female body would become a distinctive theme of the female monster cycle. Dana Polan proposes a secularization and psychologization of horror in the forties, as narratives shifted to contemporary urban settings where scientific solutions could be proffered as answers for onscreen monstrosity. This process was later arriving than Polan states within this cycle of female-centered horror texts. Starting with Irena, the nonsynthesizable bodies of the wartime female monster characters stood in for the old country as the last "exotic repository of a non-scientific knowledge, a battery of beliefs and institutions" previously embodied in the classical horror mise-en-scène of a temporally and topographically indistinct Europe.[46] This metaphorical centering of the female body as the potential site of invasion and contagion has a clear wartime resonance and was replicated in a number of American propaganda posters promoting war bonds and warning against venereal disease.[47] The simultaneous vulnerability and threat of the female body was characterized in Irena's and other female monsters' inability to synthesize and balance the multiple demands placed upon them. This has explicit links to wider wartime discourses around women's changing roles and the shifts in the perceptions of their bodies that arose from wartime contingency.

"*Since You Went Away* Disguised as a Horror Film": *Cat People* and the Home Front

In its review of *Cat People*, the left-wing magazine *The New Masses* stated that the real significance of this film (and the concurrent cross-media cycle of supernatural fiction, radio shows, comics, and newspaper astrology) was not in its aesthetic qualities, but as a "piece in the jigsaw puzzle of psychological reactions to the war." To analyze this trend, the reviewer insists, we must leave the field of literary criticism for that of psychology. She asserts, "The skilful treatment, however, is irrelevant to the value which *The Cat People* has for its audience. Its dark monster personifies the lurking terrors of a world crisis not understood; in destroying poor Simone the film points the way to a supernatural vanquishing of these terrors, and the audience feels better, not knowing why." Despite her appreciation of the skillful treatment of the film, the reviewer makes a distinction between the "healthy minds" of the *New Masses* readership—to whom Irene represents merely "a tough, gay, independent, and charmingly graceful little carnivore"—and the reaction of the typical horror audience, who possess neither "political understanding" nor a sound appreciation of the sciences.[48] Adopting a Frankfurt School–ish disposition, she draws a clear and surprisingly unselfconscious distinction between the mass audience and the *New Masses* audience. What is significant for the argument of this book is that they are differentiated through their political reading strategies: while *New Masses* readers are assumed to take pleasure in the film's characterization of its tough and independent female lead and her transgressive behavior, the mass audience is expected to take its pleasure from her symbolic destruction.

This review is interesting in that it preempts—though in some cases surpasses—the academic criticism of *Cat People* advocating that the film can be read as progressive, even feminist if you are properly versed in psychoanalytic theory, but for most people served a hegemonic, even antifeminist agenda. Most scholarly accounts place the film outside its wartime context as either addressing eternal psychological dilemmas or, if in relation to other films, decades ahead of its time. Reviewing the past criticism of *Cat People* specifically, John Berks has attempted to redress this imbalance by seeing "the film in the more historical terms of a symbolic response to a specific social context."[49] He challenges the psychoanalytic readings proffered by Robin Wood and Karen Hollinger as well as the critiques proffered by the film scholars Tom Gunning and J. P. Telotte, who in trying to bypass the limitations of a psychoanalytic framework are trapped by the same desire to find some ideological or psychological subversive essence within the film. As suggested, Wood sees *Cat People* as unusual in that it focuses on the return of repressed female rather than male sexual energy.[50] Karen Hollinger takes this further, stating that it is not Irena's "lack"—and thus the excitement and allaying of castration anxieties—but rather "the potency of female sexuality and the power of women's sexual difference" that provides a more serious threat to the male spectator.[51]

Berks claims that in the search for this potentially subversive power these critics have focused, to their detriment, on the central panther woman character. He suggests that in fact, the exotic Irena acts to displace anxiety from the real threat of the film, the other woman, Alice, who as a successful working woman represents the "new hybrid—and therefore monstrous—species" that most haunted the home front's war-torn psyche. For Berks, Irena's main function is "divert[ing] attention away from a potentially more threatening recognition, enabling the film's viewers to overlook or misrecognise the historical lesion or fault in the social fabric that Alice (seen as the true Medusa she is) would represent."[52] Although Berks's attempt to position the film in relation to its wartime context is admirable, Hollinger is right to question his use of a rather narrow historicism and his implications that the majority of the text, and its enduring central character, are a mere distraction from what is "really *Since You Went Away* disguised as a horror film."[53]

Moreover, Berks's analysis suffers from the same theoretical limitations as those he challenges, including Hollinger's, in assuming that the film is directed at the excitement and allaying of purely male fears and anxieties, though now sociopolitical rather than psychosexual ones. *Cat People*'s unprecedented box-office success (one attained largely through word of mouth) indicates, like the reception material discussed earlier, that the film was also embraced by female audience members in a way that many of its classic horror precursors were perhaps not. For example, Hollywood's earlier panther woman film *The Island of Lost Souls* (1933)—Lewton's model for what *Cat People* should not be—was characterized by *Variety* as being addressed to a solely male audience because it did not feature "the kind of chills ladies like in pictures."[54] This 1933 *Variety* article implies that there are different kinds of pleasures for female horror fans, a suggestion much psychoanalytic horror scholarship discounts or avoids. Linda Williams's account of a potentially empowering female gaze based on an affinity with the transgressive monster figure—one that in *Cat People*'s case is explicitly rather than implicitly coded feminine—is more useful for this study.[55] Though this provides a more productive model of female horror spectatorship, the nature of the female spectator's "affinity" with Irena and Alice must be historicized.

The repression of female sexuality proposed in *Cat People* has specific wartime intertexts in a number of magazines and books addressing women's sexual sublimation.[56] A March 1942 *Good Housekeeping* article questioned, "Is the danger of developing serious neuroses as the result of sex deprivation real or imaginary? If the menace is authentic . . . what are the remedies?" The best remedy according to its writer, Maxine Davis, was "transferring of energy originally designed to emerge in sexual channels into paths that are not sexual." The main paths she advised were volunteer or paid war work and/or homemaking. If successful sublimation was still not achieved she advised consulting a psychiatrist, who "as likely as not . . . will say: 'Forget it. There's nothing wrong with you a little sunshine won't cure . . . go ahead and lead your normal life, *normally*.'"[57]

These are the strategies employed by the women in *Cat People*; Alice initially sublimates her desire for Oliver by focusing her energy into her symbolic war work, while Irena, after failing to successfully channel her sexual energies into being the perfect "Mrs. Reed," is persuaded to consult the psychiatrist Dr. Judd, who delivers a speech almost identical to the one above. Through such narrative strategies *Cat People* evinces the almost irreconcilable synthesis of productivity and desirability that wartime society demanded of women like Irena and Alice. Wartime necessity "challenged conventional stereotypes regarding women's physical and emotional makeup," but it also promoted disciplinary strategies aimed at channeling these newfound corporeal energies.[58] Media, government, and scientific discourse centered the most productive use of the female body—one at once more capable and culpable—as a key transfer point for debates about wartime nationhood. This battle over the most productive use of women's bodies is made explicit in an October 1942 *Time* magazine cover story entitled "Women, Women Everywhere." Reporting on the "still incomplete social revolution wrought by World War II," it claimed that the war had proven women capable of supplanting men in all manner of previously excluded industries but concluded that "for every woman who puts on unaccustomed overalls and goes to the factory for the swing shift, another puts on unaccustomed finery (sales of black lace underwear are booming) and travels to places she has never been before to be with her man in uniform."[59] This article indicates a simultaneous masculinization and feminization, and desexualization and hypersexualization, of wartime women's bodies. This positioning of women as multiple and contradictory signs seems to correspond distinctly with *Cat People*'s metaphor of a woman's body in the process of becoming and being defined as something new, or "unaccustomed," as *Time* proposes.

Berks insists that Alice, as a working woman, represents a "monstrous mixture of previously immiscible categories," but this does not really correspond with either narrative or promotional strategies.[60] Irena is characterized as monstrous precisely because her synthesis of previously opposing categories remains immiscible, in part due to her aforementioned inability to move beyond the containment and isolation of traditional notions of a woman's role. This is not to say that Irena is villainized by the text; in fact considerable sympathy, even empathy, is extended toward her. Rather, *Cat People* laments the "contradictory tendencies, confusion, insecurity, and anxiety" generated by wartime society that placed almost insurmountable pressure on women.[61] Alice, as a wartime working woman, survives in the otherwise all-male world of shipbuilding at the cost of a stable family life, living, like many female war workers, in the temporary accommodation of the YWCA. In a line cut from the final script, the young woman behind the desk of the YWCA where Alice resides (referred to simply as Blonde) explains to a friend, "Ah, gee, I can't tonight. I got Civilian Defense work. . . . Yeah. As I was saying Brenda, them Japs and Nazis is whittling down my love life."[62] The line was cut due to an objection from the Production Code Administration (PCA)—popularly, the Hays Office. This was the division of the Motion Picture Producers Association of America (MPPDA) that enforced "the Code," a set of guidelines on acceptable movie content the industry adopted in the early 1930s after threats of external censorship. Despite the removal of an explicit war connection (in an early draft the film began with Nazi tanks entering Irena's Balkan village, the reason for her fleeing to New York), the quote above indicates that the film was conceived with a wartime setting.[63] Alice's war work, at least initially, appears to be at the cost of her relationships both in terms of romantic and familial life.

Alice works in shipbuilding, the wartime industry that saw the greatest rise in female employment: from 36 women involved in ship construction in late 1939 to 160,000 by the time *Cat People* was produced in mid-1942.[64] Alice's solitary and temporary accommodation indicates her independence, malleability, and even feminine sacrifice, implying that she is a provisional or transitional figure, very much of her historical moment in mid-1942. In contrast, Irena works in ladies' fashion, an industry whose role in wartime was highly contested. Certainly pleats, ruffles, and other unnecessary accoutrements of prewar glamour were attacked as unpatriotic and outdated in media and government discourse; as the Office of War Information's "expert on womanpower," Mary Brewster, explained at a 1943 fashion conference, "Ruffles have no place in wartime."[65] Furthermore, her artisanal, even feminine work as a fashion designer is confined (except for her initial outdoor sketching in Central Park Zoo) to the domestic sphere, in contrast to Alice's urban milieu (see figure 3).

Far from the "Unconquered Fortress: The American Home" of *Since You Went Away* (1944), the domestic realm is a site of frustration and containment in *Cat People*. While some media discourse in 1942 indicated "the kitchen and the sewing room [as] the housewife's battleground," others attacked the leisured "Mrs. Stay-at-Home" as outdated and counterproductive to the war effort.[66] A ubiquitous advertising campaign told women that if they had the nimble fingers to operate a sewing machine at home then they certainly could operate punch presses and riveting guns at a shipyard.[67] If Irena can be seen as trapped by this conflicting discourse regarding married women's roles in wartime, her hasty marriage

FIGURE 3 Irena, a fashion designer, is at the center of *Cat People*'s "strange love triangle."

could itself be seen as representative of the rush to the altar in the early 1940s.[68] Moreover, much of this urgency to marry was encouraged by the sense that women's wartime duty was purely relational in providing morale for men fighting overseas or working away. This certainly fits with Irena's almost pathological desire to please Oliver, who, as he explains to Alice, has "never been unhappy before. Everything has always gone swell for me." Revealing the weight of expectation she feels, Irena explains that she envies "every woman I see on the street. . . . They make their husbands happy." Significantly, Oliver's proposal does not disclose his love for Irena or stress their mutual dependency but sells her on the normative function of marriage in solving her (women's) identity crisis. He tells her, "You're so normal you're even in love with me. Oliver Reed, a good, plain Americano. You're so normal you're going to marry me, and those fairy tales, you can tell them to our children. They'll love them."

In this purposefully shallow polemic Oliver proposes, therefore, that she substitute her own identity for a relational marital and maternal role, at the same time as channeling her desire into a purely biological function.

In *Cat People* romance is not the answer to problems of domesticity, as it is in a number of woman's films; rather, in Oliver's proposal is the seed of what Betty Freidan would later refer to as the "problem that has no name"—the crisis in identity experienced by many postwar women who had been discursively manipulated back into the home, largely through the pseudo-Freudian glorification of women's biological role of motherhood.[69] This reading of Oliver is not purely one based on the hindsight of Freidan and Second Wave feminism, either. A number of reviews at the time noted the shallowness and ignorance of Oliver, referring to his character as "stupid," "tactless," and, at best, a "simple American boy."[70] As Friedan advocated, the scientific technology of Freudian psychoanalysis is used, through the figure of Dr. Judd, to persuade Irena to put aside the "mad legends of [her] birthplace" and "lead a normal life." Though Oliver is characterized as shallow and ignorant, Dr. Judd is characterized as egotistical and corrupt in his unwelcomed attempts to force his will—both intellectual and sexual—upon Irena. Although she warns him, "I know I should not like it if you tried to kiss me," he still does so, claiming it to be to prove her fears are unfounded, and suffers the ultimate penalty. As the *Washington Post* scoffed, "Before he can say 'psychoanalysis' [she] turns into a black panther and proceeds to claw him to death. . . . Shucks, any of us witch-doctors could have told him the gal was on the level." In congruence with such readings Judd's psychiatrist character was intended to be unsympathetic, even "delusional," as the *Post* averred.[71]

The shooting script describes him as "a harshly ugly man of early middle age. There is an arrogance in his bearing which makes some women see him as the suave, continental man, perfectly sure of his success with any woman."[72] Judd is clearly not intended to be the redemptive figure that others in his profession represent in concurrent films such as *Now, Voyager* (1942). Mary Ann Doane goes further, stating that through Judd the film reveals the "unscrupulous or suspect dimension of psychoanalysis" more generally.[73] Her reading of a more general mistrust of the manipulative and disciplinary mechanisms of psychoanalysis seems to be backed up by the film's script. The film's opening quote—taken from Dr. Judd's apocryphal text *The Anatomy of Atavism*—was attributed to Sigmund Freud in the shooting script.[74] The scientific technology of Freudian psychoanalysis is described by Judd as a "contest of wills between doctor and patient"; he even threatens to have Irena committed if she does not accept his diagnosis that her "condition" is caused by paternal abandonment rather than maternal inheritance. Furthermore, the psychoanalyst's gaze is shown to be destructive through its phallic alignment with both the King John statue's sword and Judd's own dagger, significantly hidden beneath the gentlemanly appearance of a cane.

Karen Anderson suggests that in the 1940s the disciplinary gazes of psychologists, social workers, and journalists were increasingly employed to "serve the interests of those seeking to inhibit sexual and social freedom for women."[75] Despite Judd's threat that psychoanalysis "shall discover [her] secret," Irena remains a mystery to him and ultimately proves his methods flawed. Like Judd, Oliver is compelled to objectify Irena through his gaze, but he is unable to fix her meaning. Oliver explains his attraction to Irena: "I have to watch her when she's in the room . . . but I don't really know her. In many ways we're strangers." It is perhaps in this refusal to fix her meaning by disclosing her secret that Irena represents the real threat to the ideological imperatives of wartime, rather than her sexuality specifically. After all, Irena's attitude to sex is far from empowering, and—though the Hays Office warned RKO on a number of occasions about the unacceptable "overemphasis on the fact that Oliver and Irena are not consummating the marriage"—the implication that Irena fears sex rather than kissing is fairly transparent.[76] Overall, "crazy kid" Irena's dread of her "strange, fierce pleasures" is characterized as the product of immaturity and inexperience; hence she is infantilized at the hands of Oliver and Alice, to whom she becomes almost a surrogate child. Conversely, it could be argued that the predatory Alice—"the new type of other woman"—demonstrates a sexual maturity, perhaps even experience, lacking in Irena, as evinced by her friendship with the amorous Dr. Judd, whom, after all, she recommends as the potential cure to Irena's sexual fears.

Significantly, though perhaps unsurprisingly, the greatest fears regarding the vulnerability of women to new temptations and sexual freedoms focused on the young, as later chapters will discuss. Many of these social fears around victory girls, bobby-soxers, and khaki-wackies focused upon their incorrect channeling or synthesis of bodily energies and desires, rather than their sexual exuberance per se.[77] Although Alice is able to balance and control the contradictory tendencies that society demanded of women—synthesizing her desirability and productivity, sexuality and labor, vulnerability and strength—Irena is victimized because she is so clearly marked by the bifurcated impulses that troubled societal control agents and moral guardians.[78] Irena's monstrosity arises not as a result of a robust masculinized body or ferocious female sexuality but rather from her inability to reconcile the traditional expectations and contemporary demands of society with the reality of a body in the process of becoming and being defined as something new. It is the tragic inability to reconcile the contradictory tensions between past and present, expectation and experience, patriotism and pleasure, word and world, that generates horror for the female monster cycle's conflicted heroines. Though a film like *Since You Went Away* was constrained by the ideology of wartime collectivism, the escapist *Cat People* was able to resonate with the complexities of women's lives. In the contingent and contested bodies of Irena and Alice, female spectators could identify with the limitations and liberations engendered in discovering a second self.

"A West Indian Version of *Jane Eyre*": Female Gothic and *I Walked with a Zombie*

As *Cat People* was "holding over everywhere as an 'A' attraction" and "nationally . . . passed the million mark," the *Los Angeles Times* commended the RKO unit for evolving a new cycle of "different horror pictures." The *Los Angeles Times* critic continued, "Whenever anybody evolves a new art form in Hollywood it's news. It's even news if that someone takes an old art form and just improves on it. From where I sit it looks as though Val Lewton, Jacques Tourneur and Mark Robson have turned the trick."[79] Like Berch's article for *Collier's*, the *Los Angeles Times* article associates RKO—and specifically the creative "triumvirate" of Lewton, Tourneur, and Robson—with a new horror formula that Lewton explains as "a love story, three scenes of suggested horror and one of actual violence." By placing "practical matter-of-fact folks" at the center of conjoined romance and supernatural narratives the Lewton unit intended to "make the audience participants: let them do the work."[80]

This female-oriented formula pioneered with *Cat People*, one that brought unprecedented realism and ambiguity to Hollywood horror, was even more eloquently detailed in the RKO unit's second chiller, *I Walked with a Zombie.* Like *Cat People, I Walked with a Zombie* started out as a disembodied title that had been audience-tested for RKO by Gallup and then imposed by the studio head, Koerner. For *I Walked with a Zombie*, however, Koerner also assigned a source to provide the basis for the script and a proven horror scriptwriter to write it: these were the *American Weekly* magazine article written by Inez Wallace from which the film's title was derived and the "master horror scripter" Curt Siodmak, who had penned *The Wolf Man* (1941) for Universal.[81] Despite a widely reported dejection at this triple imposition, Lewton became inspired by the idea of making the film "*Jane Eyre* in the West Indies."[82] Preempting Twentieth Century–Fox's *Jane Eyre* (1944) featuring Orson Welles and Joan Fontaine (which Lewton helped package for Selznick before joining RKO), the film significantly emphasizes and empathizes with the Bertha Rochester character while increasingly undermining the narrative voice of the Jane Eyre character. In his 1944 review of Selznick's *Jane Eyre*, James Agee bemoans Welles's film's lack of contemporary resonance and failure to evoke the novel's "feminist, ethical and erotic tensions." In this review he goes on to contrast this and other recent adaptations with the "B pictures" of Val Lewton in which such narrative and moral ambiguity were commonplace. According to Agee, Brontë's blend of "symbolic resonance," "revealing tension," and "hypnotic tone" is far more effectively captured in the narrative of I *Walked with a Zombie.*[83] It is difficult to briefly explicate its narrative, as it strives so purposefully for ambiguity, so it is necessary to give some detail in this regard. Although a brief summation of *I Walked with a Zombie* might imply a narrative that juxtaposes good and bad models of femininity—thus demonstrating different ways for women to live their lives and the potential pitfalls therein—these binaries are far more uncertain than the categories of nurse and zombie might suggest.

In *I Walked with a Zombie*, a Canadian nurse, Betsy (Frances Dee), is sent to the West Indian island of Saint Sebastian, where she is to care for the catatonic wife of the plantation owner Paul Holland (Tom Conway). He suspects his wife, Jessica (Christine Gordon), has gone insane (perhaps through his own neglect), but the doctor believes she has suffered a debilitating tropical fever. The locals, however, suspect that she is a zombie. Betsy initially mediates the spectator's position as she attempts to put together a narrative of Jessica's illness from these divergent explanations, an enigma that is never fully resolved. Paul's half brother, Wesley Rand (James Ellison), who was seemingly having an affair with Jessica, questions Betsy's motives when she encourages Paul (with whom she has now fallen in love) to persuade the doctor to attempt a dangerous shock therapy. The critic Sylvie Pierre explains that with this move from a purely observational position "Betsy has to admit to her definitive implication as an agent in the action, which, from then on, she will not be at liberty to narrate."[84] At this point her voice-over narration ends. When traditional medicine fails to kill or cure Jessica, Betsy leads her to the Houmfort, where a voodoo ceremony is under way. There Betsy discovers the voice of the goddess Damballa coming from a hut to be that of Paul and Wesley's mother, Mrs. Rand (Edith Barrett), who eventually admits to participating in voodoo rituals that led to Jessica's being transformed into a zombie. As worshippers draw Jessica back to the Houmfort with a voodoo doll, Wesley helps her to escape from Fort Holland before stabbing her with an arrow drawn from the statue of Ti-Misery (the local name for Saint Sebastian) and carrying her down to the sea, where both drown. As local fishermen carry the two bodies back into Fort Holland, Betsy and Paul are shown in a questionable romantic embrace that is further problematized by the concluding shot of Ti-Misery, the haunting iconographic reminder of the colonial misery on which the island's history is based.[85]

The film draws heavily on themes of the literary female Gothic, at the same time as it embraces the epistemological uncertainly of the genre of the fantastic; it extends the narrative hesitation between a natural and supernatural explanation beyond the film's conclusion, as Lewton had hoped to do with *Cat People*. This fits Diane Waldman's model for the Gothic romance film of the 1940s in that "this hesitation is experienced by a character (and presumably a spectator) who is female."[86] This female address should distinguish the film from the horror film according to Waldman, but the film was explicitly marketed and promoted as both a horror film and a romance addressed to the interests of female audiences. RKO exploited this dual-focus angle in publicity, announcing that "voodooism and romance are blended in *I Walked with a Zombie*, RKO's newest horror chiller film" and that "horror and romance form the themes of RKO Radio's latest chiller."[87] The studio, perhaps under the assumption that male spectators were more likely to indiscriminately attend any horror-themed film, was initially more concerned with devising the most appealing romance narrative in order to attract a more discriminating female audience. The Gallup preproduction research for *I Walked with a Zombie* focused on the audience acceptance value of two versions of the story. The variations in the story investigated by Gallup focused on the romance plot of the film—specifically variations in regard to who should be selected as Betsy's love interest—but interviews of a "representative cross-section of movie-goers" revealed little difference in popularity between the two. Seemingly "the determining factor influencing audience reaction here is the basic subject matter itself and not the plot details."[88]

The Gallup research indicated, therefore, that both male and female audiences were more interested in the voodoo theme than in the specificities of the film's love triangle. Following this research and, significantly, *Cat People*'s success, the publicity department centered on the "novel" conjoined horror and romance themes as filtered through the tragic female monster character.[89] Drawing on the tropes of classic horror advertising, the preproduction advertisement indicates the endangered Betsy as the film's protagonist; a female figure swoons at the feet of a shadowy zombie, who appears indistinct in terms of both gender and race, with the tagline "The super-startling story of a beautiful American girl who flung aside the forbidden veil of voodoo and saw the secret world of the Zombies—The Walking Dead" (see figure 4). The postproduction poster campaign brings the "doomed" female monster Jessica to the fore, however, centering the female zombie as the emotional crux with whom spectators should identify (see figure 5).

This promotion appears to directly interpellate the home-front woman, with another poster asking her to "imagine yourself perhaps hungering for love—dying for just one warm kiss . . . yet alone in a world of people . . . a part of, yet apart from, everything you hold dear." In her discussion of exploitation methods in the period, Diane Waldman stresses that "not only were women expected to project themselves into the film's situation, but they were to extrapolate from that situation to actual or hypothetical events in their own lives."[90] The poster at least calls for empathy with the "beautiful woman to who it all happened," but with many boyfriends, husbands, and potential dates either fighting overseas, undergoing military

FIGURE 4 A preproduction poster for *I Walked with a Zombie* indicates Betsy as a classic "scream queen."

FIGURE 5 The postproduction *Zombie* poster calls for empathy with the titular female monster.

training, or relocated for war work (as were a large number of women), it seems likely that the advertising was playing upon the wartime mood of emotional limbo. The explicitly male horror spectator of earlier scholarship is challenged, therefore, through this appeal to women's empathy with the taxonomically indefinite figure of the female zombie, which, as with the *Cat People* campaign, could be linked to this wider discursive positioning of wartime femininity as a distinctly borderline phenomenon in 1943.

The poster campaign instills a sense of timeliness and female identification despite the fantastic theme, successfully mediating between the political and personal. Unlike in the *Cat People* campaign, however, the pinup angle is entirely lost in favor of the focus on the female zombie "doomed to be one of the walking dead," encouraging spectators to share her emotional perspective by linking her fate to their own. This is significant in light of the aforementioned Gallup research that identified the importance of same-sex identification in advertising.[91] Although this provides evidence that the publicity department saw women as a key market for this new type of horror, their appeals to a female proclivity for romance narratives and exploitation of the idea of over-identification with the onscreen and on poster image appear intact.

I Walked with a Zombie's promotion was, unsurprisingly, at pains to stress that the film was a follow-up to the huge box office success of *Cat People*, which had confirmed the burgeoning female market for more sophisticated horror implied by films like *Rebecca*. A full-page ad for *I Walked with a Zombie* in the *Hollywood Reporter* trumpeted, "RKO launches another exploitation special" and, quoting *Variety*'s box-office report section, the "most smashing 'sleeper' of the season."[92] The trade press, like the *Los Angeles Times*, positioned the film as the successful continuation of the emergent RKO-led horror cycle. The *Hollywood Reporter* said that "having scored a smashing success at the box office with *Cat People*, producer Val Lewton turns his attention to the ever-intriguing subject of zombies for the second production for the chiller-diller cycle he has launched at RKO." It went on to say that *Zombie* "stands an excellent chance of breaking the records that *Cat People* broke."[93] *Daily Variety* concurred that the film was a "step further in RKO's current program of chillers. The film possesses every ingredient for box-office success, certainly in light of the smash scored by its forerunner *Cat People*. Lewton reaches his stride as a producer of horror pictures in this one."[94]

As suggested, the film expands on the techniques, themes, and tropes of *Cat People*, consolidating this new horror formula centering on an ambiguous love triangle in which two women's lives become tragically entwined. As in *Cat People*, the female monster character is set up as simultaneously rival and double with a symbolic war worker—in this case an independent and resourceful nurse. This character ultimately prevails over her monstrous rival because she is able to synthesize the multiple demands of productivity and desirability. The film's promotion highlights the links between the character of the trained nurse Betsy and the actress who portrays her, Frances Dee. A pressbook article explains that Dee has taken courses in Red Cross nursing—a contribution to the war effort shared by over three million other women.[95] It further says that she is a devoted wife and mother of two boys but also an outstanding dramatic actress and keen horse rider who can "shoot a bow and arrow and crack a whip." Like Betsy, Dee is celebrated for her productive synthesis of traditionally male and female roles and traits. This article is followed by one on the female journalist Inez Wallace, "a gifted writer who is petite and glamorous [and thus] traditionally the last person in the world you would suspect of knowing anything about such a horrendous subject." It goes on to stress that the narrative is based upon the direct experiences and scientific research on voodooism that Wallace, "an avid globe trotter," gathered on her research trip to Haiti.[96] Although the publicity material is still somewhat patronizing in its evocation of traditional codes of femininity and glamour, it foregrounds women's involvement in masculine heroic endeavors. These foregrounded paradoxes are in keeping with other media images in the early years of the war that broadened the range of acceptable female behavior even as they asserted more conventional norms.[97] This duality was extensively explored in the 1940s woman's film, in which, according to Basinger, the conflicting forces in women's lives were characterized through contrasting female characters.[98]

I Walked with a Zombie certainly fits this model. The film's generic hybridity—and specifically its links to the woman's film and female Gothic—confounded many critics on its release. The *Washington Post* bemoaned the conjoining of "an extravagantly far-fetched love story with the blood chilling implications of tropical voodooism," concluding that "they mix none-too-well."[99] The *Motion Picture Herald* disagreed. It saw the film as "an exceptionally well made production for its type of theme," further saying that the preview audience at the Hawaii theater in Hollywood "who were there to see a horror double bill was very much impressed." It continued, however, that "there were titters at the opening, which used off stage narration by a woman's voice, ala 'Rebecca.'"[100] The reviewer is referring to the dreamlike opening in which Betsy's voice-over announces dismissively, "I walked with a zombie. [Self-conscious laugh.] It does seem an odd thing to say." It has been widely recorded that Val Lewton was embarrassed about the studio-enforced title and that this was perhaps a self-conscious apology for it.[101] It would appear that this intertextual reference to *Rebecca* picked up in internal reports and in the trade press was an intentional production strategy.[102] It provided an immediate indication to the audience that the film was more a cousin of the literary female Gothic than a continuation of Universal's "werewolf chasing a girl in a nightgown up a tree" formula that the studio was purportedly trying to impose; Koerner's insistence on bringing in the *Wolf Man* screenwriter Siodmak might back up this claim.[103]

Lewton, who was attempting to bypass the Universal formula in favor of a literary Gothic-inspired approach, wanted a female screenwriter, Ardel Wray, for the project, as she had impressed him while involved in a Young Writers' Project at RKO. When Siodmak quit the film due to friction with Lewton over his script, the producer was able to bring in Wray to rewrite Siodmak's treatment, which, Edmund Bansak proposes, sounded more like the Lugosi vehicle *White Zombie* (1932) than *Jane Eyre*.[104] Lewton perhaps felt the script would benefit from a female perspective on the project, particularly in light of the feminine intertexts (Brontë and Wallace) upon which it draws. He eventually used Wray as scriptwriter for a number of his other films, including *Isle of the Dead* (1945); the end of the war marked the end of Wray's Hollywood career as well as the end of Lewton's contribution to this horror cycle. In a retrospective interview, Wray explained that the tension between the studio chiefs and Lewton's close-knit unit arose due to the "upstairs fears that sock-it-to-them was being sacrificed for 'arty stuff.'"[105] This creative clash found its way into the film's narrative strategies of staging a collision between official and unofficial discourse.

The film's opening reference to *Rebecca* is significant because—in addition to demonstrating how meaning is constructed by audiences intertextually—it provides a microcosm of the tension or, as Mikhail Bakhtin preferred, "interanimation" between the verbal and the visual that is at the heart of the film. The voice-over's playful challenge to the studio-sanctioned title that appears onscreen sets up the collisions of voices—official and unofficial, visual and verbal, natural and supernatural, rational and irrational, dominant and marginal, masculine and feminine—that are staged within the text. Significantly these binaries are left unresolved as the credits roll, with the key enigma of what has caused Jessica's catatonia never explained.[106] It is perhaps partially this subversive refusal to conform to classical conventions, leaving questions unanswered and refusing to tie up the moral and ideological ambiguities, that inspired such outrage in the *New York Times* reviewer.[107]

Following the film's premiere at the Rialto, the *New York Times* printed a paradoxical polemic lamenting that due to the peculiar popularity of horror at this moment, *I Walked with a Zombie* would "probably please a lot of people. But to this spectator at least it proves to be a dull, disgusting exaggeration of an unhealthy, abnormal concept of life." The combination of bemusement and ferocity (it concludes with no fewer than three question marks) with which the reviewer pulls rank with his superior cultural capital over an assumed deluded mass is atypically extreme for a *New York Times* horror review. The reviewer revealingly cites the film's transgressive ideological positioning in relation to the war, protesting that it is particularly problematic in light of the Hays Office's censorship of a number of purposeful dramas such as *In Which We Serve* (1942). He also underlines the "duty to safeguard the youth of the land" from the film.[108]

Highlighting both the success of liberalism and its promise for the future was key to complying with the Office of War Information's directive for Hollywood to represent America as an ideal democracy united against a common enemy. The OWI therefore encouraged movies that showed women and blacks as full participants in the war effort who were benefiting from the resultant gains. It was sensitive about the depiction of home-front race relations but also about the evocation of America and its democratic allies' histories of slavery and imperialism. For example, the Motion Picture Bureau objected to the script for *Battle Hymn* (1942) because of its depiction of black slaves in a Maryland household during the Civil War. The bureau's reviewer, Dorothy Jones, complained, "The fact that slavery existed in this country is certainly something which belongs to the past and which we wish to forget at this time when unity of all races and creeds is all-important."[109] As in many other such cases, the black characters were simply written out of the script.

It is not surprising, then, that *I Walked with a Zombie*, with its evocation of America's and Britain's imperialism, and particularly their shameful histories of slavery, might be perceived by the *New York Times* as incompatible with Hollywood's promotion of the democratic ideals for which the Allies were fighting. Although America's history (and present) of racial domination was a pervasive absence in most wartime films, Lewton managed to sneak through a film that provoked questions about American race and gender relations under the guise of a lurid horror shocker. The film's depiction of the results of imperialism and slavery was particularly contentious because the United States had ended its occupation of Haiti less than ten years earlier and was still in control of its external finances.[110] RKO was aware that *I Walked with a Zombie* might have serious problems gaining approval and therefore, according to OWI's Overseas Branch, played a "'hide-and-seek' game" with the film to get a government blessing before it was viewed by the BMP.[111] Ulric Bell, the Overseas representative in Los Angeles, centered the film as his key example of studio chiefs' circumvention strategies. Bell "tried to get a look at the film for six weeks but was always told it was not ready." It was not until February 4, 1943, that the studio invited the OWI to screen it—one day after the Censorship Office had approved it for export.[112] RKO's sidestepping of the OWI/BMP could certainly be related to Bell's fears around the film's address of potentially controversial racial and colonial subject matter.[113]

In *Icons of Grief* (2005), the only book to attempt to purposefully link the Lewton films to their wartime context, Alexander Nemerov states that the black zombie character Carrefour "suggests the violent subjugation *and* the emergent power of blacks during the war."[114] He further says that the evocatively named Carrefour shows "America again at the *crossroads*," positioned at the threshold of the past of slavery and lynching in America and the emergent self-reflexivity regarding the nation's legacy of racial discrimination. This was initiated by the convergence of the tactical move to distance the Allies' ideology from that of the Nazis and the reality of social changes engendered by wartime manpower shortages. As the events of 1943 showed, however, this transition would not be as smooth as many hoped. The film came at a period of overt hostility and aggression when the partial desegregation of the American workplace necessitated by manpower shortage and subsequent influx of black and Hispanic workers into more affluent urban areas was inflaming white racism and black dissatisfaction at poor living conditions in major cities.[115] This tension eventually resulted in the infamous race riots in Los Angeles, New York, and Detroit in the summer of 1943. Nemerov fails to associate this historically specific situation of shifts in the labor force and the subsequent backlash to the comparable experience of women in America and the resultant conflation of these two forms of patriarchal domination in the film. The symbolically dominant but narratively marginalized Jessica, who is doubled with Carrefour throughout the film, is finally herself lynched by a white male believing he is acting in her best interest as Carrefour looks on mournfully.

In his best-selling book *An American Dilemma* (1944), the Swedish economist Gunnar Myrdal stresses the similarities in the techniques of social control employed to keep women and blacks in America in a state of relative powerlessness vis-à-vis white men.[116] He explains that the development of an industrial economy had not brought about the integration of women and blacks into society; rather, white patriarchal hegemony had, through the concession of illusionary rights, encouraged these subordinate groups to respect their proposed "natural" inferiority and enjoy their subordination at the hands of the white paterfamilias.

> As in the case of the Negro, women themselves have often been brought to believe in their inferiority of endowment. As the Negro was awarded his "place" in society, so there was a "woman's place." In both cases the rationalization was strongly believed that men, in confining them to this place, did not act against the true interest of the subordinate groups. The myth of the "contented women," who did not want to have suffrage or other civil rights and equal opportunities, had the same function as the myth of the "contented Negro."[117]

Myrdal evokes the Foucauldian model of (modern) power relations, with social inequality normalized through self-perpetuating discourse that is so ingrained that it comes to appear natural to all parties involved. Although this sex/race analogy has been rightly challenged for being reductive, it provides comparative examples of how social control is experienced in America (both using a physical foundation for denying rights and subsequently maintaining this domination through the restriction of economic opportunity), and thus it is a fairly useful starting point for societal critique and certainly a provocative metaphor for a 1940s horror film to employ.

This naturalization of gendered and racial inequality Myrdal proposes, however, was somewhat denaturalized by the social dislocations and shifts necessitated by war. Although, as Myrdal predicted, in the long term racial and sexual inequality remained after the war (and many of the minimal wartime advances in terms of employment opportunities and pay were reversed), "the vicious cycle of social control which had compelled obedience to traditional patterns as the price of survival was at least partially broken by the massive jolt of full-scale war."[118] The resultant realization and expectation of alternative economic and social relations—the possibility of things being otherwise—contributed heavily to the preconditions for the emergence of the American civil rights and feminist movements of the 1960s and 1970s. J. P. Telotte argues that Fort Holland becomes a "fortress of the rational . . . a conservative force which shuts out, as a way of denying existence to, that with which it cannot adequately deal."[119] This also includes shutting out these historically specific challenges to the previously unchallenged domination on which this society had run.

The myth of the family's hegemony is unsustainable beyond the walls of Fort Holland, a point revealed when the trickster figure Sir Lancelot—intended according to the director, Jacques Tourneur, to act as a "sort of ancient Greek chorus commenting upon the action"—challenges the dominant myth of the family through a calypso song about the "shame and sorrow" of the Holland family that undermines their official history.[120] *I Walked with a Zombie* reflects the liberalist views of contemporary critics such as Myrdal through this realization of the illusionary power structures that have historically dominated women and blacks (both domestically and imperially), but at the same time the film is instilled with a well-founded skepticism that the postwar future will promise to be any more egalitarian.

The shadow of "shame and sorrow" surrounding the Holland family's narrative of colonial exploitation lingers in Paul Holland's attempts to dominate women through language. As Valentin Voloshinov explains, "Each word, as we know it, is a little arena for the clash and criss-crossing of differently oriented social accents. A word in the mouth of a particular individual person is a product of the living interaction of social forces."[121] In *I Walked with a Zombie* the clash of competing voices is staged, in microcosm, over the meaning of the word "beautiful." This recurring motif is introduced in the opening scene when Paul challenges the validity of Betsy's narrative voice by responding to what appears to be her flashback narration, to which she in turn responds, "You read my thoughts, Mr. Holland." He discredits her interpretation of the sea by interrupting, "Everything seems beautiful because you don't understand," a position he backs up through scientific discourse. He continues, "That luminous water—it takes its gleam from millions of tiny dead bodies. It's the glitter of putrescence. There's no beauty here—only death and decay."

Rather than acting as the "site of knowledge" who reveals the truth of this unfamiliar world, the "most logical or rational of people [prove to be] the greatest threats that emerge from the Lewton films."[122] Although Paul Holland, as the logical or rational character, is not finally proven as malevolent or wrong (as is Dr. Judd in *Cat People*, for example) the spectator is expected to infer his threat to Betsy and thus his complicity in Jessica's condition. Following a scene when Paul mocks Betsy for "thinking [herself] beautiful," the prophetic Wesley warns her that "one of these days he'll start on you like he did on her. You think life is beautiful, don't you, Jessica. You think you are beautiful, don't you, Jessica. What he could do to that word beautiful. That's Paul's weapon, words. He uses them like other men use their fists." The word "beautiful" has already been codified as representing the Hollands' colonial domination over the slaves they brought to the island. When the carriage driver explains that the Hollands' ancestors brought their "long ago fathers and long ago mothers of us all here chained to the bottom of a boat," the initially naïve Betsy responds, "They brought you to a beautiful place, didn't they." The carriage driver replies, with an ironic laugh, "If you say so, miss, if you say so." Through the linguistic sign of "beautiful," Paul's subjugation of Betsy and, previously, Jessica is encoded as a form of colonial domination maintained through the monologizing voice of the family patriarch.

The competition of official (centripetal) and unofficial (centrifugal) voices within the text is finally undecidable, most significantly the dispute over a rational or irrational explanation for Jessica's "illness." Todorov explains that through "the hesitation it engenders, the fantastic questions precisely the existence of an irreducible opposition between real and unreal."[123] As one of the purest cinematic examples of the inherently dialogic genre of the fantastic, *I Walked with a Zombie*, through this undecidability, calls into question absolute claims to truth. This includes the biologically deterministic old-time concepts of good and bad femininity that conservative postwar critics bemoaned had been lost during the war.[124] Juxtaposed to the professional and resilient wartime working woman Betsy, Jessica can be read as a critique of prewar conceptions of femininity, a monstrous exaggeration of the unpatriotic "Mrs. Stay-at-Home" who favored traditional glamour and domesticity over the productive calling of war work.[125] In a line cut from the shooting script, Paul attacks Jessica's narcissism and selfishness (in contrast to Betsy's "selfless" role as nurse), saying that she "lived in a world with room for nothing but her own image and her own desires."[126] This was perhaps considered too indicting to remain, but in the film her maid tellingly describes her as a "beautiful doll," and her doctor describes her as "a woman without any will power, unable to speak or even act by herself."

The narrative works to instill doubt in the spectator as to Betsy's motives and provide a sympathetic voice for Jessica, even in her silence, and despite the insinuations of infidelity. Although she remains mysterious, the final shooting script hints at the producers' conception of Jessica's history and thus culpability. The screenplay's poetic description of Jessica's room, calling for a mannerist mise-en-scène that Lewton hoped would embody her pre-zombie state, provides a useful insight into the film's moral positioning toward this potential transgressor: "It is a beautiful woman's room, feminine but with no suggestion of the bagnio; elegant rather than seductive, and reflecting a playful yet sophisticated taste. . . . The empty chair and wind-stirred glass curtains give a dual effect of elegance and loneliness."[127] In his direction to avoid any "suggestion of the bagnio" (brothel) and to give the sense of "elegance and loneliness" he makes it clear that he wishes to avoid having her misread as sexual predator and instead hopes to inspire some sympathy with the character's situation—the product of domination or neglect by her husband rather than calculated transgression. In congruence with this reading the film instills serious skepticism about Betsy and Paul's future as a couple, intimating that Betsy will suffer the same fate as Jessica if she is to remain with him. The antiquated Rochester figure admits his culpability in the system of subjugation of women he perpetuates, warning Betsy, "I was trying to hurt you. It was the same way with Jessica. I had to hurt her. Everything she did or said made me lash out at her." He continues, "You think I love Jessica and want her back, it's like you to think that, clean decent thinking. I wish it were true for your sake." At this point, in the background, heavy drums begin to beat.

These drums imply the threat of domination, both sexual and colonial, and we have heard them before. They were first introduced as Wesley explains to Betsy that Paul's father was a plantation owner and his was a missionary, thereby revealing the dual economic and ideological domination of the island by the Holland/Rand family. Wesley teases her about "the jungle drums, mysterious, eerie," but then dispels her fear by explaining, "That's the work drum over at the sugar mill. Saint Sebastian's version of the factory whistle"—symbolizing not the threat of voodoo but rather the economic exploitation upon which the island is built. They sounded again following Paul's revelation of "an ugly scene" in which he told his wife, "driven mad by her own husband," that "she couldn't go. That I'd keep her here by force if necessary." The ominous drumming is a subtle aural motif that works as historical return of the repressed—an interruption of verbal over visual that intimates the suppressed or repressed meanings behind the dominant discourse.

In her book *Divine Horsemen* (1953), the experimental filmmaker Maya Deren, who went to Haiti in the 1940s to record voodoo rituals, writes, "I have come to believe that if history were recorded by the vanquished rather than by the victors, it would illuminate the real rather than the theoretical means to power."[128] Like the statue of King John in *Cat People*, the polyvalent figurehead of Ti-Misery remains a silent yet all-signifying presence in the film; it symbolizes the histories of "shame and sorrow" that lie behind dominant historical accounts. When Jessica is finally sacrificed in the manner of the iconographic Ti-Misery, the narrative comes full circle, as the fatalism of beauty turned to misery is represented in the film's final haunting utterance. Like Deren's *Meshes of the Afternoon* (1943)—introduced as a film from "Hollywood 1943"—*I Walked with a Zombie* subverts Hollywood's wartime purpose of showing the home as "the place that we are fighting for." Instead it represents Fort Holland as "an alien, even evil environment, ultimate site of the loss of self, a vibrant *agon* in which aggressivity and sexuality come bursting out in a virulent fashion."[129] If in *Meshes of the Afternoon* and *I Walked with a Zombie* the "home has become a nightmarish place [of conflict] where women can only destroy or be destroyed," then in Lewton's *The Seventh Victim* the home front becomes so nightmarish that death provides women's only real escape from its "repetition of victimization."[130]

"Sister of Satan! Marked for Death!": Sex and the City in *The Seventh Victim*

Following the huge box-office successes of *Cat People* and *I Walked with a Zombie*, Val Lewton was offered an A-class budget for his next film, *The Seventh Victim*. This was retracted prior to the commencement of production, however, because Lewton refused to remove the novice director Mark Robson from the project.[131] As a result, certain elements in the script had to be cut or reduced to bring the film in around the one-hour mark typical for "B" pictures. Although this is often given as the reason for some of the film's confusions and ambiguities, many of the same scholars see the film as a "masterpiece" to rival *I Walked with a Zombie*.[132] *The Seventh Victim*'s repetitive structure and fatalistic tone are typically attributed to Lewton's poetic and pessimistic worldview, one clearly informed yet rarely attributed to his feelings on the world's "return to barbarism—the savage wars that mark the end of a cycle of civilization."[133] It would be reductive to attribute the film entirely to Lewton as auteur, but a resignation to the barbarism and fatalism of World War II certainly informs *The Seventh Victim*'s cyclical and cynical narrative.[134] Following the disappearance of a young businesswoman, Jacqueline (Jean Brooks), her younger sister, Mary (Kim Hunter), travels to New York to try to find her. Mary's investigation, aided by Jacqueline's husband, Gregory (Hugh Beaumont), reveals that Jacqueline is a member of a cult of Greenwich Village Satanists called the Palladists. The Palladists have condemned Jacqueline to death for disclosing their secrets to the psychiatrist Dr. Judd (Tom Conway)—the same Dr. Judd we met in *Cat People*—and they make a series of failed attempts on her and her sister's lives.[135] Jacqueline ultimately commits suicide, however, leaving Mary and Gregory, who have fallen in love, to console each other.

The Seventh Victim received mostly poor reviews in the mainstream press and, perhaps in part resultantly, did comparatively poorly at the box office despite its positioning within the industry as a continuation of the successful RKO-led horror cycle. The trade press insisted that the film "fits snugly into the groove of RKO productions which have had unusual and in several instances phenomenal success" and was a "chiller in best RKO tradition. The fourth in the series of psychological horror dramas Val Lewton is producing at RKO favorably matches up with its predecessors."[136] Critics identified the film's narrative ambiguities and inconsistencies on "the problematic nature of perspective" as, at best, unnecessary pretension or, at worst, the result of "a particularly poor script."[137] Bosley Crowther of the New *York Times* professed himself bewildered: "This writer claims with modest candor to have an average amount of brains, and we make it a point to pay attention whenever reviewing a film. But, brother, we have no more notion of what *The Seventh Victim*, at the Rialto, is about than if we had watched the same picture run backwards and upside down."[138] Although these characteristics came to be admired in later female monster texts and reappraisals of Lewton's "canon," this new horror formula was initially seen as unnecessarily confusing or pretentious by middlebrow critics such as Crowther.[139]

In contemporary reception, therefore, *The Seventh Victim*'s excessive ambiguity and its resultant poor reception were mostly blamed for its limited box-office success, but Bansak blames its lack of a blatantly exploitable female monster character. He argues that "unlike the Tourneur films, *The Seventh Victim* offered nothing that the publicity department could tag as a monster for the poster ads, no feline terrors."[140] The promotion department did make some attempt, however, to exploit similar marketing techniques based upon the bifurcation of the central female monster and the conflation of horror and romance themes. All the poster images and taglines focus on the tragic Jacqueline character, emphasizing "Sister of Satan Marked for Death! Robbed of the Power to Love by Devil Cult!" and "Helpless Victim of Strange Pagan Beliefs! Beautiful Victim of the Devil's Cult . . . Robbed of the Power to Love." The more transgressive bifurcated appeals of Irena's panther woman and Jessica's female zombie (simultaneously monster and victim) are rejected in favor of Jacqueline's more passive solitary role of victimhood.

Despite the absence of such internal bifurcation for promotional purposes, the narrative maintains its focus on female doubling as in Lewton's previous films. Telotte states that Mary and Jacqueline "resemble light and dark versions of the same character, different potentials" just like the female doubles in *Cat People* and *I Walked with a Zombie.* He continues, "The final destruction of this particular doubling, which occurs with Jacqueline's suicide and Gregory's avowal of his love for Mary, underscores the tragic component of this fantasy formula."[141] The narrative focuses again, therefore, on a tragic love triangle—or "eerie threesome," as the pressbook tagline says—in which female doubles compete for the same man. Likewise, Bansak details Lewton's use of female doubles, or "flip sides if you will—held together by a common bond. In *Cat People* we have the mystical Irena and practical Alice bound together by their common interests in Oliver. In *I Walked with a Zombie* we have the vibrant Betsy and comatose Jessica Holland, the common element Paul Holland. . . . In *The Seventh Victim* we have two sisters who fall in love with the same man; one sister, Mary, is innocent and optimistic, the other, Jacqueline, is worldly and despairing."[142] Both critics point out the centrality of themes of female duality, or doubling, and the triangular romantic structure in which the light version of the female character ultimately wins out. They both fail to explain the purposeful blurring of these light and dark characters, however, and the relevance of this strategy to these films' wartime contexts. These auteurist accounts of Lewton's visionary approach to horror mark his aesthetic and thematic choices, including his characters, as ahead of rather than of their time. Bansak, for example, proposes that Lewton's "admirable" female roles are "closer to the kind of 'liberated' feminine roles we expect today."[143]

As the *Seventh Victim* promotion suggests, Lewton saw this new type of horror as specifically reflecting a contemporary state of mind in which "normal people—engaged in normal occupations" in the modern world—suddenly encounter "extraordinary things." The *Seventh Victim* pressbook, quoting Lewton, explains that the new RKO horror school's approach is based on the assumption that "it would be much more entertaining if people with whom audiences could identify were shown in contact with the strange, the weird and the occult."[144]

Nemerov proposes that Lewton's films "suggest" the unseen horror and tragedy lurking behind the everyday home-front experience, expressing the anxiety and sadness experienced by Americans during the war.[145] As this chapter has argued, however, these films also evoke the feelings of excitement and adventure in encountering the new and unfamiliar—an experience wartime audiences could also identify with. Specifically, these are narratives of female experiences of the strange and extraordinary, whether working as a nurse on a remote island or relocating to an overwhelming urban metropolis.

The bewilderment, terror, and excitement experienced by the small-town sisters Mary and Jacqueline on relocating to New York can certainly be equated to those of female war workers, discovering for the first time what lies "behind the teeming life of our great cities," as the *Seventh Victim* posters promised to reveal. The film's labyrinthine structure and narrative dead ends could be seen to reveal the experience of initial encounters with these complex urban environments. Beyond the obvious presence of Dr. Judd, the similarities to *Cat People* are most distinctive in regard to the female doubles and their relationships to New York. As with Irena who works in fashion, Jacqueline works in cosmetics, a career choice problematized through its attachment to prewar modes of femininity as with Irene's vocation in *Cat People.* Like *Cat People*'s Alice, the resilient Mary is distinguished from her world-weary double by her ability to navigate and thus survive the mystifying landscape of New York. This is also the case for the heroine of *Phantom Lady* (1944), which will be discussed in a later chapter, particularly in relation to the issue of the discursive construction of New York, and especially Times Square, as a site of contradictory wartime experiences for women.

A central scene in *The Seventh Victim* richly demonstrates the twin pleasures and terrors of the city for women. When Jacqueline flees the cozy Greenwich Village coven of the Palladists, she finds herself on the shadowy streets of New York at midnight, pursued by a would-be assassin as she heads toward the lights of Fifth Avenue. Again replicating one of *Cat People*'s most effective scenes, *The Seventh Victim* employs the renowned "Lewton walk"—crosscutting between the shoes of victim and pursuer—and three "bus" moments that provide anticlimactic shocks. Following the first bus moment, a dustbin lid falling, the shadowy figures in an alleyway are revealed as merely a couple petting. Jacqueline then meets her assassin in a similarly shadowy alleyway. As she reaches her fingers around the wall, their hands caresses while the assassin readies his blade (see figure 6). At that moment, a crowd of actors bursts out of the backstage door of a theater; one of the actresses' gleeful screams provides the final bus moment and Jacqueline's opportunity to escape her assassin's clutches. Jacqueline runs over to a large, jovial actor who is dressed in Roman half armor to represent the god Gambrinus—the Roman god of fecundity and good humor.[146] She pleads, "Please help me, there's a man following me," to which the actor responds, "I shouldn't wonder, babe, I shouldn't wonder." What Jacqueline interprets as danger and threat, the actor interprets as seduction and sexual frisson. Women's relocating or commuting to downtown centers such as New York for work and entertainment provided complex and contradictory experiences for them, none more complex and contradictory than their experiences of sex. It was a period in which sexual codes were disrupted, and while many women found that war work exposed them to the threat of sexual harassment, others "discovered a new freedom that many found irresistible."[147]

When Jacqueline persists with her seemingly correct interpretation of events, the actor succumbs: "I'll help you to beer and a sandwich. Come on, babe." When they arrive at Cleary's Tavern, however, Jacqueline escapes his embrace and wearily walks away toward her eventual doom. This scene perfectly encapsulates the simultaneous pleasures and horrors—or comedy and tragedy, as the masks painted on the backstage door represent—of wartime experience. Jacqueline is unable to see beyond the bloodshed and misery lurking behind home-front daily life, but other women in the film choose to embrace the excitement of the big city.[148] When Jacqueline returns to her hotel to take her own life, she encounters the "sickly" (or hypochondriac) guest Mimi (Elizabeth Russell) on the landing. Conversely Mimi has made the decision to embrace the unprecedented quest for pleasure going on in the booming downtown districts of New York, "where the war defense industry and patriotic activities of woman had changed the entire picture" of entertainment life.[149] Appearing in evening dress—before, she has been seen only in a dressing gown—Mimi explains, "I'm going out, I'm going to laugh and dance and do all the things I want to

FIGURE 6 Jacqueline experiences the dangers and excitements of New York in *The Seventh Victim*.

do." Jacqueline asks, "And then what?" Mimi responds, "I don't know." To which Jacqueline retorts, "You will die."

In the face of "the specter of a world that doesn't know when it will be free," Mimi, unlike Jacqueline, ultimately makes the decision to embrace the contingent pleasures of New York's nightlife.[150] As Mimi descends the stairs toward the frivolous pleasures of the city, Jacqueline's voice-over reiterates John Donne's (c. 1572–1631) "Holy Sonnet," which appeared on the film's opening intertitle: "I run to death and death meets me as fast, and all my pleasures are like yesterdays." As in *I Walked with a Zombie*, with this shift from the visual to the verbal Jacqueline reclaims this canonical patriarchal text; she sees her only strategy as one of embracing her annihilation at the hands of a barbaric world. Mimi and Mary, however, choose to embrace an alternative interpretation, one that foregrounds the excitement rather than tragedy of home-front life. The film does not side with either of these female coping strategies; rather, it presents them as equally viable attitudes to an uncertain world.

In *Cat People, I Walked with a Zombie*, and *The Seventh Victim*, the orchestration of multiple voices and perspectives infuses the characterization of the female characters, revealing the conflicting forces in real wartime women's lives. They represent the cinematic essence of Voloshinov's theory of literary dialogism, exploiting the "layering of meaning upon meaning, voice upon voice" and the combination of voices that converge and become socially meaningful at the point of individual spectatorship.[151] In his 1951 obituary of Lewton, Manny Farber said approvingly that it was this dialogical "use of multiple focus" and centering of the audience as the ultimate authors of these texts that made his horror unit's "minor approximation[s] of *Jane Eyre*" so appealing to wartime audiences.[152] Though some middlebrow critics saw Lewton's films as an unpatriotic and "perverted kind of escapism," they provided democratic spaces for audiences to engage with the complexities and contradictions experienced in their own lives on the American home front.[153] Widespread reporting of the extraordinary popularity of *Cat People* and *I Walked with a Zombie* with wartime audiences encouraged the other Hollywood studios (with the exception of Warner Bros.) to incorporate the easily imitated features of Lewton's films into their horror programs.[154]

2

Series, Sequels, and Double Bills

The Evolution of the Female Monster Cycle, 1943–1944

In this country there is a cult which is gaining force by leaps and bounds. . . . And so, because Hollywood is ever ready and willing to fill the needs of audiences everywhere, the horror films have taken a sudden upsurge recently. And out of it all is emerging a set of horror queens who are anything but horrible to look at.

—Dee Lowrance, *Oakland Tribune* (March 19, 1944)

In her article "Shebas of Shudders," Dee Lowrance rejoiced that "the screen now offers a great variety in horror queens." Pointing to the evidence of both the Lewton films discussed in the previous chapter and a number of the Universal films discussed below—including *Weird Woman, Son of Dracula*, and *The Mummy's Ghost*—she demonstrates that "zombies, werewolves, bats and ghouls[are] all in the day's work for these heroines of horror films."[1] Like Donald Kirkley of the *Baltimore Sun*, Lowrance sees this phenomenon as a bottom-up movement, with Hollywood responding to audience demand rather than directing it. Instead of seeing this as a symptom of an alarming wartime mindset as Kirkley does, however, the *Tribune*'s female Hollywood correspondent sees this representational shift as a positive development for women in both the industry and the audience—while offering a concessionary novelty for men to "look at" too.

This chapter will analyze how the representational shift instigated by Lewton at RKO was assimilated by other studios—particularly the horror specialists Universal and Columbia—turning the female monster film into a Hollywood-wide cycle. Rick Altman suggests that once a new cycle has been initiated by a studio successfully bringing a "new type of material or approach [to an] already existing genre," assuming these new features (character types, plot elements, stylistic traits) can be imitated by other studios and that "conditions are favorable," then "other players in the industry [will] adopt the model for development of their own projects."[2] As this chapter will explain, with market conditions favorable, the horror stalwart Universal responded quickly, introducing new proprietary characters (*Captive Wild Woman*) and incorporating female monsters into ongoing series (Dracula, Sherlock Holmes, the Mummy). Columbia and other studios soon followed suit (or hirsute), however, with critical reception recognizing female monster films as a distinct Hollywood cycle, perhaps even a subgenre, by mid-1944.[3] Furthermore, reception and marketing revealed the female monster film as not merely a generic innovation but also a more general indication of the expansion of wartime women into male roles both on screen and off.

"And Now a Lady Joins the Boo Clan": The Transformation of *Captive Wild Woman*

On March 31, 1943—as *Cat People* held its grip over audiences nationwide, including extending its run at the Hawaii in Hollywood into its eleventh week—*Variety's* Jim Cunningham chewed over the phenomenal box-office success of "horror pictures, horror in whodunits, and just plain whodunits." He continued, "The chillers are cleaning up in most spots around the country, even getting first-run and downtown bookings in unprecedented manner. . . . Chalk it up to the war!"[4] With a parallel decline in grosses for romance and war themes, both major and minor studios were racing chillers into production. Universal was reportedly positioned to pounce first. Cunningham noted that the studio had two pictures "finished, but unreleased, *Son of Dracula* in which Lon Chaney horrifies, and *Captive Wild Woman*, to be billed as the first woman horror (in films), with the gal known only as Acquanetta, who is turned into a gorilla."[5] Although these two films (in preproduction before the realization of *Cat People*'s success) look back to precursors in the shape of Universal's classic horror of the 1930s, their marketing and reception were certainly shaped within the context of the female monster films' engagement with women's wartime experiences.

In July 1943 the *Dallas Morning News* announced, "Frankenstein's Monster, the Wolf Man and others of the Boo clan can move over and make room for a lady, *Captive Wild Woman*, Universal's new monstrous problem child, who is part chimp and part human." The reviewer went on to link this shift in women's roles onscreen in horror to the wider "manpower shortage which has brought the female of the species into all sorts of jobs usually filled by men."[6] Rather than being purely a product of its wartime context, however, Universal's new monstrous female had a precursor in the classic horror pantheon of the 1930s. The reviewer pointed this out, specifically highlighting Universal's "gorilla girl" as the progeny of the "panther woman" of *Island of Lost Souls* (1933)—Paramount's adaptation of H. G. Wells's novel *The Island of Dr. Moreau*, in which Charles Laughton (as Moreau) uses surgery to transform a panther into a woman.[7] This classic horror spawned few if any comparable female characters in 1930s horror and was perceived by the trade press as having an entirely male address because it did not feature "the kind of chills ladies like in pictures."[8] *The Island of Lost Souls*'s almost "high concept" strategy—centered on marketing it through its "panther woman angle rather than as a chiller"—appears to have had a positive influence on *Captive Wild Woman*'s casting and other preproduction decisions, however.[9]

Universal announced its intention to produce *Captive Wild Woman* in the trade press two years before its eventual release. A preview advertisement placed in the *Hollywood Reporter* on June 29, 1941, accompanied a picture of a leering female face with the promise the "strange figure of femininity to capture the interest of the nation's sensation loving moviegoers! *Captive Wild Woman* featuring The Wild Woman [and] introducing the surprise star of the year."[10] This hype around the "surprise star of the year" who would play the Wild Woman replicates the rhetoric around *Island of Lost Souls*'s nationwide competition to find the "Panther Woman of America" in 1932; Kathleen Burke, a secretary from Chicago, eventually won the role and was hyped as "a star before she starts" in the film's pressbook.[11] The *Captive Wild Woman* ad proposes a release date of November 7, 1941, which would have preempted the release of *The Wolf Man* (1941) by over a month (and *Cat People* by over a year). The corresponding advertisement for *The Wolf Man* uses a picture that looks very much like Jack Pierce's final creation, hailing it as 1941's "figure of grotesque horror" who would "outdraw Frankenstein and Dracula," but the ad for *Captive Wild Woman* makes no reference to horror.[12] A subsequent trade paper advertisement for the film from 1941 featured an exotic female figure, knife in hand, running through the jungle, introduced again as "The Wild Woman." This intimated a jungle adventure movie about a female Tarzan-type character in the mold of Universal's popular *Jungle Girl* (1941) serial.[13] There was no implication of the eventual horror narrative of a gorilla-woman produced by a mad scientist that eventually materialized in 1943. This mutation in the script was a later development, perhaps inspired by the success of *The Wolf Man*. Fittingly the *Captive Wild Woman* idea appears to have been transformed into two separate entities.

The film was initially reported as a George Waggner production, but by the time it finally went into production on December 10, 1942, Universal had brought in its specialist horror producer, Ben Pivar, who had recently completed his second *Mummy* sequel, *The Mummy's Tomb* (1942). Waggner took the *Jungle Girl* elements of the initial concept and produced *White Savage* (1943), which featured an exotic heroine (portrayed by Universal's popular star Maria Montez) battling plunderers and shark hunters on a South Seas island. Therefore, surprising as it seems, the initial idea promoted in the trade press in 1941 was deemed rich enough to produce two films for Universal, although *Captive Wild Woman* supplements its story by doing a little plundering of its own, reusing animal footage from the jungle adventure *The Big Cage* (1933).

Captive Wild Woman, released June 4, 1943, features John Carradine as Dr. Walters, a mad scientist—in fact, a mad endocrinologist—who injects human glands into an ape in an attempt to create a new "master race." Walters's treatment of young Dorothy's (Martha Vickers) "glandular problem" takes a bizarre course when he discovers that her sister's fiancé, Fred (Milburn Stone), is an animal trainer in possession of a particularly brainy ape.[14] Walters injects his patient's glandular secretions—ones that significantly contain an "abnormal amount of the sex hormones"—into the ape, and it takes on human form. The resultant creation Paula's (Acquanetta) "animal instincts" and hypnotic gaze allow her to help Fred (whom she has had a crush on since her ape days) with his animal taming act. Unfortunately, she transforms into a gorilla-woman hybrid when she becomes inflamed with jealousy toward his fiancée, Beth (Elizabeth Ankers), with whom she becomes involved in a somewhat bestial love triangle. When Beth confronts Walters regarding his bizarre medical practices, he attempts to transplant her brain into his hybrid creation, which has now fully reverted to gorilla form. The ape escapes, however, killing its cruel master and returning to the circus, where it is shot dead while saving its beloved trainer Fred from a lion.

Daily Variety noted the film's generic hybridity—explaining "Universal injects a female werewolf into a circus melodrama"—but most reception, including the *Dallas Morning News*, identified the film as part of a recent horror cycle aimed at the "substantial market for screen chiller-dillers."[15] Following his paradoxical attack on *I Walked with a Zombie*, Bosley Crowther referred to *Captive Wild Woman* as the continuation of a "weary succession of . . . metamorphosis tales" instigated by "gentle items such as *Cat People* . . . and a daub such as *I Walked with a Zombie*." As with Lewton's films, he discounts the "inconsequential" nature of *Captive Wild Woman* while insisting that "there is reason to mutter against [its] clinical unpleasantness"; he derides both its ape-into-woman premise and more specifically its use of lurid pseudo-scientific dialogue.[16] Crowther points out the films' links to the female monster films but concludes by stressing their inability to match up to Universal's and RKO's "awesome freak pictures" of the 1930s, specifically *Dracula* (1931) and *King Kong* (1932). Despite Crowther's misgivings and its earlier marketing as a jungle adventure, *Captive Wild Woman* was exalted as a "Universal horror classic" in its release campaign and promoted as an extension of the studio's classic horror franchises. The pressbook cover tagline explains: "AGAIN! . . . Universal climaxes its record as the master makers of the imaginative master piece! Dracula . . . Frankenstein . . . Wolf Man and now Captive Wild Woman! . . . Screen's newest and most startling of all creations of Horror!"[17] Nevertheless, the poster campaign's central focus is the film's unusual female monster and the mysterious woman who would be portraying her, rather than the studio's legacy of other horror classics.

Although *Cat People*'s unimaginable box-office returns would not have come to light until *Captive Wild Woman* had commenced production, the film's release campaign was designed with the foreknowledge of the success of Lewton's film. Almost two months before the film's release *Variety* noted that "an unusual number of hit and run pictures are being steamrolled into big coin under impetus of circus stunt exploitation." Horror films aimed at war workers were benefiting most from "old-fashioned stunting," it continued, with a recent unnamed chiller aptly demonstrating the wartime "looseness of coin."[18] The Hawaii's and Rialto's elaborate storefronts and lobby displays for *Cat People*—with its aforementioned advertisements featuring lines of female war workers at the theaters—and its resultant extensive runs may well have been what the *Variety* reporter was referring to here.

It is therefore unsurprising that the Universal publicity department should also look to *Cat People*'s sensational campaign as a productive model for *Captive Wild Woman*'s promotion. An article in the pressbook headlined "Sensationalize! That is the Key Word of Your Campaign!" encouraged exhibitors to convert "one complete side of [their] lobby" into a jungle-cum-laboratory scene with branches, potted palms, colored spotlights, and "a beautiful girl [lying] under a sheet with hairy leggings made by a local furrier."[19] As *Variety* demonstrates, this type of ballyhoo was not unusual during the war years—particularly in theaters like the Hawaii and Rialto—but the *Captive Wild Woman* campaign places the corporeal conflict of the female monster ("gorgeous body hiding the horrors of a jungle giant") at the center of its appeals.

In doing so the poster campaign specifically imitates the bifurcated taglines and pinup imagery from the *Cat People* campaign. The posters for *Captive Wild Woman* feature Acquanetta in the same pinup pose Simone Simon holds in the *Cat People* poster, but with the direct replacement of the encroaching panther with a snarling ape, while its sexualized tagline of "Torn by strange desires!" has direct parallels with the "strange, fierce pleasures" from which Irena cannot escape in the *Cat People* campaign (see figure 7). The bifurcation of the *Cat People* promotional discourse is reiterated—perhaps in even more lurid form—in taglines such as "Flesh of rapturous beauty! . . . Fury of an untamed beast!" and "She monster! Beautiful body . . . fury of an untamed beast breaking loose!" As explained in relation to *Cat People*, this bifurcation emerged at a time when the media was struggling with the classificatory confusion engendered by the woman war worker. The *New York Times*'s case history of a war worker named Alma celebrated "her strong but extremely feminine build" but stressed the resultant pressure upon her to synthesize the multiple demands upon her body, "between the war work and the housework."[20]

Like *Cat People*'s, *Captive Wild Woman*'s narrative draws upon Freudian psychoanalytic discourse, or at least popularized 1940s versions of it,

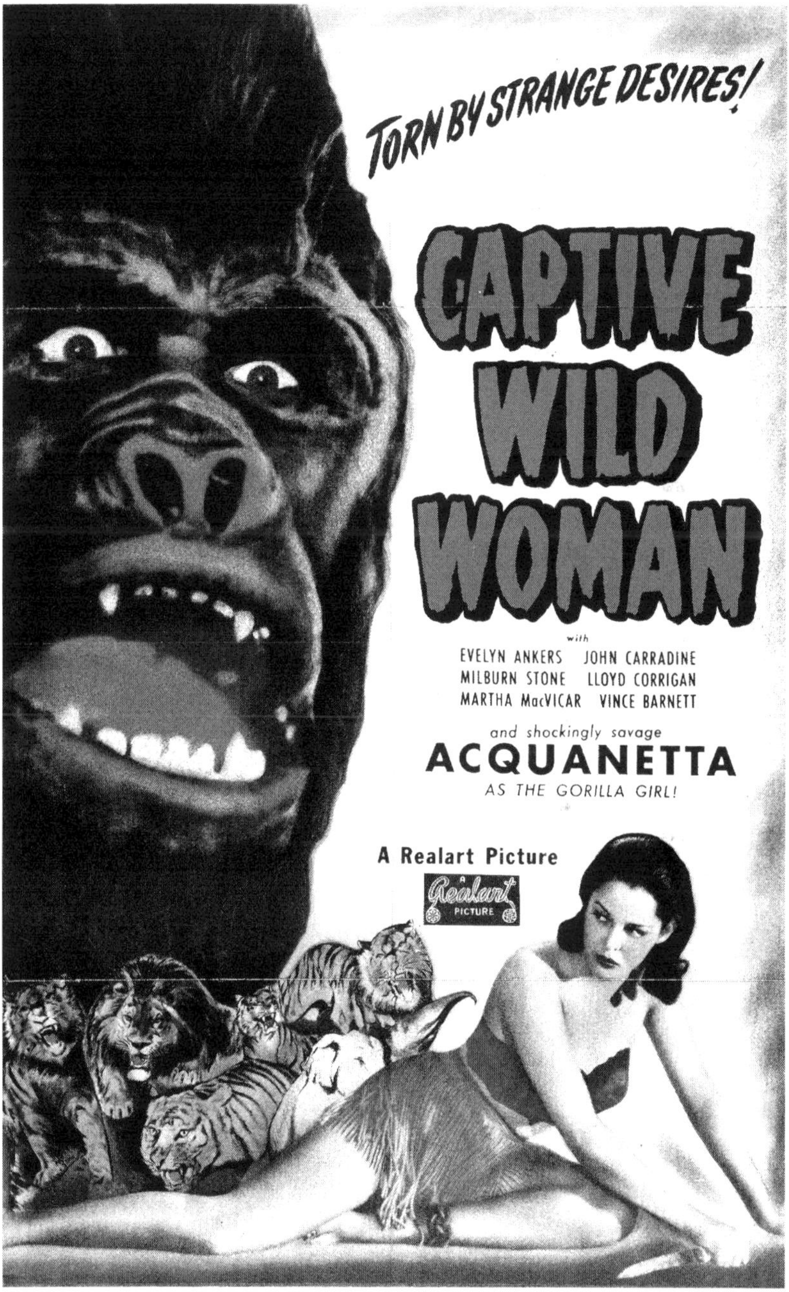

FIGURE 7 *Captive Wild Woman* apes *Cat People*'s poster campaign.

while evincing considerable mistrust of the figure of the psychoanalyst. As Dana Polan states, in *Captive Wild Woman* "the psychiatrist and the mad scientist become interchangeable figures, equal violators of the rules of normality."[21] Dr. *Sigmund* Walters—who is prepared to sacrifice a number of innocent lives in order to further science—is aligned with Nazi ideology in his wish to "create a race of supermen" through the hybridization of human and animal. His uncontrollable desire for power is interchangeable with Paula's sexual desire; he tells her, "Your mind is my mind. Your every though is my thought." This indicates a suspicion of psychoanalysis; in Walters's hands it is a form of sexual mastery and self-suggestion.

Despite such skepticism, *Captive Wild Woman* also draws on psychoanalytic discourse in shaping its narrative strategies. The film actualizes the metaphorical accounts of female patients recorded in Freud's early studies in which their bodies become "the battleground in the hysterical repression of the grotesque form."[22] In *The Politics and Poetics of Transgression* (1986) Peter Stallybrass and Allon White recount how the repression of female sexual desire and concomitant deprivation of "appropriate discourse" to discuss the female body, and thereby "own it comfortably," encouraged the women in Freud's studies to turn "to the carnivalesque and the circus for the images through which [they] may recognize [*themselves*] without disgust." The authors contend that following the demonization and repression of popular carnival and festive forms—ones that were perceived to be incongruous with the individualist ego ideal of the emergent middling classes—circus and carnival imagery took on a symbolic role in the middle-class unconscious as that which should be expelled in order to define one's self as respectable. They continue, "It is not the analyst but the patient who reached out to the showman and the circus. [The patient] *reproduces* the iconographic sensationalism of freak shows at the fair" as a fetishistic stand-in for the unmentionable "lower bodily stratum." Because of this symbolic link with "unspeakable" desires, these images would "return at the level of subjective articulation, as both phobia and fascination, in the individual patient."[23]

Captive Wild Woman enacts this overt link between the repression of female sexual desire and the eruption of circus "terrors" in the everyday world through the nervous and neurotic figure of Dorothy—a clear contrast to her confident and forthright sister, who is able to synthesize work and home life. Walters diagnoses Dorothy as having a "rare case of follicular cyst which induces secretions of unusual amounts of sex hormones." This dialogue appears to consciously draw upon Freud's discourse employed in his most famous hysteria case, in which he attributes Dora's "neuroses" to an "abnormal secretion of the mucous membrane of the vagina [that] is looked upon as a source of disgust."[24] By transferring these secretions to a circus ape that becomes "a human form of animal instinct," as the film describes it, Walters enacts a Freudian reversal. He transposes the sexual hysteria that he himself has diagnosed back into the metaphorical terms of the circus and the freak show that were used by Freud's patients. The film erases the distinction between the circus and the surgery by cutting between these two otherwise antithetical spaces, while at the same time linking them by way of a dialogue overlap that showcases a form of carnival barking that applies to both situations: "You are about to see what no human has seen before."[25] In *Captive Wild Woman*, Walters's scientific methods amount to a form of diabolical showmanship that is enacted on the female body.

Walters is unable to prevent the return of Dorothy's repressed desire, which once embodied in the gorilla-woman is able to run amok to the anticipated excitement and terror of the spectator.[26] Freud's accounts of the contradictory emotions experienced by the hysteria patients could be linked to Noël Carroll's theory regarding the pleasure derived from "art-horror." He sees it as a "curious admixture of attraction and repulsion" experienced simultaneously at the category violation inherent to monstrous figures.[27] As discussed above, the bifurcation of the gorilla-woman in narrative and promotional strategies (centering upon her "gorgeous body hiding the horrors of a jungle giant") fits both Carroll's model (we are simultaneously attracted to and repulsed by the horror monster) and Freud's (the hysteria patient is simultaneously afraid of and fascinated by her body's "strange desires").

This conflation of "jungle giant" and women's emergent desires is also inherent to the jungle adventure films of the 1930s, according to Rhona Berenstein. She asserts that films such as *Trader Horn* (1931) and *The Blonde Captive* (1932) "associate awakening female sexuality with women who make their way through the jungle."[28] It could be suggested that in *Captive Wild Woman* the jungle adventure film's metaphorical locale is internalized in the body of the gorilla-woman—the materialization of Dorothy's awakening female sexuality. The two readings are not mutually exclusive, however. The jungle adventure films' brand of colonial discourse, which conflates the geographical and sexual other, was also appropriated by Freud in his metaphor of the "dark continent" of female sexuality.[29] Disturbingly this process of othering was imposed not only on *Captive Wild Woman*'s gorilla-woman but also on the actress who portrays her. The pressbook conflates Acquanetta with the "savage" character she portrays, describing her as "Acquanetta—A Sensation in Savagery!" and "the shockingly savage screen beauty Acquanetta."[30] This extension of the "dark continent" metaphor to Acquanetta can be linked to her disputed ethnic status, as exploited in the film's promotional campaign. A pressbook article explains that "unpredictable Acquanetta furnishes another surprise for film fans. She is the surprising young lady who, posing as Venezuelan, captured Hollywood as she captured Broadway." The article refers to the fictional ethnic identity of the "Venezuelan Volcano" that the Native American actress was encouraged to adopt, allegedly by William Randolph Hearst. This was the image that got her a contract at Universal in 1942.[31]

This latinization of Acquanetta's image was in keeping with wider developments of the "Good Neighbor policy" era, when Hollywood's output increasingly invested in Latin American (or seemingly) stars and locales in order to attract this market that was unaffected by the war.[32] Ella Shohat and Robert Stam argue that this discursive linking of Latin American women with "verbal epithets evoking tropical heat, passion and spice"—other examples include Lupe Velez, the "Mexican Spitfire," Olga San Juan, the "Puerto Rican Pepperpot," and Marie Antoinette-Pons, the "Cuban Hurricane"—plays into the aforementioned discourses that link the colonized to the biological rather than the cultural, evoking protean images of a (sexually) ungovernable force of nature.[33] This is certainly part of the story, though the most popular Latin stars such as Velez and Carmen Miranda infused the tempestuous and fiery stereotype with a theatricality, excessiveness, and self-consciousness that drew attention to the distinctly cultural dimensions of these representations. Although this type of exoticization was seen as a productive wartime ploy, certain sections of the critical community condemned the racism of *Captive Wild Woman*'s narrative as counterproductive to the Allied war effort. Despite the film's attempt to condemn the megalomaniac Dr. Walters through his alignment with Nazi science, the liberal newspaper *PM* protested that the film draws upon those same "Nazi race theories." If the proposition that the only partially successful experiment should produce a woman of ambiguous ethnic origin were not offensive enough, the *PM* reviewer suggests, the film goes even further by inserting a transformation scene that "changes a Hollywood glamour girl into an ape and vice versa with the Negro stage inserted right where Hitler says."[34] The film was also challenged in at least one letter to the Bureau of Motion Pictures, but that body ultimately refused to condemn the movie officially.[35] These race theories, which tied sexual instinct with heredity—and hence also with eugenics and various forms of racism—drew upon the perversion-heredity-degenerescence system in a manner that Michel Foucault has since argued was rigorously opposed by Freud himself.[36] The film's generic hybridity is therefore tempered with this corresponding hybridization of scientific methods, which was seen, even on release, as "morbid and neurotic—as . . . in some pre-Nazi German films."[37]

In addition to the increasing popularization of Freudian psychoanalysis—including its incorporation into Hollywood's narrative strategies—*Captive Wild Woman* was produced at a time when women (particularly young women like Beth's younger sister, Dorothy) were being inundated with contradictory discourses about their bodies and their roles in social life.[38] They were encouraged to imitate sexualized pinups that would inspire soldiers to win the war overseas but simultaneously accused of being the oversexual creatures who were losing the battle at home. The images of the cheesecake pinup and war worker (embodied in the symbolic figure of Rosie the Riveter) were celebrated, but their hybrid manifestation in the figure of the "victory girl" was seen as a direct threat to the war effort. For example, the *Dallas Morning News* protested that "teen-age girls are losing the fight for the future in the camouflaged battlegrounds of juke joints, midnight streets, hotel rooms and highways."[39] Therefore, the issue of young women's sexuality and bodily discipline became intimately conjoined with vociferous debates about women's contributions to winning the war; of course, the double entendre of "losing it" extends the metaphor of the pinup girl waiting virtuously for the soldiers' return. This deployment of discourse told women to see themselves as simultaneously objects of fascination ("beautiful body") and disgust ("hiding the horrors of a jungle giant"); they were constructed as both hero and villain of the home-front war effort.

Though *Cat People* extends considerable sympathy toward the tragic Irena—unable to synthesize these twin demands of desirability and productivity—*Captive Wild Woman*'s female monster is characterized as the result of sexual dysfunction rather than the inability to balance the contradictory requirements of wartime. Correspondingly, the gorilla-woman's rival, Beth (played by the more typical scream queen Ankers), represents a more traditional sense of femininity than Alice, the strong and independent "other woman" in *Cat People*. While Alice is engaged in war work in the shipping industry, Beth is employed as a secretary at the circus (a more feminine leisurely role), and it is made clear that she is incapable of replacing her man in the ring. When she overreacts to the potential danger posed to Fred, a passing cleaner tells her, "Don't get panicky, that's the first thing to learn in animal training." The emotional Beth does not know the first thing about lion taming, but the supernaturally strong Paula is more than able to take on this masculine occupation. As explained, though, her ability to take on this most male of roles is codified as the product of female sexual dysfunction, not wartime contingency.

Correspondingly, media discourses celebrating the realization that women's bodies were equally strong and capable as men's when it came to heavy industry were reversed in a sinister backlash. Rumors were spread in factories in 1943 that riveting caused breast cancer and a condition called "riveter's ovaries," thus aligning these unfeminine jobs with female sexual dysfunction and sterility.[40] Such discourses attempted to reinstate the myth of the unreliable and vulnerable female body while simultaneously threatening to withdraw women's biological function of childbirth. On a narrative level, *Captive Wild Woman* appears to correspond with this discursive construction of a biologically determined proper feminine role and therefore, arguably, the gender politics of earlier horror and jungle adventures. The film's later promotion, however, like that of *Son of Dracula*, attempts to stress the expansion of women's roles as a positive and productive wartime development.

"The New Temptress of Terror": *Son of Dracula*'s Gendered Power Inversions

In his aforementioned review of *Captive Wild Woman*, the *Dallas Morning News* reviewer identifies the link between shifts in women's roles onscreen and wider changes in women's jobs in the workforce on the American home front. Although, as suggested, the narrative inspiration for the film may lie in generic precursors in 1930s horror and jungle adventures, the publicity department was keen to promote the timely angle of women's changing roles both on screen and off. The pressbook for *Captive Wild Woman* boasts that Acquanetta is "the first Hollywood actress to undergo 'horror treatment' in a Hollywood studio plaster shop," a selling point emphasized in half the featured articles.[41] The pressbook also highlights that "no feminine star has essayed the parts dared by this new heartquake of thrills and beauty!" The implication is that this depiction of monstrous femininity breaks new ground for women and is yet another daring wartime occupation of a previously exclusively male role.

This angle is pushed much further in the campaign for *Son of Dracula*, which was produced at roughly the same time as *Captive Wild Woman* but was not released until the end of 1943. The pressbook heralded the infiltration of women into more important roles in perceived male genres during the war, proffering, "There are two feminine leads—Louise Allbritton and Evelyn Ankers, in Universal's 'Son of Dracula,' a horror drama which once would have been considered exclusively a male province." Attributing the phenomenon partially to wartime movie manpower shortages, this publicity article, entitled "Movie Doors Now Open to Taller Actresses," claims that statistical evidence backs up the assertion that leading ladies are "taller than several years ago" and that "height has become almost a prerequisite for those parts."[42] This article makes explicit the link between wartime transformations in the American social body and the literal transformation of women's bodies onscreen and beyond. The media's celebration of the increasingly capable and corporeal wartime woman is literalized here in a proposed physical transformation toward the Amazon ideal; the article continues, "Measuring up to a screen role has become a physical as well as professional qualification of Hollywood's leading woman."[43] In a number of further pressbook articles this extension of female leads in horror films is constituted as positive and appealing to prospective audiences. A suggested lobby card for *Son of Dracula* introduces Louise Allbritton as "The New Temptress of Terror," whose "unusual role in this picture is Box Office Bonanza and should be played to the hilt."

A comparable article from the "Showmanship" section commends that while most performers rise to stardom through "beauty, personality or ability[,] Louise Allbritton possesses all three of these. And she adds a fourth . . . a deep and realistic quality of MENACE!" This article proposes that Allbritton's characterization represents a supplement rather than merely a shift, an expansion of the multiple and complementary possibilities of female representation. Furthermore, an article in the "Publicity" section celebrates Allbritton's "refusal to confine herself to romantic roles," stressing that this "sensational role" is in keeping with her previous choices of "lawyer, aviatrix, radio writer and enemy agent."[44] These new roles for women in horror are codified as progressive and promoted as a unique selling tool that differentiates this new horror cycle from previous generic utterances. Such discourses appear to actively interpellate female spectators by linking their own experiences of expanding employment opportunities to the actresses' choices to portray monstrous characters typically played by men.

As the previous chapter explained, shifts in female employment—particularly women relocating or commuting to urban centers for war work—had effects on female cinemagoing, encouraging Universal to embrace the wartime phenomenon of the "unescorted femme" in marketing its films. A *Variety* advertisement to promote the held-over *Frankenstein Meets the Wolf Man* (1943) centers the staging of a nationwide exploitation stunt in which a prize was offered to any woman who dared watch the midnight screening of the film alone. Although Diane Waldman claims that this "ominous" contest exploited female fears and experiences of harassment and attack, Rhona Berenstein questions her reductive analysis. She agrees that this stunt plays on conventional assumptions about women in patriarchal culture but argues that in doing so it exploits, and to an extent subverts, gender stereotypes pertaining to horror spectatorship.[45] Berenstein's more playful interpretation of the stunt is backed up by a subsequent ad that features the contest held at the Fox Theater in

St. Louis, where the winner was an eighty-year-old grandmother, Margaret McHale. Below a picture of her sitting alone in the auditorium is a copy of her contest-winning letter that mocks, "In fact, if Frankenstein and the Wolf Man were there in person, it wouldn't make any difference to me. You could get Dracula too, and I'd sit and we'd have a good poker game. I'm not squeamish and I like to play poker."[46] Like the St. Louis exhibitor, the marketing department chose to embrace the carnivalesque spirit of gendered and generational inversion provoked by McHale's letter, rather than select a story connoting genuine threat or menace. This wartime promotional ploy—coming at a time when more women were visiting urban cinemas such as the Fox on their own—directly interpellates women by challenging them to disprove gender stereotypes.

The "dare to see the movie alone" stunt encourages the subversion of gender assumptions pertaining to horror spectatorship—albeit through the exploitation of these very assumptions—but Universal also attempted to expand its "woman's angle" for other horror narratives by hybridizing them with perceived female genres. In August 1943 *Film Daily*'s lead story detailed that "with the percentage of feminine film patrons considerably increased under war-time conditions" and the subsequent success of "femme appeal pix during the 1942–1943 season," such as RKO's *Cat People*, "Universal [had] fortified many of its recent attractions to score with women patrons, and was repaid via large accruing 'takes.'"[47] The story pointed to the Universal Technicolor remake of *Phantom of the Opera* (1943)—a $1.75 million "combination of splendor, terror and musical drama"—as one such film "which women would enjoy in the coming weeks."[48] The trade paper's subsequent review reiterated that Universal had "widened [*Phantom of the Opera*'s] appeal to women and those who are not out-and-out shocker fans."[49]

As a result, Universal attempted to replicate *Phantom of the Opera*'s generically hybrid "femme appeal," though minus the budget and the splendor, with *The Mad Ghoul* (1943), which was double-billed with *Son of Dracula*. *The Mad Ghoul*, perhaps surprisingly, combines a mad scientist narrative and backstage musical plot; the *Washington Post* saw this as "an innovation in corpse operas"—a generic demarcation that, perhaps unsurprisingly, did not catch on as a local genre.[50] In the film, the eponymous character's murder spree is crosscut with his ex-fiancée's (Evelyn

Ankers again) celebrated concert tour, allowing her to perform three full classical songs and realize a new romance with a fellow musician. The gendered appeals of the two narrative strains are embodied in two reporters, a female culture critic and a male newshound, whose stories become entwined because, as the male reporter reveals, "your girl and my ghoul have been playing the same tour." Although *The Mad Ghoul* and *Phantom of the Opera* do not contrast their independent career women (albeit with careers coded as distinctly feminine) with female monsters, the infusion of tropes from the musical genre and tragic romance narratives indicates a wider shift toward the purposeful targeting of female audiences *Film Daily* suggests.[51]

Though *Son of Dracula* does not make the concession of songs, its tragic narrative of doomed love could perhaps more purposefully be defined as a "corpse opera" than *The Mad Ghoul.* It updates the Dracula myth by transferring its narrative to a contemporary setting in the American South, as well as by centering a manipulative femme fatale figure who plays off the affections of her two lovers; it has been characterized in contemporary criticism as "inspired equal measures by Bram Stoker and James M. Cain."[52] The film's trailer lured spectators with the promise "You'll shudder at the screen's most fascinating woman vampire luring men with cold beauty and the promise of immortality," while barely mentioning the tepid threat of Count Alucard, whose reversed moniker (Dracula backward) almost self-consciously prefigures the film's gendered power inversion.

The publicity for *Son of Dracula* is significant in that Louise Allbritton's "Temptress of Terror" character is centered in the poster campaign—both visually and in the taglines—over the title character played by the film's biggest star, Lon Chaney Jr. (see figure 8). Although the film was seemingly conceived with Chaney and his eponymous role in mind, he is forced into the background of the posters. Instead, Allbritton is centered in a pinup shot that, like those exploited in the *Cat People* campaign, ambiguously positions her as simultaneously victim and threat. The empathy afforded to the female monster character is reiterated in the most prominent taglines of "Blood on Her Lips! Doom in Her Eyes!" and "Bride of a Vampire! Cursed by the Kiss of her Monstrous Mate! . . . To Live Forever! . . . To Kill Forever! . . . A Beautiful Beast!" Despite the film's title, both publicity articles and poster campaign build up the female monster

FIGURE 8 *Son of Dracula* promotes its central "Temptress of Terror."

character at the expense of Dracula's son and Chaney's admittedly flawed performance of him.

Despite the centrality of the female monster in promotional and, to some extent, narrative terms, the script (devised before *Cat People*'s success) does not adopt the triangular structure of two women competing for the same man. Instead it "is more of the same," reviving Universal's classic horror model, established in *Dracula* (1931), of two men competing for the soul of one woman—at least initially, until her soul is deemed as irredeemable.[53] It is appropriate, however, that Chaney should be relegated in the promotional campaign, as he is outacted and outwitted by Allbritton's opportunist female vamp(ire), Kay Caldwell. Kay, having supplanted her father as the head of the family plantation, manipulates Dracula's progeny into doing her bidding, with the intention of later killing him and gaining eternal life for her and her fiancé. The shift in the balance of power from male to female vampire is realized when Kay's hypnotic gaze wills the count to glide across a misty swamp toward her; he is drawn to her by a desire powerful enough to cloud his usually supernaturally acute judgment. Although the love triangle centers, at least initially, on Kay and her male rivals, she is still doubled with another woman, her sister, Claire, thus fulfilling this trope of the female monster model. Again Evelyn Ankers portrays the contrasting good model of femininity, one characterized as more practical and progressive; Ankers's usual tailored knee-length suits are juxtaposed to Allbritton's impractical flowing gowns. Kay is notably infantilized in the film through her refusal to leave the family home, Dark Oaks. She has changed her father's will so that Claire receives the significantly greater assets of cash and security, and Kay, upon her own request, gets only the plantation house where, she wants to "live forever."[54]

Ultimately, however, Kay fears she may have to kill Claire, and in doing so the last remnants of her own good self, in order to "consummate what might be called an unholy alliance [that] will destroy her own soul and Frank's." It is an alliance that is codified in sexual terms and made more unholy for its adulterous overtones. When Kay appears supernaturally in Frank's jail cell—following his accidental shooting and killing of her—she explains, "Count Alucard is immortal. Through him I gained immortality. Through me you will gain immortality." Frank, who is more shocked by the prospect of adultery than vampirism, responds, "But you're married,

Kay," refuses this libidinous ménage à trois, however. Of course Kay must eventually face her hegemonic elimination, in this case on a funeral pyre tended by her ultimately incorruptible but seemingly inconsolable fiancé. But for seventy-eight of the film's eighty minutes, Kay controls the destiny of all involved. Through Kay—a character so resourceful and powerful that she even outwits a Dracula—the film provides, as Basinger asserts, a "device for telling a woman that she ought to conform to the roles society approves for her at the same time as it allowed her the freedom to see and possibly identify, however temporarily, however tangentially, with a female character who did not conform or follow the rules."[55] In this regard the film certainly fits the female monster model, and, as explained, the attractions of this transgressive female character were central to the film's marketing.

Though the film's marketing identifies Allbritton's character as a sign of wartime progress in regard to expanding female representation, the film's narrative links Kay to the degeneracy, both epistemologically and ideologically, of a premodern era. Kay's "morbid" interest in the occult is not characterized as the necessary, even productive female counterdiscourse of Lewton's films and the 1944 prestige productions they inspired. In fact, it is characterized as an infectious and emasculating threat to America's war effort. Although the Bureau of Motion Pictures insisted that *Son of Dracula* "has no bearing whatever on the War Information Program, domestic or overseas," the film's central tenet of a woman's fear of her fiancé's impending death and its final message of sacrifice for the good of the wider community has implicit wartime allusions.[56] Count Alucard accepted Kay's invitation to come to America because his Hungarian homeland is "dry and desolate. The soil is red with the blood of a thousand races." A visiting Hungarian professor concurs that "what was once a happy productive region is now barren waste"; that is why Alucard has come to America, to "drain it dry like he did his own home land." Kay's wish to prevent harm coming to her fiancé has allowed a foreign threat—one explicitly linked to racially inspired conflict—to infiltrate American soil. As in other female monster films, the penetrated body of the female lead stands in for the old country as the last "exotic repository of a non-scientific knowledge, a battery of beliefs and institutions" previously embodied in the classical horror mise-en-scène of old Europe.[57] This metaphorical centering of the female body as the site of potential invasion by a foreign threat has a clear wartime resonance and was replicated in a number of journalistic columns.[58] As Agnes Meyer wrote in her wartime column for the *Washington Post*, the "sex epidemic . . . infects the whole community. . . . The girls, moreover, are the aggressors, and pursue not only sailors but war-workers."[59]

Kay's actions are constituted as a threat to the virility of the masculine American nation—as Dr. Brewster (Frank Craven) explains, "a younger country, stronger, more virile" than its European counterparts—and therefore counterproductive to the war effort. This female vampire's unpatriotic infection of the nation could be related to the aforementioned fears about young women spreading STDs and also, albeit in reverse, the aforementioned debates about the possible sterility of wartime women's bodies. Beyond these specific allusions, *Son of Dracula* links Kay to a morbid and outdated metaphysics that does not correspond with the wartime reconstitution of womanhood. The film proposes that women on the home front must willingly and maturely be guided by the same spirit of sacrifice as their partners on the battlefields. Through its narrative of an old-country threat lurking behind the facade of the everyday, *Son of Dracula* invokes what could be described as the art-horror experience of war on the American home front—more conceptual nightmare than lived reality for most. This obviously provides a somewhat patronizing image of women's war involvement, considering that tens of thousands of women had volunteered for the armed services by this point and that the female corps had received full army status from the War Department in mid-1943. This metaphorical centering of the female body as simultaneously threat, weapon, and motivation for the home-front battle discloses *Son of Dracula*'s dialogue with its early wartime context.

Universal's Other Weird Women: Serial Production of Female Monsters

The year 1944 saw Universal expand its offering of "horror queens" through sequelization of its proprietary characters (*Captive Wild Woman*) and incorporation of female monsters into other franchises, including the Mummy and Sherlock Holmes films. It also experimented by incorporating female monster tropes into adjacent genres such as mysteries and fantasy films.

As a result, critics stressed that Universal was "deviating considerably from established horror formula" by, for example, introducing a sympathetic female mummy character and a supernatural romance narrative into its Mummy series in 1944.[60] In *The Mummy's Ghost* (1944) Ramsay Ames plays an Egyptian college student (curiously researching ancient Egypt in Massachusetts) whose body is taken over by the soul of a three-thousand-year-old Egyptian princess, Ananka. Reception highlighted Ames as representative of Universal's increasing "variety in horror queens," spanning traditional victims, resilient heroines, and tragic monster characters.[61] Princess Ananka was reincarnated six months later in the form of Virginia Christine in *The Mummy's Curse* (1944). Universal also demonstrated its commitment to the female monster formula through its consolidation of its gorilla-woman horror franchise. The genetic hybrid Paula, a.k.a. the Captive Wild Woman, appeared in two sequels in 1944 and 1945, making her at least as persistent as other stock horror characters in the wartime schedule of Universal's horror unit.[62] The first sequel, *Jungle Woman* (1944), was promoted in publicity material and the trade press as the follow-up to the "earlier, successful horror tale," "picking up where *Captive Wild Woman* left off in the shenanigans of an ape who (or which) turns into a beautiful girl by the injection of special serum."[63] *Jungle Woman*'s posters also reiterated its precursor's bifurcated taglines—"flesh of beauty . . . soul of Satan" and "In love . . . a rapturous beauty! In fury . . . a murderous beast!"—and the "cheesecake" poses of Acquanetta in leopard-print sarongs. Resultantly, the *New York Herald Tribune* condescended to say that "Universal has left the door open just a tiny bit for another sequel—in case the devotees of the supernatural demand an encore of the ape woman's life and loves."[64] Addressing an issue far more serious than this calculated attempt to create a new female monster series, *PM* again attacked the "annual moral outrage" of the ape woman series for its racism and opined that, instead of further sequels, the film should inspire "a law against propounding Nazi race theories."[65]

The female monster character also infiltrated less controversial series and neighboring subgenres produced by Universal's other studio-based units. These included those produced by the Sherlock Holmes unit under the supervision of Roy William Neill, the Inner Sanctum Mysteries (1943–1945), and the Technicolor jungle fantasy *Cobra Woman* (1944).

In January 1944, the "luridly titled picture" *The Spider Woman* confounded critics who discovered that "this is nothing more than a new turn with Sherlock Holmes."[66] The *New York Journal-American* warned, "Don't be misled by the title. . . . I don't know why they took Sherlock Holmes out of the billing. It may have been because they thought *The Spider Woman* would better attract the thrill trade."[67] The titular focus on the female monster character was seen, therefore, as the film's key selling point, particularly at a moment when "horror pictures are so hot at the box office they've had to water cool theatre cash registers."[68] Universal even upped the budget for the Holmes pictures from *The Spider Woman* onward "to give them added production value and a wider appeal."[69] Rather than dismiss the movie's generic hybridity as merely a calculated ploy, *Daily Variety* commended it, asserting that "Universal's new Sherlock Holmes film carries the imprint of past successes plus chiller action all its own."[70] Others concurred that while Holmes "lurk[ed] behind" the title, the film downplayed his "uncanny powers of deduction. . . . This time the entertainment springs from horror thrills."[71] The *New York Post* commented, "These murders are 'feline' not 'canine.' It is a 'female Moriarty,' a 'femme fatale.'"[72] What's more, in congruence with other female monster characters, this female Moriarty was celebrated for her complexity and ambiguity, with the *Hollywood Reporter* musing, "How Miss Sondergaard can screen so beautifully and yet so menacingly is one of the delights of the film."[73] The film set a precedent for Holmes's increasing encounters with horror and ambiguous femme fatales, including the eponymous *Woman in Green* (1945) promoted with the question "temptress of pleasure or mistress of murder?"

Elements of the female monster film were also central to Universal's Inner Sanctum (1943–1945) series of mysteries. The name was licensed from Simon and Schuster, whose 1930s suspense novels had been adapted and popularized for the high-rating radio drama *Inner Sanctum Mysteries* (1941–1952). The show employed Hollywood horror stars such as Boris Karloff and Peter Lorre and horrific sound effects pioneered by the earlier *Lights Out* (1934–1947) radio serial.[74] Universal used only the name of the popular radio program, however, instead commissioning new screenplays from contract players such as Edward Dein (also *Jungle Woman* and *Soul of a Monster*) and occasionally adapting other sources such as Fritz Leiber's debut novel, *Conjure Wife* (1943). Nearer to the RKO model than Universal's other horror output, the films relied more on psychological horror or, as the distorted head floating in a crystal ball that introduced each film suggested, "a strange, fantastic world controlled by a mass of living, pulsating flesh: the mind." In addition to its more subtle or psychological approach the series, at least initially, adopted the triangular structure of two women competing for one man—in all cases the ubiquitous Lon Chaney Jr. In so doing these initial films set up an antagonism between two competing women, with the category of good and bad woman in the struggle significantly blurred. In the first film, *Calling Dr. Death* (which went into production in mid-1943, well after the box-office success of *Cat People* had been realized, and was released in December), Chaney plays Dr. Steele, who suffers a blackout following his cruel and unfaithful wife's murder. He fears that he may have killed her himself but ultimately reveals under hypnosis that the murderer is his secretary, Stella (Patricia Morison), who is in love with him.

It is the second title in the Inner Sanctum series, *Weird Woman* (1944), that most blatantly assimilates the tropes of the female monster cycle into an existing text (Leiber's aforementioned novel) and its promotion. In the film Chaney is miscast as the sociology professor Norman Reed—a "mental giant" according to one of his colleagues—who becomes embroiled in a fatal love triangle after returning from a research trip in the South Seas with his new bride, Paula (Anne Gwynne). Paula is the daughter of American missionaries but was raised and trained in "weird pagan rituals" by the high priestess of a tropical island. When Norman rejects his old flame and work colleague Ilona (Evelyn Ankers), she conspires to convince everyone, including the recently wed couple, that Norman's recent success is due to the magical powers of his "witch wife." Ilona's manipulations result in the suicide of an elderly professor and manslaughter of a jealous student, but the elderly professor's wife (Elizabeth Russell) ultimately discovers the deception and tricks Ilona into confessing. She does this by taking Ilona into her confidence, explaining a dream she had that the one responsible for the deaths would die in thirteen days, at one minute past twelve. Ilona is "accidentally" strangled by vines while attempting to flee as the clock ticks down to this precise fated moment, thus fulfilling the promise of the supposedly fabricated dream.

The presence of the Lewton regular Elizabeth Russell is but one debt to RKO's female monster films. *Weird Woman* also transposes Leiber's novel to a Caribbean setting, at least initially, and incorporates extensive scenes of voodoo ritual, a fantastic resolution, and ambiguous female characterization, all highly reminiscent of *I Walked with a Zombie*. Resultantly the *Hollywood Reporter* mused, "Due to the conduct of several feminine members of the cast there may be some doubt as to which is playing the title role, since all qualify."[75] Likewise the New York papers saw the film as part of a recent "series of psychological horror pictures that send real thrills and chills up and down one's spine," clearly aimed at "the 'horror' picture addicts—and there appears to be plenty of them."[76] The *New York Times* also saw the film as heir to the suggested psychological horror of Lewton but bemoaned its derivative nature, commenting, "It certainly is weird what some women—and some film studios—will do in a fit of desperation."[77]

Universal was also prepared to invest big budgets into female monster narratives in order to cash in on the cycle. The Technicolor jungle fantasy *Cobra Woman*, via split-screening, pits Maria Montez against herself as good and bad twin sisters battling for the affections of Ramu (John Hall). This love triangle between identical twin sisters—one a "snake dancing high priestess," the other "her kindly twin sister"—and the male hero replicates the sexual dynamic of the female monster film.[78] The thematic centrality of the "Pagan Cobra Cult" and the obfuscation engendered through the split-screen technique reproduce the supernatural overtones and ambiguity surrounding the bifurcated female lead(s) of the other films in the cycle. The film was marketed with the taglines "Pagan Witch or Weird Woman of Rapture?" and "Temptress of Terror . . . As Quick on the Kiss as the Kill." In addition to the female bifurcation, animal transmutation themes, and romantic triangulation representative of the cycle, *Cobra Woman* brought in Universal horror personnel in the form of Robert Siodmak (as director) and Chaney (in a supporting role). The film was produced by George Waggner, fresh from his success with the aforementioned Technicolor horror-crossover *Phantom of the Opera*, thus stressing Universal's financial and creative commitment to such projects.

Resultantly the *Hollywood Reporter* pointed out the film's "double-barreled box office draw. . . . *Cobra Woman* combines two formulas that have coined fortunes for Universal. Into the lush, tropical backgrounds where Maria Montez is accustomed to distort herself in eye-watering

Technicolor, a definite note of horror is strongly injected."[79] The *New York Post* reviewer was more critical of the film's calculated generic hybridity, mocking, "I wouldn't mind seeing a boxing kangaroo, a polar bear and Bela Lugosi, quite mad and scientific, in the next one, just to make it complete."[80] In addition to the film's acknowledged incorporation of themes and tropes from popular horror cycles, it can also be seen, like the other female monster films, to be reflecting wider concerns and contradictions surrounding wartime womanhood. Lucy Fischer proposes that the film's theme of a tyrannical matriarchal society reflects male anxieties during the war "when women were alone on the home front, left to function collectively without their men."[81] Preempting Fischer's retrospective claims, in 1944 the Universal publicity department made specific reference to the film's allegorical transposition of a totalitarian wartime threat onto the categorically unstable female body. The pressbook emphasizes the "parallel between the situation in *Cobra Woman* and any occupied nation[;] it is worth noting that before the final fadeout, the forces of Good in the person of Maria Montez . . . triumph over Evil, also in the person of Montez."[82] In congruence with earlier discussions, the publicity material explains how the split-screen technique allows for the metaphorical centering of the female body as the battleground where the war will be won or lost, to be literalized through the bifurcation of Montez's good and bad sisters. *Cobra Woman*'s allusions to American women's symbolically central wartime role were, therefore, clearly understood, at least by the team working on the film's postproduction publicity.[83] Following the release of the Universal productions discussed in this section *Variety* reported, "It pays to horrify according to statisticians at Universal where approximately $10,000,000 profits have been made by the company's chiller dillers."[84] Embracing these financial incentives, other studios reoriented their production schedules in order to reproduce the successes of Universal and RKO.

"Two Queens of Horror" for the Price of One: Columbia Consolidates the Cycle

Columbia's 1944 "horror double-bill" of *Cry of the Werewolf* (1944) and *The Soul of a Monster* (1944) is a clear indicator of the consolidation of the female monster cycle. As the pressbook for the two films explains, "For the many fans who have been clamoring more and more of late for their favorite film-fare, the horror story, Columbia Pictures is currently offering . . . two queens of horror who pierce the mysteries of the half world."[85] Perceiving a favorable market for female-centered horror, Columbia shelved its planned sequel to the Bela Lugosi vehicle *Return of the Vampire* (1943)—a shameless Universal imitation that had double-billed with the Boris Karloff comedy-horror *The Boogie Man Will Get You* (1943)—in favor of these titles showcasing "two female monsters."[86] Realizing that horror names previously assumed to be bankable were no guarantee of success, Columbia instead borrowed heavily from the plots and style of Lewton's two hits, *Cat People* and *I Walked with a Zombie*, promising "outstanding realism . . . despite the supernatural themes" of ancient gypsy rites and zombies, while focusing its poster campaign on the "fiendishness" of its female leads.[87] Moreover, both films reflect the female monster cycle's transformation of the dominant horror film dynamic: the triangular structure of two women competing for the same man. Both films also strive for the subtlety and ambiguity that had become associated with Lewton's films, appropriating his use of ambivalent introductory quotes, albeit ones that paradoxically made identical statements about their supposed dialogic intentions. *The Soul of a Monster* opens with the prelude "To many of you [the story] may be a grim reality, to others, perhaps just a dream"; *Cry of the Werewolf* reiterates, "Perhaps our story is something that has lived on in a person's memory or perhaps just a legend." Both appropriate other stylistic touches introduced in *Cat People*; most blatantly, the famous bus technique is exploited at extraordinary length in *The Soul of a Monster*, where a derivative scene features three bus moments before the stalker finally (and anticlimactically) reveals himself. This scene encouraged one reviewer to complain that the "suspense is supposed to be unbearable. Actually the length of the walk is exhausting."[88] Despite the clearly derivative nature of these films in drawing on the style, plots, and character types from Lewton's films, few links have been made in horror scholarship.

In *Monsters and Mad Scientists* (1989) Andrew Tudor groups *The Soul of a Monster* together with *The Seventh Victim* (1943) as examples of wartime texts with supernatural, external, dependent threats but states that "apart from some ambiguity about the nature of supernatural forces involved . . . and a tendency to feature women as central characters, there is no real pattern apparent within this group."[89] Although he hints here at some of the key tropes of the female monster cycle, Tudor's preoccupation with categorizing films by types of threat—supernatural/secular, internal/external, dependent/autonomous—means that he fails to grasp wider trends across the period independent of the specificities of threat. Like David Skal, Tudor sees *Cry of the Werewolf* as "spawned" by *The Wolf Man* (1941) rather than the more recent female-centered transmutation films that reviewers at the time perceived as its influences.[90] Tudor's account of the forties as a period of decline for horror in which the only innovation in the genre was in the "literary" films produced by Val Lewton is, as has been explained, fairly representative of horror scholarship. Although it is difficult to disagree with his comments about the poor quality of some of the films he selects, he is wrong in contending that the Lewton films "hardly represent a dominating and influential genre development."[91] On its release the reception of *Cry of the Werewolf* clearly positioned the film in relation to the ongoing female monster cycle—one initiated by the success of *Cat People* and exploited by Universal in its subsequent sequels and series.

In her review for the *New York Journal-American* Rose Pelswick sees *Cry of the Werewolf* as part of recent genre developments, identifying the film as part of an ongoing cycle. She comments that "it seems like just the other day that the Rialto Theatre concerned itself with the story of a gorilla that turned into a girl named Acquanetta and went around killing various members of the cast."[92] The *New York Post* is even more explicit about the derivative nature of the film and its position within a female-centered horror cycle instigated by *Cat People* and *Captive Wild Woman.* Commenting upon the final transformation scene from wolf to woman, the reviewer condescends: "What a novelty it would have been, and really mysterious, to fade back to a gorilla or a black panther, though possibly an infringement of copyright on Universal or RKO Radio properties."[93] Unlike modern critics, none of the contemporary reviewers mention *The Wolf Man* in relation to *Cry of the Werewolf*; rather the film is positioned as the continuation of the cycle of female monster films.

As with the contemporary reception, the films' billing, publicity stories, star biographies, and story outlines foreground the self-styled "queens of horror" as the films' most marketable features. Congruently, the *Cry of the Werewolf* and *Soul of a Monster* double-bill posters center the female monster characters in the taglines and images, mostly with extreme facial close-ups. The representative bifurcated tagline "Terrifying . . . fascinating. Two female monsters in two chilling horror dramas! One . . . half woman, half wolf! One . . . ghostly leader of the ghastly dead!" stresses the films' contradictory appeals. This ambiguity is pushed even further, however, for these wartime female monster characters, becoming a conscious selling ploy in studio marketing. Another split-screen poster shows a melancholy Nina Foch, looking more likely to kiss than kill Stephen Crane, under the slogan "As a werewolf she wanted blood," and a glamorous close-up of Rose Hobart (albeit with an unrepresentative catchphrase that refers to Jeanne Bates's character). In combination with the images, the main tagline of "Two queens of horror explode a double dose of TNTerror in your heart!" exploits the ambiguity of the connotations of "heart" to again propose the simultaneous emotional attraction and disquieting horror that these women will provoke (see figure 9). Opening up the intended dual appeal of this metaphor further, the "Publicity" section explains that "reports from preview audiences [for *The Soul of a Monster*] say that in your wildest dreams you have never seen a woman so beautiful . . . and so deadly. Rose [Hobart] plays this fiendish female with her hands on the audience's throat and heart."[94]

Cry of the Werewolf's typically bifurcated tagline "As a woman she wanted love! As a werewolf she wanted blood!" perfectly encapsulates Altman's assertion of studio marketing's simultaneous appeal to both sexes—"something for the men" (blood) and "something for the women" (love).[95] As discussed in the previous chapter, this mode of bifurcation appeared to tap into the simultaneous tragedy and excitement of women's lives on the home front, particularly the new opportunities that had arisen for women due to the horrors of war. Of course, many of the resultant employment opportunities involved leading a transitory double life, often of housewife by day and war worker by night, while relocation and loss of partners overseas meant, in many cases, a reorganized social life that was at the same time distressing (because of the absence of loved ones) and enlivening (due to new leisure opportunities). Although the marketing makes these nods toward the potential romance angles of the plot, the multiple genre labels used to describe earlier films in the cycle are discarded in favor of *Cry of the Werewolf*'s blatant positioning, both singly and as part of a double

FIGURE 9 This Columbia double-bill poster highlights the contradictory appeals of its "queens of horror."

bill, as an unequivocal horror text.[96] This less deliberate attempt to incorporate "something for the women" in terms of non-horror-based attractions indicates a change in the studio's perception of women's generic tastes and perhaps even a wider conception of wartime womanhood.

In a variation on a perennial exploitation stunt, the *Cry of the Werewolf* pressbook encourages exhibitors to "challenge a local newspaper woman to sit through the picture alone at midnight" prior to the film's release, with the provoking question "Can she take it?" This stunt continues to play upon gender stereotypes—though of course encouraging women to disprove them—but it is now a female journalist rather than audience member who is challenged. Although clearly patronizing, particularly considering that 127 female war correspondents were risking their lives overseas by 1944, this "challenge" references the increasing prominence of "newspaper women" (particularly those covering home-front issues, including writing entertainment stories and reviews) who had found new opportunities due to wartime manpower shortages.[97] In a similar vein the "Exploitation" section proposes holding a special afternoon matinee for women; "if women cannot come to the special matinee, they should come at night, only in small groups or with a male escort." Again this patronizing tone is intended as a provocation to women, who, wartime exhibitors reported, were mostly attending cinemas alone or in all-female groups. Though these exhibition ploys draw upon traditional gender assumptions, the "Can she take it?" stunts use the same provocations to target the "hardened" horror fans of both sexes. The pressbook asserts that this double bill would "shock even the most inveterate mystery fans," and "even the hardened addicts of horror films amongst preview audiences have shivered as death stalked an eerie museum." Women and horror fans are interchangeable in the marketing campaign, centered as those most likely to be attracted to the extreme shocks of these female monster films, rather than those who genuinely need alerting to the fact that they may be unable to "take it"—a strategy that would be highly counterproductive.

This purposeful blurring of gendered and generic distinctions caused confusion for some critics. The *New York Times*'s shock at *Cry of the Werewolf*'s "rare reversal of social (and melodramatic) form" in introducing a female werewolf character was specifically triggered by a woman transforming into a wolf—an animal so linked in film and folklore to male (sexual) aggression—rather than a more feminine, feline creature.[98] From Freud's case history of the "Wolf Man" (1914) to Lon Chaney in the 1941 film of the same name to Michael J. Fox as a hereditary hirsute in *Teen Wolf* (1985), lycanthrope narratives have been typically read in scholarship as an analogy for the simultaneous horror and fascination experienced by adolescent males at the physical and mental transformations of puberty. *Cry of the Werewolf* utilizes the werewolf myth for a distinctly female oedipal story, however, with a young Romanian woman attempting to escape a shapeshifting curse passed on through the matriarchal line—a narrative clearly informed by *Cat People.* Like Tudor, Robin Wood argues that the Lewton films are "outside the mainstream development of the horror film [and] have little direct influence on its evolution." *Cat People*, he stresses, "is centered on the repression of female sexuality, in a period where the monster is almost invariably male and phallic."[99] As in Lewton's film, however, the shape-shifting curse in *Cry of the Werewolf* is codified in terms of unleashed female sexuality, though Wood would probably question whether this film highlighted repressed female sexuality as the cause of the horror, as in *Cat People*, or identified female sexuality itself as the problem, thus relegating it to a group of more "reactionary" horror texts.[100] The tragic dimensions of Lewton's earlier female monster characters—namely their inability to incorporate the twin demands of productivity and desirability—are certainly present in the character of Celeste, though; as the *New York Post* lamented, Celeste "is not a particularly despicable werewolf. She doesn't want to harm anyone."[101]

In *Cry of the Werewolf* Celeste, a gypsy princess (Nina Foch), kills a leading scholar of the occult, Dr. Morris (Fritz Leiber), because he is about to publish a manuscript that will reveal her werewolf ancestry, on her mother's side. She then becomes involved in a love triangle with the dead professor's son, Bob (Stephen Crane), a scientist doing suitably patriotic chemical research for the government, and the dead professor's female assistant, Elsa (Osa Massen). Elsa is initially the chief suspect (largely because, as one of the policemen puts it, "I get it, she's from Europe") and even confesses when she, like Bob, becomes entranced by Celeste. Following the revelation of her guilt, however, the tragic Celeste is killed by a policeman, who laments, "We're looking at a real phenomenon. An ancient legend come true . . . that wolf used to be a beautiful gypsy girl."

The film's "rare reversal of social form," in its interrogation of issues of female sexuality (whether in a progressive or reactionary sense), can be linked to the specific discursive context of the American home front in 1944.[102] Jane Gaines explains that the slang term "wolf," which had been used to refer to a sexually promiscuous male since World War I, was joined by the female derivative "wolfess" during World War II.[103] Correspondingly, in March 1944 a *Dallas Morning News* headline revealed that "Women Can Be Wolves Also, Police Aver." The article echoed, "All wolves are not men—at least these days, Dallas police are discovering." Most women they picked up on moral charges were not the widely reported teenage victory girls but "older married women—women between 25 and 30 years old." The article went on to explain that "after a few weeks or months, some stay-at-home wives bec[a]me lonesome" and thus sought the "company of servicemen in Dallas taverns, hotels and tourist camps."[104]

The unproductive body of the stay-at-home wife was juxtaposed to the patriotic female war worker, who was considered to be doing all she could to get the American hero home. As discussed in relation to *Son of Dracula*, these debates about the disciplining of the female body became intimately linked with women's contributions to winning the war. Women were encouraged to view their bodies as weapons that could be deployed to either win or lose the home-front battle. In autumn 1943 the American Social Hygiene Association held a conference on female sexual delinquency. It concluded that wartime promiscuity, or "sex hunger," was often motivated by misplaced patriotism and desire for wartime adventure.[105] That same year a U.S. Army medical report stated that American girls in their late teens and early twenties were the army's biggest problem in terms of spreading disease: "While mothers are winning the war in the factories, their daughters are losing it on the streets."[106] Other commentators disagreed. For example, although Agnes Meyer of the *Washington Post* saw these girls as "the aggressors" in this "sex epidemic," she ultimately complained that their mothers, sometimes referred to as "gypsy war wives," were "the children's worst example of intoxication and sexuality, women who before earning high wages were law-abiding citizens."[107] *Cry of the Werewolf*'s depiction of a nomadic girl who turns into a wolf when overcome by primeval urges inherited from a similarly inclined mother would have had a topical resonance for media-savvy spectators. As the *Cry of the Werewolf* poster explains from Celeste's tragic perspective: "My mother terrorized millions. Because of her sins I can never marry. I can't love . . . I must kill!" Her mother is the consummate bad role model.

As these contradiction-fraught newspaper reports indicate, the media increasingly attempted to separate women's wartime experiences, bifurcating the office worker by day and sexual adventurer by night into distinct and separate entities—one feminine yet productive, the other sexually aggressive and unproductive. This bifurcation is made explicit in *Cry of the Werewolf* through the moral contrast of Elsa and Celeste. The night watchman at the museum challenges Elsa, saying, "Why not give up the night work. You're too nice a girl not to be out having a good time. There's plenty of time to be going to work when you're my age." She retorts, "Thank you, Max, but there's some jobs that can't wait until we are older." As with Alice in *Cat People*, whose work in shipbuilding often means late nights at the office, Elsa's war work is clearly contrasted to her double's predatory nighttime pursuits. Celeste is encoded as transgressive both in her predatory pursuit of the engaged Bob and in her blatant adoption of the male role in the proceedings. Having persuaded Bob to drive her home, Celeste flirts with him, asking, "Do you think I'm beautiful, like you'd say, easy on the eye?" She continues, "Bob, you're a little afraid of me. . . . A women likes to have a man a little afraid of her." The female leads in *Cry of the Werewolf* are doubled, but ultimately differentiated, through their relationship to their European homelands. As discussed above, the threat of the old-world European setting of 1930s classic horror becomes internalized in the female body in these 1940s female monster films; this can be, and in *Cobra Woman* was, linked to the wider discursive centering of the female body (specifically the balancing of its proper sexual use) as the battlefield where the war will be won or lost. Significantly, like the good twin in that film, Celeste's good double, Elsa, escaped the irrational belief systems and consequent totalitarian threat of her ancestral home. As Elsa explains, "My father was a magistrate, he asked Dr. Morris to bring me to America. He said there would be a lot of trouble in Europe."

A different but comparable message about women's wartime role is encoded in the Faustian *The Soul of a Monster*. In the film a mysterious woman, Lilyan (Hobart), turns up to revive a famous surgeon on his deathbed after his wife calls on another power to save him. The wife, Anne (Jeanne Bates), has lost her faith in God because her philanthropic husband (George Macready) looks certain to die, even though "murderers who torture and kill millions of people, monsters, live." Although Lilyan saves the doctor, Anne realizes the selfishness of her call for her husband's life to be spared at any cost, thus rediscovering her faith. Anne persuades him to confront Lilyan and ask to reclaim his soul by receiving a "justifiable death." Lilyan shoots him, and the film inexplicably cuts to her being hit by a truck. In a celestial flashback to the opening scene (via a cloudscape) the entire film is revealed as a trompe l'oeil—seemingly Anne's own internal dialogue while on vigil. As a result, she decides against calling upon evil forces, a decision confirmed by her husband's dying words: "When I was a little boy I read something in the Bible, 'for we wrestle not against flesh and blood, but against principalities, against power, against the rules of darkness in this world.' Pray for me, Anne."

Lilyan is clearly intended to be the similar-looking Anne's double; she is constructed visually as her mirror image in a number of scenes, and the two characters are conflated in the poster campaign. At the end of the film, it is revealed that Lilyan is actually a projection of Anne's imagination or, more accurately, her potentially guilty conscience. Anne must come to terms with, and in a way sanction, the necessary sacrifice of her husband for the greater good—a sacrifice justified through explicit religious discourse. Clearly the film's immediate juxtaposition of the philanthropic surgeon who "did nothing but good" and "monsters [who] murder and torture millions" has explicit propagandistic overtones. Anne's refusal to accept her husband's untimely death allows the manifestation of this very evil in her own community; on discovering her husband's murder of a friend she exclaims, "It's my fault. I brought it about. I wanted him to live." Having reclaimed her faith, she prays to a statue of the Virgin Mary (who replaces Lilyan in a similar mirrored image), saying, "Help him to buy back his soul. If necessary he'll die for it. He won't be afraid to fight. He won't be alone." The film, therefore, attempts to address women's wartime experience by providing a moral justification and spiritual redemption for husbands and boyfriends who have died or may yet die fighting overseas; the war is codified as a holy crusade for the redemption of mankind that is worth the loss of individual lives. This admixture of propaganda, theology, and B horror is perhaps a little unusual, but it can be linked to a wider interest in spirituality in 1943 and 1944 that the media put down to anxieties about loved ones overseas and to a search for meaning in the horror of wartime.[108] Resultantly the media acknowledged a "new spiritual resurgence in Hollywood . . . due to the war," but one manifested in A-class pictures such as *Song of Bernadette* (1943) and, as the following chapter will discuss, Paramount's *The Uninvited* (1944), rather than low-budget "chillers" such as *The Soul of a Monster*.[109]

Universal's sequels and franchises indicate the consolidation and escalation of the cycle, perhaps even into subgeneric form, but Columbia's derivative "queens of horror" also provide an early indication of the female monster reaching saturation point. At this point it is no longer in the economic interest of studios to utilize the model in this undifferentiated form.[110] Likewise, though Lewton's films for RKO (and *The Uninvited*) allude to witchcraft, occultism, and even Satanism as providing alternative coping strategies for women, these options are ultimately closed off or refuted in films like *Son of Dracula* and *Cry of the Werewolf.* As this chapter has argued, this corresponds with escalating media and government discourses warning against women's excessive freedoms and dangerous counterhegemonic strategies as the tide of the war turned in 1944. Universal's and Columbia's female monster films were able, at least to some extent, to evoke the complexities and contradictions of wartime women's lives, but ultimately they stressed that the primary female role is waiting faithfully for loved ones to return.

3

A-Class Monsters

The Escalation into Prestige Productions, 1944–1945

This new horror cycle is being launched on a far more ambitious level than the forerunning vampire, werewolf and Frankenstein chillers. Starting with such pictures as *The Uninvited, The Phantom Lady*, and *Gaslight*, the fresh psychological efforts are being dressed in full Class "A" paraphernalia, including million-dollar budgets and big-name casts.

–Fred Stanley, *New York Times* (May 28, 1944)

Due to the waning popularity of war films, the critic Fred Stanley explains, "Hollywood, temporarily at least, has all but shelved martial projects" in favor of this cycle of A-class horror productions.[1] The RKO, Universal, and Columbia female monster films discussed previously would be positioned somewhere between routine B and near-A status, in the production category Richard Maltby classifies as programmers that could play either half of a double bill.[2] The inflated budgets, investments in presold properties, and casting of established and emergent talent in prestige productions like *The Uninvited* and *Phantom Lady*, however, demonstrate the escalation of the female monster cycle, in Rick Altman's terms.[3] Although these films were discussed as horror in their critical reception (a fact that challenges both assumptions about the quality of horror in the forties and women's historical relationship to the genre), they are largely excluded from horror scholarship today. This is perhaps because they center on female protagonists and are therefore deemed woman's films (or, in *Phantom Lady*'s case, sometimes film noir) in contemporary scholarship.[4]

It is precisely because these classy horror films were centered upon and confirmed female perspectives that they are so valuable to the argument of this book. *The Uninvited* and *Phantom Lady*, the main focuses of this chapter, were heavily promoted and celebrated in their reception due to their introduction of strong, resilient women—including the latter's producer, Joan Harrison—who were seen to represent the wartime ideal.[5] Furthermore, through their central female characters, these films explore women's wartime experiences and coping strategies. *The Uninvited* was discussed in relation to the wider wartime revival of the occult in America—a phenomenon that was displaced onto women's anxieties about loved ones overseas and at times exploited for patriotic purposes. *Phantom Lady*, marketed as the first "mystery from the woman's perspective," foregrounds the phenomenological experiences of female war workers in urban centers like New York. Complaints by censors and critics regarding *The Uninvited*'s and *Phantom Lady*'s negative influences on women indicate potentially counterhegemonic strategies in these films and the cycles within which they are situated.

"First Serious Story of Spirit Influence": *The Uninvited* and Wartime Occultism

In 1944 the *New York Times* reported that Hollywood, Broadway, and popular literature were "haunted as never before. . . . It's an odd sort of escape from a world in which evil and terror are, objectively, literally, so important, but not unexpected."[6] Stanley's class-A horror cycle can be situated, therefore, not only in relation to the female monster films but also within an expansion of interest in the supernatural across media platforms. Furthermore, it came in the wake of a barrage of serious media forms, beginning in mid-1943, that reported the popularization of all manner of spiritual and psychic practices and practitioners, including séances, astrology, telepathy, spiritualist mediums, and tea leaf readers.[7] This revival in occult rituals was not attributed to a desire for escapism; rather, it was understood as an attempt to engage with the emotional and epistemological uncertainties of wartime.

In September 1944, the *New York Times* reported on this phenomenal shift in wartime communication. It explained that between February and June one New York department store alone had sold more than fifty thousand Ouija boards to "credulous customers." This was "clearly a

1944 development since last year there were few calls." Manufacturers, the article reports, were unable to keep up with this boom in demand.[8] The *New York Times* consulted Dr. Woodworth, emeritus professor of psychology at Columbia University, who identified the renewed "popularity of the Ouija board [as] a typical manifestation of wartime anxiety." He pointed out a comparable interest in the occult by the anxious and bereaved back home during World War I but differentiated "today's Ouija board fans" from these predecessors by emphasizing that they take its answers with "a grain of salt." Despite his skepticism, Woodworth posited that "anyone feels more confident to have it say that a husband or fiancé will be home by Christmas."[9] As this article suggests, these media discourses largely attributed this wartime revival to women, claiming that it reflected their anxieties about loved ones overseas and occasionally their wider epistemological uncertainties resulting from the war. A follow-up article in the *Dallas Morning News* patronizingly titled "Ouija Board, Ouija Board, Where's My Soldier Boy?" made the New York paper's gendered implications more explicit by characterizing "the new interest as a typical manifestation of worry about men overseas." This article also sought the testimony of psychologists—seeking both the reason for this "upswing of interest in mental phenomena" and a logical explanation for how Ouija boards work—but ultimately concluded dismissively that "your own subconscious answers through the board."[10]

These media reports emphasized the potential morale-boosting power of these alternate belief systems, while distancing themselves somewhat through recourse to scientific testimony. More problematically this "new occultism" was often linked to a female propensity for consumption. One headline exclaimed, "First it was women's panties, now it is Ouija boards that are in demand."[11] As these articles reveal, the nation's anxieties about the legitimacy of the rationalist principles upon which it was built, and the subsequent experimentation with alternative belief systems, were typically displaced onto women, in this case explicitly the female body. Paradoxically, these antirationalist principles were simultaneously appropriated in order to shore up the dominant belief systems for which the country was fighting—in this case consumerism, traditional gender roles, and heterosexual coupling.[12]

In his 1947 article "Theses against Occultism," Theodor Adorno leveled this very criticism at the wartime popularization of the occult. He saw it is an attempt to recover an objective reality, at a time when people "no longer trust[ed] their own reason." It was precisely the seriousness of modern occultism that Adorno saw as problematic. Following his wider thesis of modernity's basis in "authoritarian irrationalism," he asserted that this tendency to occultism was, like capitalism and even fascism, a manifestation of unquestioning investment in something not fully believed. He continued, "The horoscope corresponds to the official directives to the nations, and number-mysticism is preparation for administrative statistics and cartel prices."[13] Adorno described capitalism's cultivation of false needs and their reification into consumables as the "phantasmagoria" of commodity production—a metaphor that evokes both the supernatural and the cinematic apparatus. Following Adorno's reasoning it is possible to see how the supernatural narratives of these class-A horror films—with their call to suspend disbelief for the duration—rather than providing an escape from the reality and ideology of wartime America, might be harnessed as the ideal medium for disseminating an unspecified propaganda message. The head of the Office of War Information, Elmer Davis, asserted that "the easiest way to propagandize people is to let a propaganda theme through when people do not realize they are being propagandized."[14]

It can be seen, therefore, why Hollywood might combine supernatural themes with explicitly patriotic plots in a film like *A Guy Named Joe* (1943), in which a deceased American bomber pilot (Spencer Tracy) stationed in Britain is given the final mission of returning to earth as a ghost, in order to pass on his expertise to a young protégé. As Manny Farber of the *New Republic* explained, "Hollywood has been fighting a tremendous battle with the problem of death in the war and *A Guy Named Joe* is the most elaborate statement of its conclusion on the subject."[15] Following Adorno's and Davis's reasoning, Farber's assertion that *A Guy Named Joe* was Hollywood's most successful attempt to date to deal with "the problem of death" in wartime makes perfect sense. *Variety*, however—in parallel with Adorno's opinion on the occult generally—saw the film's seriousness as its key flaw. The reviewer complained that *A Guy Named Joe* shunned the "sharp wit and dry humor" of prewar ghost stories such as *Here Comes Mr. Jordan* (1941) and *Topper Returns* (1941), instead transferring "the mood . . . to the realm of metaphysics"—a "metaphysic of dunces" according to Adorno.[16]

This representational shift was highlighted in trade and mainstream presses as a "developing cycle . . . of pictures with ghosts in starring roles."[17] This Hollywood production strategy was seen as "apace with [the aforementioned] widespread wartime revival of public interest in other manifestations of the mysterious," but also as an attempt by Hollywood to provide a substitute for the increasingly unpopular cycle of war movies.[18] From 1942 onward, *Variety* was reporting that women—assumed by the industry to be Hollywood's key market—were "shying away from war pictures" in favor of escapism and romance.[19] By mid-1943 the trade and mainstream presses were confirming that the "war film cycle [was] now over with."[20] Instead, "all manner of the eerie" was finding great popularity, particularly with female war workers in defense plants and war industries.[21]

Along with *A Guy Named Joe* and *The Canterville Ghost* (1944), Warner Bros.' *Between Two Worlds* (1944) was identified as representative of this "logical evolvement of the cycle."[22] Bosley Crowther of the *New York Times* wrote that in opposition to the "popular comedy line" of previous Hollywood ghost stories, "this study of the hereafter is notoriously wistful and grim." He concluded that this is "probably because [Warner Bros.] figured that these are troubled times in which people are more than commonly interested in their spiritual destinies."[23] *Between Two Worlds* was based on Sutton Vane's 1924 Broadway hit *Outward Bound*, which had been produced as a film under that title by Warners in 1930. In the play and film of *Outward Bound*, a disparate group of passengers aboard an ocean liner slowly come to the realization that they are dead, and sailing toward their eventual destination of heaven or hell. In adapting the play for the home-front market in 1944, however, the screenplay was transposed to a contemporary setting, and characters were introduced or adapted to give the film "a new war slant."[24] The setting was shifted to wartime London, where the establishing shot of "A Port in England—1944" is interrupted by an overhead speaker informing the audience—both inside and outside the film's diegesis—"you are reminded that we are traveling to America under wartime conditions, and England is still very much a battle area." Most of the characters introduced in this opening scene are subsequently killed in a bombing raid as they flee the port's departure lounge. The other two are suicide victims and are therefore initially condemned to sail the "metaphorical sea" for eternity; they are ultimately redeemed, however, through a trompe l'oeil narrative device that allows the lovers a second chance at life.[25]

In developing this "war slant" the screenplay also introduces a new character of a thrice-torpedoed American merchant seaman, who is ultimately reconciled to dying through the knowledge that he dies for a cause. This allowed the screenwriter, according to the *New York Sun*'s somewhat dismissive review, "to work in the usual war speech," one that valorizes the American sailor's noble death and resultant "joyous and contented" afterlife.[26] The film therefore consolidates Anglo-American relations—while reconciling Britain's class-obsessed past to hell through the figure of the snobby social climber Genevieve Cliveden-Banks (Isobel Elsom)—through the noble sacrifices and shared destinies of the Allied nations.[27] It is clear to see how the public's more than common interest in their "spiritual destinies" was able to be channeled into rationalizing and perhaps softening wartime casualties.[28] The marketing subtly played down the film's explicit wartime allusions, though—selling it as "a romance that was out of this world." Warners tapped into women's perceived mood of emotional limbo at the same time that it implicitly promoted faithfulness to men overseas. As the film's tagline explains, "Her devotion stayed the cold hand of death and lighted his path to the world of hope and promise."[29]

To reduce the heterogeneity of experience of divergent texts, intertexts, and their individual consumption to this type of hegemonic reading would surely be to employ the universalizing identity thinking that Adorno so opposed, however. Feminist critics have condemned Adorno—and mass culture theory in general—for reinforcing hierarchical gender relations through the linguistic characterization of mass, consumer culture as feminine.[30] Replicating the popular media discourses on wartime occultism, Adorno invokes perceived feminine qualities—emotion, escapism, romance, sentimentalism, passivity—as key descriptive categories in his discussions of the occult phenomenon and its relationship to consumer culture. The intention here is not to provide an application or critique of Adorno's theories on modern occultism and wartime ideologies, but rather to highlight these types of debates as historically pertinent within the academy as well as the media at this time. Furthermore, research into the production, critical reception, and exhibition of Paramount's

The Uninvited alludes to the potential counterhegemonic strategies these maligned occult practices, and even their Hollywood representations, might have held for women struggling to make sense of the epistemological and emotional uncertainties of wartime.[31] Far from a trivial and therefore, by this logic, a discursively feminized generic product, the film was seen as a serious, even contentious, creative intervention.

Targeting wartime women's preferences for adaptations of books with spiritual and supernatural themes, *The Uninvited* was adapted from Dorothy Macardle's novel *Uneasy Freehold* (1941), the Christmas bestseller for 1942.[32] In the film version, siblings Rick and Pam Fitzgerald (Ray Milland and Ruth Hussey) come to suspect that their new clifftop home in Cornwall is haunted when they hear strange wailing and experience icy chills and the smell of mimosa. They are informed by a local girl, Stella (Gail Russell), that this ghostly presence is her mother, Mary Meredith, who died seventeen years earlier. Stella's blossoming romance with Rick becomes subordinate to her obsession with the house and her desire to rekindle a relationship with this maternal presence. Stella goes into a trance during a séance in which her mother seemingly appears to her. On hearing this, her grandfather (Donald Crisp) has her confined to an asylum run by Miss Holloway (Cornelia Otis Skinner), a family "friend" who idealizes Stella's dead mother. Rick and Pam realize that they have two ghosts, the other being that of Carmel, a "Spanish gypsy" who was Stella's father's mistress. It is revealed that Carmel was actually Stella's mother, and that her ghost is trying to guard Stella from the malevolent spirit of Mary Meredith, who died attempting to push Stella over the cliff and has returned to finish the job. With the revelation of Stella's real heritage, both ghosts are banished, seemingly restoring a heterosexual equilibrium with Rick and Stella, and Pam and the local GP, Dr. Scott (Alan Napier), embracing as the titles roll.

Like the subsequent film, the novel bears close similarities with du Maurier and Hitchcock's *Rebecca* (1940), a connection repeatedly exploited in the film's poster campaign and stressed by reviewers (see figure 10). In *The Uninvited* the "icy" Mary Meredith, who "feared and refused motherhood," is the film's Rebecca figure, but the implications of a lesbian relationship with the Mrs. Danvers character, Miss Holloway, are made even more explicit than in Hitchcock's film.[33] *The Uninvited* also goes further than its precursor in actualizing the female Oedipal narrative and

FIGURE 10 The poster for *The Uninvited* sells the film as a supernatural *Rebecca*.

supernatural overtones of Hitchcock's earlier hit, while drawing on the conventions of the female monster film, especially the subtle, restrained approach of Lewton's influential *Cat People* and *I Walked with a Zombie*. The film's amalgamation of the female Gothic and Universal approaches to horror, a generic hybridity characterizing the female monster cycle, are suggested by Cornelia Otis Skinner's description of her character as "a female Frankenstein, a new Mrs. Danvers."[34]

Embracing the bifurcated model of the female monster cycle, the *Uninvited* poster reveals, "Out of this World—two women fought for her . . . the malignant evil of *The Uninvited* and the protecting spirit of her mother! In this world—he fought . . . to take her away from the fascination of *The Uninvited*." Although these opposing female role models are competing for Stella's soul, rather than the heart of the male lead, as the poster explicates, Rick's romantic destiny depends upon Stella's chosen path. As *Motion Picture Daily* explained, however, the film's "sordid, triangular episode," the structuring relationship of the female monster film, is actually "revealed in the past tense" through the backstory that comes to light of the two women's ultimately tragic battle over Stella's father.[35] The female monster narrative has arguably already played out, and we witness only its haunting aftermath and Stella's attempts to reconcile it.

Lewton's earlier female monster characters provide a haunting presence in *The Uninvited* that was registered in contemporary criticism as well as more recent scholarship.[36] In an article following the release of the film, the *Los Angeles Examiner* suggested that it was appropriate that Elizabeth Russell, "a fixture in Lewton's films" and a self-confessed "female Bela Lugosi in constant zombie state," should haunt *The Uninvited* as a "semi-materialized and totally unrecognizable ectoplasm." Although Russell is all but unrecognizable in her role of the semi-materialized ghost, it stressed that her presence in the film is informed intertextually by her roles as Irena's mysterious "sister" in *Cat People*, the "morbid, strange woman who makes life so unpleasant . . . in *Curse of the Cat People*," and, in her own words, "the Ophelia-like creature who wandered through *The Seventh Victim*."[37] In addition to Elizabeth Russell's semi-materialized presence as Mary Meredith, Gail Russell's more tangible performance as Stella fits the mold of the female monster film's heroine, and her portrayal garnered considerable praise in the press.[38]

Manny Farber commended Gail Russell as the ultimate model of movie femininity in 1944, because of her ability to negotiate and synthesize the multiple demands that the war placed upon women. Referencing her role in *The Uninvited*, Farber hails Russell as the epitome of a new crop of heroines who will "show soldiers the type of girl they should wait for, look for or expect when they get back." Farber continues that this hybrid heroine has "something from all the former Lady categories. This includes the ambition of the great acting ladies like Bette Davis, the body of the bathing beauty, the face and the wholesomeness of the girl who plays Sister in the family movies, and the free-swinging, sexual lustiness of the vampire woman."[39] Farber sees Russell's success, like that of the working women characters in the female monster films, as due to her onscreen ability to negotiate and reconcile these various modes of femininity. Rather than being exceptional, however, Russell was promoted for her perfect, though at the same time attainable, fit with the all-American-girl ideal. Appealing to other young women's desire for stardom, the pressbook proffered that "the most recent proof that the Cinderella myth has counterparts in real life is demonstrated in Gail Russell's role in *The Uninvited*"; she was discovered "by accident" only a year before while studying to be a commercial artist in Santa Monica.[40]

The Uninvited was distinguished from most horror films, though significantly not Lewton's, through the subtlety and seriousness it brought to the genre. As with the more positive reviews of *Cat People* and *I Walked with a Zombie*, the film was praised for its restrained and therefore "doubly effective" use of horror devices, its "blending of the everyday with the inexplicable," and its commingling of high and low culture.[41] The *Los Angeles Times* reviewer compared it to a literary "masterwork" such as Henry James's *Turn of the Screw* but stressed that the film's "all-out triumph" was in "arousing reactions of excitement and horror. . . . The audience screamed and yelled and virtually had conniption fits."[42] Reviewers also pointed out the film's atypical sincerity and seriousness as its most outstanding features. The *New York Herald Tribune* enthused, "Its chief attraction is its sincerity—it is an honest ghost story, with no attempt made at the end to explain away the phenomena on logical grounds."[43] The *New York World Telegram* further stated, "*The Uninvited* takes it for granted that you believe in ghosts, and even shows a couple to convince the wavering skeptics."[44] Echoing these sentiments, the *Washington Post* explained that the film was "no cheap, run-of-the-mill 'shocker' aimed at the easy susceptibilities of 'horror' lovers [but was] seriously aimed at adult audiences."[45]

These reviewers suggest that seriousness and the supernatural were no longer mutually exclusive, thus permitting "adult audiences" to answer in the affirmative to the poster's provocation "Do you believe that the spirit of a mother can stay behind to guard her daughter from the malignance of the un-dead?" without feeling stupid, or childish. In all Paramount's promotion, in fact, *The Uninvited* was explicitly marketed as "the first serious story of spirit influence" and "the first serious ghost story in which the hauntings are never explained on natural grounds."[46] Like the more explicitly war-themed ghost films, wrote John McManus in *PM*, *The Uninvited* was distinguished from Hollywood's "ghost stories of the past—such as *The Ghost Goes West*, the *Topper* films, [and] *Here Comes Mr. Jordan*. . . . The new way with ghosts, as with children, is the progressive approach. Instead of chasing after them with holy water, you try to understand their problems."[47] The film's serious treatment of the occult and spiritualism is therefore tied to American society's wider attempts to engage rationally with these alternate belief systems, as reported in newspapers and magazines during the film's production and release. Reports on its exhibition indicate that audiences were perhaps initially confused by the film's overturning of generic expectations. The *Motion Picture Herald* noted that the downtown Los Angeles audience "tried to find in the previewed film the cues for laughter usually spotted in chiller-dillers and, failing to find them, laughed uneasily in some wrong places and then relaxed into absorbed attention."[48]

The Uninvited's serious consideration of the occult, and specifically its characterization as a potentially disruptive feminine counterdiscourse, is represented most explicitly in the controversial séance scene, which was identified as the film's key set piece and was specifically promoted for its authenticity. The studio publicity stressed that it had hired a top spiritualistic medium, Reverend Pearl Barnes, as a technical adviser to oversee this Ouija board sequence and even encouraged exhibitors to recreate it by staging lobby séances in their theaters.[49] Following *The Uninvited*'s success, other studios adopted exploitation marketing that played into the public interest in the occult. For example, Cleveland's Loews Ohio

Theater doubled its average weekly business by having "two professional fortune tellers" situated in the lobby during *It Happened Tomorrow*'s (1944) theatrical run; the trade press noted that "women lined up for readings all during the fortune tellers' engagement."[50]

The Uninvited's séance sequence demonstrates, somewhat self-consciously, the gendering of these alternate beliefs as feminine, and a patriarchal appropriation of them on the grounds of placating women's anxieties. Just before this scene, Rick warns that Stella is "on the edge of a nervous collapse." This follows her grandfather's assertion that "Stella suffers from a general delicacy" and her eventual institutionalization. The men in Stella's life therefore attempt to diagnose her belief as hysteria. This follows a number of patriarchal attempts to use faux-scientific discourse to unconvincingly explain the ghostly wailings. After his first experience of the ghost, a terrified Rick tells his unruffled sister, "There's nothing to worry about, Pam. This can be scientifically explained. It's probably a loose wire hidden around the house somewhere acting as an aerial picking up some woman in the village crying." Both the doctor and Stella's grandfather insist that it is merely "an echo from a cave, probably," while Rick—performing in a style reminiscent of Cary Grant's screwball roles—provides comic relief through his attempts to appear brave in the face of abject terror.

All the women in the film, however, both believe and embrace their supernatural encounters. Pam, who intimates her belief in psychic phenomena at the film's outset when she tells Rick that she has "just had one of [her] feelings" that they would buy the house, explains to her brother that she'd be "interested, not scared," to have a ghost in the house. This juxtaposition of Rick's nervous disavowal and Pam's intellectual engagement with the occult is acted out in the séance scene. Rick scoffs at Pam's suggestion of holding a séance, saying such practices are only believed in by the "idiot fringe," but Pam counters, "Rick, you have no right to say that. Many intelligent people believe in spiritualism," including, it seems, herself. Pam's superior intelligence and reasoning are stressed throughout *The Uninvited*, something the film attempts to also achieve through casting and extratextual discourse. A publicity article entitled "Ruth Hussey Able to Hold Own Even with Professors" maintains that the star has such a "noble air about her that many people have been misled into believing that she holds a PhD degree."[51] Rick agrees to go along with the séance idea, but only in order to fake it, thus tricking Stella into following their wishes. Dr. Scott alludes to Rick's potentially self-serving intentions, saying, "What are you going to tell her? Entrust your life to a tall, dark man, excruciatingly handsome."[52]

Having constructed a makeshift Ouija board and explained how it works, Pam gets the séance under way. Like the film's posters, Stella stresses from the outset that "the important thing is that we all believe," though Rick and Dr. Scott remain the "wavering skeptics" of the earlier review. It soon becomes apparent to them, however, that they have no control over the proceedings; realizing the Ouija board is really working, they try to stifle its "voice" by holding the glass to keep it from moving from letter to letter. Stella becomes aware of what they are doing and forces them to drop out. This leaves just her and Pam to navigate the board, and they reveal a message stating that Stella's mother is protecting her from some "malignant force." In this scene the séance is clearly demarcated, therefore, as a mode of female communication that is closed off to or denied by men. This could be potentially seen as a counterhegemonic strategy that disrupts, perhaps even short-circuits, the dominant (patriarchal) belief system; in the film it is the rational that is clearly irrational. This representation of the occult as an alternate female language system draws historically on essentialist ideas—women's intuition and the female irrational.[53] It also offers a microreversal of the power dynamic that could be seen very much to relate to the wartime shifts in women's roles in the workforce and leisure.[54] Wartime necessity had showed dominant beliefs about women's capabilities and social wants to have been an elaborate ruse, a case of a patriarchal hand on the glass.

The idea that the occult, even in its watered-down Hollywood form, could provide a counterhegemonic voice is suggested by the heated correspondence to the Hays Office regarding the possible dangers of *The Uninvited.* On May 10, 1944, the National Legion of Decency sent a letter to Will Hays drawing his attention to "a situation that exists regarding the Paramount film *The Uninvited.*" Namely, "in certain theaters large audiences of questionable type attended this film at unusual hours." The letter goes on to center "certain erotic and esoteric elements" of the film as the key attraction for this demographic, pinpointing seven instances where a lesbian relationship between Miss Holloway and Mary Meredith is implied. Although this is a concern for the Legion, they explain that their original objection to the film, and the reason for their B rating, is the "the spiritualistic séance sequence," which is "so constructed as to convey the impression of credence and possible invitation to spiritualistic practices."[55]

Although Paramount's head of foreign and domestic censorship dismissed the claims of lesbian overtones as "a figment of their imagination, that may have led them to believe they saw things which did not exist (after all, it was a ghost picture you know)," Joseph Breen followed up these claims by sending the Hays Office's representative from the Catholic Church to see the film.[56] In the end, Father Daniel Lord fed back that his only concern was that "it might interest people in what is a dangerous device," the Ouija board. He continued, "Aside from the Ouija exhibit which had only the element of exciting curiosity, I got nothing but enjoyment out of the film."[57] His and the Legion of Decency's fears were reiterated in a March 1944 letter to the *New York Times* that emphasized the potential dangers of this "unprecedented cycle" of "psychism emanating from the film capital." It linked this cycle of Hollywood "movies that truck in psychic phenomena and . . . human emotions that are 'out of this world'" to wider wartime trends, stressing that "any sane minded person can perceive that Hollywood is only reflecting a state of mind" but that the studios should be more responsible in addressing "a public eager for substance and realities in place of illusions."[58] These concerns around female audiences of a "questionable type," and around the séance scene's "invitation" to occult practices and ungrounded emotions, indicate the moral fears around what wartime women were getting up to while men were away. The communities of women involved in war work, and their increasing disposable income, meant that many women came into contact with lifestyles, options, and support mechanisms that they had not encountered before. This resulted in the early war years not only in shifts in women's attendance practices at urban cinemas but also in a burgeoning lesbian scene in major cities such as New York, where the Legion's concerns were raised.[59] The truth of these reported "questionable" audiences is not really important to the argument herein; what is significant is this increasing discussion and concern over women's solo and communal pastimes, and their perceived hegemonic challenge to traditional morals and ideals.

In *The Uninvited* the temporary community of women—living and dead—is disbanded at the film's conclusion as it is revealed that the couples present at the séance will marry and that Stella's mother(s) is(are) "gone forever." Stella's final reminder of Rick's feminine behavior—"you're still shaking, Rick"—is counteracted with a mother-in-law joke: "Well, I've had a lucky escape. She might have been my mother-in-law." This alternate belief system, which admittedly shakes up the men, could be seen as a temporary expedient to bring about the restoration of order, much like the dominant view of women's wartime roles. This would perhaps position the film within the realm of the other patriotic ghost stories, like *A Guy Named Joe*, in which the female lead overcomes her fiancé's death to assume the male role of war hero, but with the ultimate aim of saving another man to whom she is attracted, thus restoring a heterosexual coupling following the war.

The two reading strategies proposed in this chapter are not necessarily irreconcilable, and, as with much of the aforementioned wartime discourse, the film offers a range of multiple and contradictory positions that spectators are able to assume, perform, or reject. In 1945 Bosley Crowther mused, "Why should the mind be stimulated—or relaxed—by frankly horrifying films when we know a certain audience-resentment is felt towards candid pictures about war?"[60] Crowther is correct to stress the simultaneous ability of these films to engage with and escape the horrors of wartime. In a film like *The Uninvited*, the physical absence yet psychic presence of these earthbound spirits addresses issues of memory and loss, at the same time that it draws attention away from the violent eradication of bodies.

This serious dialogue between movies and wider social trends was intensified following *The Uninvited*'s success, inspiring further financial and critical investment in the spiritualist debate in film. Despite *Variety*'s fears that *The Uninvited*'s "unusual and controversial subject" would affect its box-office performance, the film was popular with audiences as well as critics.[61] As the *Motion Picture Herald* explained, "*The Uninvited*, according to three independent New York circuits, did business approaching top Paramount releases," thus inspiring the aforementioned cycle of classy "spook pictures."[62] The *Herald* subsequently highlighted *The Uninvited* as instigating a "developing cycle" of profitable "pictures which treat, in both whimsy and seriousness, with disembodied spirits, messages from the beyond, zombies, reincarnation and other spiritualistic phenomena."[63] It discusses a number of texts with "psychic overtones" that came in *The Uninvited*'s wake but identifies *The Curse of the Cat People* (1944) as the *key* thematic and financial benefactors of its success.[64] The precedent set by *The Uninvited* ultimately forced RKO and the smaller studios to increase the budgets and talent expended on their female monster films, including Val Lewton's loosely related sequel to *Cat People*, in which Irena (the feline shape-shifter of the title) returns, but this time as a benevolent "ghost."

Combining "'A' Pictures with a Good Screamie": RKO Escalates Its Budgets

In his review of *The Curse of the Cat People*, Archer Winsten of the *New York Post* links the film to the wider media phenomena discussed above, by asking with condescension, "You don't suppose there's anything in all this twaddle about ghosts, apparitions, and incredibly visible spirits that blow in the window curtains or darken the electric lights of a house, do you? Because there seems to be an unusual amount of it lately in the movies."[65] Though *The Uninvited* was forgiven its sincere treatment of ghosts because its production values raised its cultural status from "catch-penny fabrication of thrills and chills for the horror-picture trade" to "a piece of distinguished product," the lack of comparable traits in *The Curse of the Cat People* was construed as a key "selling problem" by contemporary critics.[66] The *Showmen's Trade Review* warned exhibitors that "it is too highbrow in theme for the average 'horror film' audience and the cast lacks box-office names to attract the more discriminating or arty fans."[67]

Released just a month after *The Uninvited*, the film was perceived by many critics to be a cynical and flawed attempt to "cash in on RKO's phenomenally successful *Cat People*."[68] *The Curse of the Cat People* was attacked (though also in a few cases praised) for not replicating the tropes of its successful precursor and the promises of its horrific promotional campaign (see figure 11). The *Los Angeles Times* took RKO to task for "developing a positive affection for their monsters and menaces."[69] Half of the reviews followed this reviewer's lead in attacking the film as a tame follow-up to the "horrific opus" *Cat People*.[70] The others complained that its "accursed title," again forced on Lewton by RKO, was unrepresentative of

FIGURE 11 A contradictory lobby card highlights the mis-selling of *The Curse of the Cat People*.

"one of the nicest movies of all time."[71] The *Los Angeles Times* continued that the film "has little to do with either curses or feline folk. . . . The film is really a psychological study of this child."[72] Almost all newspaper critics, including this one, read the Irena character as an imaginary playmate, not a ghost, thus making the film a "psychological study" rather than a horror film.[73] Only two of the New York reviews concluded that the film was a ghost story, and these were written by the film's two female reviewers. Kate Cameron of the *New York Daily News* explained that Irena was a "lovely and sympathetic ghost," and Rose Pelswick of the *New York Journal-American* declared that the film "does have a ghost, but the ghost is a friendly spirit."[74] This film, like *I Walked with a Zombie*, is certainly ambiguous in regard to the epistemological status of its supernatural female character, and the hesitation it engenders is extended beyond the film's conclusion; this again underscores Lewton's debt to what Tzvetan Todorov characterizes as the literary genre of the fantastic.[75] This inherent ambivalence would explain the reviewers' generic confusion, but it is worth considering that only the female reviewers, when faced with this hesitation, were open to the supernatural reading of the film; the male reviewers opted universally for the rational, psychological solution to the narrative.

Although the film received mostly poor reviews in the press (though notably not from the *New York Times*'s longtime horror skeptic Bosley Crowther), some more esteemed critics praised the film for its un-Hollywood tendencies. James Agee and Manny Farber celebrated *The Curse of the Cat People* for bringing sophistication and sincerity both to horror and to movies generally. In his column for the *Nation*, Agee wrote approvingly that while "masquerading as a routine case of Grade B horrors—it does very well at that job—the picture is in fact a brave, sensitive, and admirable little psychological melodrama." The Times Square horror audience, perhaps "the finest audience in the country," was captivated by the film, he said; "as long as such an audience exists, no one in Hollywood has a right to use stupidity of the public for an alibi."[76] Likewise, Farber found the film "so sincerely adult minded in its whole approach as to make it the least Hollywood-like film from Hollywood this year."[77] *The Curse of the Cat People* was praised for its sincerity and sophistication by certain specialized audiences and their celebrants, but it was not perceived as possessing the high production values and talent to tap the wider target market of adult moviegoers interested in supernatural themes that *The Uninvited* was seen to be addressing.[78] RKO and other studios (including MGM and Fox) were soon to follow Paramount's lead, however.

In mid-1944, *Film Daily* noted that Hollywood was boosting its output of horror fare and the budgets of those films as a result of their wartime popularity. Citing examples spanning *Laura* (1944) to *Cry of the Werewolf* (1944), it concluded that "there will be no lack of entertainment for horror fans and budget makers." It went on to say that "RKO is contemplating making 'Carmilla' one of the first horror offerings to be done in Technicolor. It is a costume horror story dealing with the Salem, Massachusetts witch trials of the 18th Century," with Val Lewton assigned to produce.[79] Although this idea for a big-budget, Technicolor adaptation of Sheridan Le Fanu's classic 1872 Gothic novel about a female vampire was never fully realized, RKO did boost the budgets and production values for Lewton's films following *The Curse of the Cat People*, including a loose adaptation of *Carmilla* titled *Isle of the Dead* (1945).[80]

Some of the themes and plot elements of *Carmilla* were realized in *Isle of the Dead*, which in early production correspondence was titled *Camilla* and featured a central female character called Catherine.[81] Attributing the whole film to Lewton, "who started all this kind of thing with the 'Cat People,'" and stressing its ambiguous status, the *Hollywood Reporter* positioned *Isle of the Dead* as "definitely for those who like to balance their 'A' pictures with a good screamie."[82] The film extends the earlier Lewton films' ambiguity around seemingly monstrous female characters, but with enhanced production values and in a setting far from the American home front.

Isle of the Dead is set in Greece during the Balkan War of 1912. Boris Karloff plays a general who moves from a position of skepticism to belief in vampires (or the "Vorvolakas" of Greek legend) as the death toll rises on the island where he has gone to visit his wife's grave. As a septicemic plague decimates the island, the general succumbs to a peasant woman's belief that a young maid, Thea (Ellen Drew), is the vampire-like "wolf-spirit" responsible for spreading this "contagion of the soul," and he therefore sets out to kill her. Ironically, Thea is suspected because she "looks so full of life," a clear contrast to the other key female character, Mary, a British diplomat's wife who suffers from catalepsy and is resultantly buried alive in the belief she has died. Mary escapes her tomb but is driven insane by the ordeal; she attacks the general, who in his death throes mistakes her for "the Vorvolaka!"

J. P. Telotte explains "how, in attempting to exorcize monsters from our thoughts and world, the film implies we always run the risk of becoming that sort of monstrous, disintegrative force we fear."[83] The film's themes of reason pushed to its limits becoming unreason, and mystery and myth's potentially beneficial effects due to their recognition of "inexorable and unpredictable forces" in the world, have some clear wartime resonances.[84] *The Isle of the Dead*'s narrative of mankind searching for supernatural answers in the face of a crisis of faith in rationality can certainly be linked to the wartime revival of the occult that this chapter has outlined. Unlike in *The Uninvited*, in which the female character's belief in the occult is confirmed, in *Isle of the Dead* the central male character's temporary embrace of this irrational feminine belief system is a psychotic impulse brought on by the horrors of war, which is ultimately proven as destructive and delusional (see figure 12). The film's favoring of a scientific solution to the

FIGURE 12 Boris Karloff's general is driven to an irrational belief in vampires in *Isle of the Dead.*

island's mysterious deaths compelled contemporary critics to position it generically "halfway between a horror film and a thriller."[85] This generic hybridity was also emphasized in the film's promotional campaign.

Like the aforementioned "alleged horror" *The Curse of the Cat People, Isle of the Dead* indicates the drive toward the secular narratives and psychological solutions to the female monster problem that were beginning to be played out in adjacent subcycles such as the "women's mystery film," discussed below, and would be fully realized in the "psychiatric picture" cycle following the war.[86] In a *Los Angeles Times* interview following the release of *Isle of the Dead*, Val Lewton predicted that the current profitable wartime horror cycle in film and literature would give way to a postwar "philosophical cycle" as it did after World War I.[87] Similarly, in 1944 Manny Farber, a Lewton fan, linked the "mysterious demand" for horror pictures to the "curious atmosphere that wartime is to some extent vacation time, a transition period in which life is not quite the same as it has been before." He particularly linked this to women "living outside the settled equilibrium of home" and the effects of this situation on their employment and leisure time.[88] These female-centered horror films tapped into the epistemological and emotional uncertainty of wartime—including the uncertainty around what it meant to be a woman—at the same time as they evoked the concomitant sense of liberation and empowerment that this engendered. This is nowhere more apparent than in Universal's *Phantom Lady*.

"The Female Mystery Drama": *Phantom Lady* and Women War Workers

Phantom Lady is a clear example of Hollywood bringing in female expertise in order to target a newly realized female market for horror and mystery films. Universal appointed Joan Harrison, a former protégé of Alfred Hitchcock, who had progressed from a secretarial position in Britain to coscreenwriter of *Rebecca* (1940) and *Suspicion* (1941) in America before reaching an executive position. The announcement of her appointment in mid-1943 sparked considerable media interest. Barbara Berch of the *New York Times* introduced the "Hitchcock alumna" Harrison as "Hollywood's only full-fledged woman producer." She would specialize in mystery films "from the woman's angle," Berch said, going on to suggest that her gender and her experience with the "master of horror" put her in a unique position to fill this role. Harrison posited a gap in the marketplace for such texts, commenting that "women must have something to pull for, you know, whether it's a dog, a horse, an old beggar—or even another woman."[89] Subsequently, the Universal publicity department marketed her first production, *Phantom Lady*, as "a mystery story from the woman's point of view, a formula which has never before been translated for the screen. Love stories yes, thousands of them . . . but not a single mystery film based on feminine psychology for its essential appeal."[90] Hitchcock himself might have questioned this assertion, but certainly the appointment of Harrison was intended to bring a profitable female perspective to the burgeoning horror and mystery market.[91]

In order to construct a woman's mystery story, Harrison reconstructed the source material for *Phantom Lady* to privilege a female protagonist's point of view. In Cornell Woolrich's novel (under the pseudonym William Irish), the secretary Carol "Kansas" Richman is a marginal figure—only the suspect's girlfriend, not his work colleague. In the film, however, she takes on a traditionally male investigator's role.[92] Like most other reviews, the *New York World-Telegram*'s pointed out that the film was not a mystery story, as the identity of the murderer is revealed early in the film; instead, "the whole story is the girl's quest."[93] Reviewers stressed that the film subverted the typical investigation narrative of the mystery genre, instead attempting to reveal "actual life in actual settings, and to project the psychological states of both its people and events."[94] It is in these attempts to draw out the phenomenological and psychological experiences of the female characters that the film is most successful in addressing women's lived experiences on the American home front. Rather than privilege the linear trajectory of most mystery stories, *Phantom Lady* attempts to actualize the temporary social and sexual liberations experienced by the wartime women Harrison was aiming to address. Although the film concludes with the female protagonist perhaps ready to relinquish her professional and independent status, it is her ability to navigate and overcome her tough urban environment that is *Phantom Lady*'s central tenet. Like Harrison herself, Kansas (Ella Raines) transcends her role as secretary to excel in the perceived male world of mystery and terror because of, rather than in spite of, her gender.[95]

In *Phantom Lady*, Kansas swaps secretarial duties for hard-boiled detective work when her boss, Scott Henderson (Alan Curtis), a civil engineer, is sentenced to death for murdering his wife, Marcella.[96] She sets out to track down his alibi—the eponymous woman with whom he shared the night in question but did not exchange names. Mysteriously no one remembers the "phantom lady" despite the elaborate hat that she wore, which seemed to get her noticed at the bar where she met Scott and the show she attended with him. This represents a chief clue to her identity. Kansas is plunged into a corrupt underworld of lies, payoffs, betrayal, and murder. She initially haunts the bar where Scott first met the "phantom lady," in the hope that the owner will change his story. However, following a sequence reminiscent of the stalking scene in *Cat People*, he is killed by a car while attempting to escape her. Masquerading as a "hep kitten" called Jeannie, Kansas seduces the show's lascivious drummer, Cliff (Elisha Cook Jr.). After some drinking and jiving in an underground jazz club they return to his apartment, where she gets Cliff to reveal that he was paid "five hundred smackers" to keep quiet about the woman. After

Kansas is forced to flee, her cover blown, the real murderer arrives and strangles Cliff.

The serial killer is Jack Marlow (Franchot Tone), Scott's "best friend," who was having an affair with his wife; this revelation comes just over halfway into the film. Jack subsequently pretends to assist Kansas in an attempt to sabotage her investigation, but she is still able to discover the name of the milliner who made the hat and thus track down the mysterious woman. On arrival at her Long Island home it is discovered that the "phantom lady," Ann Terry (Fay Helm), is under psychiatric supervision, having suffered a nervous breakdown following her fiancé's death. Kansas manages to persuade her to relinquish the hat, which represents vital evidence to back up Scott's alibi. Back at Marlow's apartment, Kansas realizes he is the killer and alerts the police. On their arrival, Marlow throws himself out of the apartment window, following a failed attempt to strangle Kansas. Scott is cleared of the crime and returns to work, where he makes an offer to Kansas over the Dictaphone to have dinner with him "tonight, the next night, then every night after that."[97]

Although film scholarship has acclaimed *Phantom Lady* as one of the original and epitomic films noir, it was discussed mostly in terms of its positioning in relation to the horror genre in contemporary studio and critical discourse. As we have seen, it was identified by the *New York Times*, along with *The Uninvited*, as part of a new prestige horror cycle in mid-1944.[98] Likewise, the *New York Sun* stressed that "Loew's State is the place for horror fans this week. *Phantom Lady* is a killer-diller of a horror yarn," and *Daily Variety* ranked the film as a "chiller of top proportions. . . . The picture, as directed by Robert Siodmak, belongs to the chiller school."[99] Aspiring higher, however, the Universal pressbook asserted that the film is "in no sense a horror film, nor is it just another 'whodunit' of the cops-and-robbers pattern." Correspondingly, *Motion Picture Daily* advised that "exhibitors should not be misled by the title *Phantom Lady* into pegging it as just another horror film."[100] Whether or not the reviewers thought the film deviated from conventional horror, it mostly received positive reviews, typically using Hitchcock, the master of horror, as the benchmark for its success or failure. Echoing a number of other trade journals, the *Motion Picture Herald* enthused, "The pupil equals, perhaps even outdistances, the master."[101] The dismissive *New York Times* review did not agree, however, stating that "something was bound to happen when a former Alfred Hitchcock protégée and a former director of German horror films were teamed up on the Universal lot—something severe and unrelenting, drenched in creeping morbidity and gloom."[102] The reviewer pinpoints the unremitting dark tone and stylization that would become synonymous with film noir but bemoans these tropes as a relic of "German horror" rather than recent generic innovation.[103]

Though the film is typically discussed as a seminal noir, the female archetypes of femme fatale and stay-at-home nurturer, proposed by Janie Place as a key structuring binary, are significantly blurred in *Phantom Lady*.[104] Like her counterparts in Lewton's earlier films (*Cat People, I Walked with a Zombie, Seventh Victim*), the spider woman character is defined by her overattachment to the domestic realm rather than her desire for independence and public life. The "phantom lady" is problematic not because she attempts to transgress traditional modes of femininity but because she is unable to move beyond these outdated gender ideals. As the hypersignification of the hat (both textually and extratextually) suggests, women's clothing choices are integral to the film's quite sophisticated investigation of the contradictory discourses shaping definitions of female identity in wartime America.

With particular reference to *Now, Voyager* (1942), Mary Ann Doane explains how the despecularization of the female body is used as a signifier for women's ailing mental health in a number of 1940s women's films. In contrast to *Now, Voyager*, in which Charlotte's (Bette Davis) recovery is marked by her increasing investment in female glamour, in *Phantom Lady* the titular character's overindulgence in traditionally feminine accoutrements, most significantly her elaborate hat, is actually the symptom of her pathology.[105] The hat was to be worn at her wedding, but her fiancé died two days before they were to be married. It is this traumatic death of her partner, a tragedy with obvious wartime resonance, that triggers her nervous breakdown. The narrative and metaphorical significance of this fetish object is clear in *Phantom Lady*'s opening shot, which zooms out from an extreme close-up of the all-important hat. The pressbook's proposal that theaters exhibit in the lobby a replica of the "hat of horror" created by a local milliner highlights its positioning as an object of simultaneous fascination and horror; this ambiguity demonstrates the precarious and ambiguous status of traditional modes of femininity during the hiatus of wartime.

When Scott and his mysterious date visit the "boom-boom musical revue" at the Casino Theater, the Latina performer Miss Montero (played by Carmen Miranda's sister Aurora) is infuriated to discover that she is wearing the same hat. Although the hat is at home in this performative sphere (significantly linked to the desexualized exoticism and theatricality of popular Latino stars in this Good Neighbor era), it is deemed inappropriate or overindulgent when removed from this realm.[106] When questioned, Montero says, "What woman other than me could wear hats like those without looking ridiculous?" Antonia Lant discusses the symbolic resonance of a similarly decorative hat used to represent the "Problems of 1945" on the cover of the British *Picture Post*—it shows a woman in military dress trying on a clashing tutti-frutti hat. Lant proposes that this Carmen Miranda hat "works as a synecdoche both for pre-war notions of femininity—notions of frivolity and attention to decoration—and for the woman's desire for an end to austerity conditions."[107] With the war still raging in early 1944, Ann Terry's inappropriate headgear is clearly codified as a problem in the text, an anachronistic relic of the conspicuous consumption and impractical adornment of prewar notions of femininity.

As discussed in chapter 1, due to government restrictions on fabric usage, Hollywood was encouraged to tone down its own lavish costuming for the duration of the war.[108] This shift toward utilitarian fashions allowed Hollywood to exploit the unpatriotic connotations of excessive pleats, ruffles, and unnecessary accoutrements to characterize certain female characters as transgressive, most blatantly in classic femme fatale characters such as Phyllis Dietrichson (Barbara Stanwyck) in *Double Indemnity* (1944). While the stereotypical femininity of the "phantom lady" is clearly juxtaposed to the internally and externally unruffled Kansas, she is far from a femme fatale figure.[109] Christina Lane insists that Ann Terry is not "a specter of monstrous femininity—the insane and degenerate alter ego of the bride-to-be—and she neither frightens nor intimidates Kansas."[110] As in Lewton's films, this "phantom lady" is far more tragic and elusive than the typical femme fatale, but she certainly has elements of the spectral and monstrous characters in *Cat People* and its sequel, for example, though more the peripheral characters played by Elizabeth Russell than the central roles played by Simone Simon.

As Lane argues, Kansas's relationship with her is one of sympathy, not conflict. In fact, rather than being frightened or intimidated, the assertive heroine is able to provide hope for Ann Terry's recovery by getting her to give up the hat, and thus her unhealthy attachment to the moment of trauma—as with the child's influence on Russell's haunted character in *The Curse of the Cat People*. On a more symbolic level, the relinquishing of the hat cuts the link to an anachronistic mode of female identity based on overinvestment in traditional glamour, marriage, and suburban domestication. In the novel, Ann Terry never meets and befriends Kansas, as it is she, not Marlow, who throws herself out of a window. Harrison chose not to mark her out as beyond redemption; these conflicting modes of femininity were reconcilable in her treatment of the story.

The *Collins Dictionary* definition of "phantom" is "1: an apparition or specter . . . 2: the visible representation of something abstract"; it is this second definition that defines the phantom lady's symbolic resonance in the text.[111] She is an abstraction of traditional femininity, one that must be reconciled with the realities of wartime. This reality is portrayed by the resourceful Kansas, who is philosophical in the face of scarcities and sacrifices on the home front. According to the pressbook, Joan Harrison explained to Ella Raines that "the nature of her character would not permit her to be beautiful. That her clothes would be ordinary, some of them downright shabby." Raines responded, "I didn't work so hard for years and years just to be pretty."[112] Her costuming is hardly shabby, but she is outfitted in the plain, straight-cut suits favored at the time by career women. The image of Raines as privileging professionalism over glamour is clearly intended to inform her character extratextually; another pressbook article conflates the "svelte and spirited young woman" with the "wholly unstereotyped" heroine she portrays.

Her wartime work ethic is stressed in her unfaltering commitment to her new detective role—"a man's job" according to Marlow. She takes to this traditionally male role with ease, remaining undaunted by the tough urban milieu, while utilizing disguises and hard-boiled dialogue. (When the police question why she followed the barman she replies, "Maybe I needed the exercise.") What's more, her emotional strength is contrasted to that of Scott, who is shown crying in despair. In fact, Kansas reveals that she loves Scott for "how soft he really is"; the film therefore explicitly subverts traditional gender expectations. Also, in her relocation from Wichita to New York in order to find employment mirrors the feted mobile women who moved from rural areas to major cities to work in wartime factories. As she tells Marlow, she moved to New York without a job offer or financial backup and "lived for a whole week on sandwiches."

She is at home in a "man's world" but also exploits her sexuality by masquerading as the good-time girl Jeannie in order to gain information from a key witness, Cliff. Back at the Casino Theater an upward camera tilt reveals Kansas's transformation; the spectator appropriates Cliff's point of view as he scans her legs adorned in fishnet stockings, her tacky jewelry, and her decorative hat. Unlike Cliff, however, the spectator is aware that this is an elaborate ruse to entrap the predictable drummer. Harrison herself was well aware of the advantages her sexuality might offer in the male-dominated world of Hollywood. In an article on *Phantom Lady* in *Time* magazine, she differentiated herself from other producers by saying "I use my sex," even exploiting "some leg art" in her studio publicity photographs. The article continues, "Besides using a pair of ah-inspiring legs, she also uses a mind trained at the Sorbonne, Oxford, and by England's shrewdest director."[113] Like Kansas, Harrison suggests, she was able to get ahead by manipulating the male gaze.

In a *Chicago Tribune* article on Harrison titled "Glamour Galvanic," Hedda Hopper describes her as "a 33-year-old, golden-haired ball of fire with a temper of a tarantula, the purring persuasiveness of a female archangel, the capacity for work of a family of beavers, and the sex appeal of a No. 1 glamour girl." Hopper characterizes "Hollywood's most successful lady" as a hybrid creature—simultaneously aggressive spider woman and ethereal innocent, desirable pinup and desiring predator. Embracing the imagery of the female monster cycle, Hopper represents her as a unique amalgamation of opposing gendered spheres, a female Frankenstein created through a supernatural galvanic process. Hopper still struggles to negotiate this synthesis of perceived active masculine and passive feminine traits, however, noting that Harrison's labor (the "hardest, most exacting toil a girl—or a man—ever put in") does not correspond with her demeanor ("pert, pretty and piquant"). She continues, "Today Joan Harrison makes me think of a man—why do I keep recurring to the masculine?"[114] Almost all articles discussing Harrison's role at Universal celebrate her overturning of gender expectations but stress that she had succeeded in spite of being female, rather than because of it. Following her appointment at Universal, *Collier's* reported that "Hollywood's only femme producer thinks like a woman, is very pretty, and is sure there's nothing lovelier than a nice, juicy homicide. . . . She is not, as you might suspect from all of that, a huge, hearty, masculine woman. She's small, hoydenish, and wears an evening gown with the same eye-filling éclat as Lana Turner." The article goes on to challenge the idea that "she got to be the first woman producer because of the war. . . . Joan Harrison would have been a producer if Hitler had been a jockey."[115]

Similarly, in a February 1945 article for *Modern Screen* entitled "It's a Woman's World Too," Ann Daggett points out, "It isn't because Joan is beautiful enough to be a movie star herself, nor yet because she is a woman with a woman's winning ways that she is today one of Hollywood's top producers in a field exclusively for men. Rather she has succeeded in spite of these two factors." Harrison somewhat challenges Daggett's caveats, stating that "today there is more recognition of women's talent than ever before. Those who want a career can certainly have one." But Daggett concludes with a note of caution, suggesting that though the pioneering producer proves it is possible to attain an executive position in Hollywood, "the fact remains that she's one of the few women who has so far."[116] Significantly, to the right of the article is an advertisement with the tagline "You'll steal his heart in 'Flight Command' slack suit." This ad showing the RKO screen star Rita Corday posing in the "captivating version of a Flight Officer's uniform with definite feminine touches" indicates how women's ability to adopt male roles had to be supplemented with a traditional sense of desirability and femininity. This is a reality that Harrison seemingly knew all too well, using "her sex" as well as her talent, as she reveals in *Time*.

Like Harrison, her fictional alter ego Kansas is able to negotiate the simultaneity of functions that are traditionally bifurcated into opposing gendered terms—namely, active (male) spectator and passive (female) spectacle. Like our female movie monsters, the "phantom lady" is dislocated from society because of her inability to embrace her divided self; she is purely spectacle and thus only spectral. She is the pathological extreme of the figure of "Mrs. Stay-at-Home" or the female slacker who was a threat to the war effort, as characterized in wartime media reports. It is the multiple and material bodies of Harrison and Kansas that are characterized as uniquely adaptable to American home-front life. As with the confusion of noir female archetypes, their representative chronotopic spaces of a dangerous urban landscape and idealized pastoral idyll are subverted. Place insists that it is the "sexual, dangerous woman [who] is comfortable in the world of cheap dives, shadowy doorways and mysterious settings."[117] In *Phantom Lady*, however, it is the utilitarian heroine Kansas who becomes master of this tough urban landscape. It is through mastery of the gaze, at least initially, that this reversal of gendered power relations is played out. In the opening scene Scott Henderson explicates his panoptic control over the city to his mysterious date. As the couple travel by taxi along Forty-second Street, Scott turns and asks, "Ever walk down Broadway and watch people's faces? It's fun." Real footage of Broadway is back-projected as the taxi passes through Times Square, significantly taking in the Rialto's marquee, but Ann Terry neither takes in the scenery nor maintains eye contact with her date. Her self-consciousness is clearly juxtaposed to Scott's self-assuredness, but this is to be short-lived. Scott's omniscient gaze is shattered as key witnesses deny seeing the "phantom lady"; he eventually resigns himself to the possibility that "maybe there never was a woman. . . . Maybe she doesn't exist." Kansas dismisses this possibility and sets out to gain the visual mastery of the city that Scott overconfidently assumed he possessed.

Unlike the male detectives, Kansas refuses to accept the bar owner's assertion that he does not remember a woman drinking in the bar on the night in question. She therefore returns to the bar on three consecutive nights to sit silently staring down the barman until he acquiesces. Her persistent and unremitting eye contact makes the barman increasingly nervous; he is unable to return her gaze and becomes fidgety, eventually smashing a glass. He confides in some regulars, "She's been sitting there all night, like last night, and the night before, staring at me." When he turns back, however, she is gone, calling his own vision into question. Subsequently she tracks him through the streets of New York, refusing help from male bystanders when the panicky bar owner confronts her. Later, in the scene in which she masquerades as Jeannie (supplanting the position previously taken by Ann Terry), her manipulation of the relations of looking is even more sophisticated. She now takes control of the easily manipulated Cliff's gaze through her masterful performance; as Marlow tells the doomed Cliff, "She was magnificent. She loathed you but went with you." She later spots the clues leading to the whereabouts of Ann Terry (a hatbox) and the identity of the murderer (her own handbag that she left at Cliff's apartment). Through her use and manipulation of the gaze, Kansas overcomes the mysteries and dangers of downtown New York.

Kansas is linked to the pastoral idyll through her eponymous home state, but she is more at home now in this urban environment, refusing calls by the two male leads for her to return to Wichita; the film, like Kansas, clearly chooses the urban over the pastoral. Her love interest, Scott, is linked to progress, modernity, and city living through his job as a civil engineer; alternately, the psychopathic Marlow reveals, "I never liked cities; noise, confusion, dirt. And the people in them; they don't like me because I'm different." Therefore, just as the gendering of the gaze is reversed, the potential dangers and terrors of the city are displaced onto a non-city-dweller rather than being a symptom of the urban condition. In fact, the key pleasures of the film arise precisely from the excitement and revelry of New York City life, a point that clearly split contemporary reviewers.

The critical *New York Times* review went on to say that the film's failing was its privileging of sensation over narrative coherence, concluding, "Sensation is specious without reason. And reason is what this picture lacks."[118] More "hep" reviewers considered this privileging of autonomous sensational sequences over narrative economy the film's chief success. As Manny Farber commends, *Phantom Lady* "works much harder than most modern movies to turn up some actual life in actual settings." The scene garnering most attention in the film's reception is the sequence when Kansas, masquerading as Jeannie, visits an underground jazz club with Cliff, which Farber praises for "actively enter[ing] the event and tr[ying] to get over to the audience the heart of the moment."[119] This frenetic montage sequence utilizes disorienting camera angles and close-ups as it cuts between the musicians performing and Kansas dancing, pouring liquor, kissing Cliff, and applying makeup. It culminates in a frenzied drum solo that cuts back and forth between Cliff's increasingly sweaty, manic face and Kansas's feigned ecstatic expression.

The *Nation*'s James Agee contends that the "jam session [is] used as a metaphor for orgasm and death—which in turn becomes a metaphor for the jam session. [It is a] good, physically vivid metaphor; but it is juvenile delinquent jazz."[120] The liberal New York newspaper *PM* also identified the jazz scene as the film's best sequence, stating, "There is no dialogue; just the hottest of hot music, one drink of what looks like gin, a madder-than-mad flight on the drums, and at the end of it the drummer is hopped up like a reefer addict. For *aficionados* of hot jazz, this scene alone makes a session with *Phantom Lady* worthwhile."[121] Reviewers almost universally celebrated the phenomenological essence of this scene, disregarding its position in the film's overall cause-and-effect narrative. When the script was sent to the PCA this sequence caused the most concern for Joseph Breen. He recommended, seemingly unsuccessfully, that the "jive sequence" should be "handled with the greatest of care to avoid any intimation that Cliff and the rest of the musicians are dope addicts. Furthermore in this sequence, the relationship between Carol and Cliff should be handled carefully; especially the business of Carol dancing, to avoid any offensive sex suggestiveness."[122] From this initial reading of the script Breen could not have foreseen Siodmak's orgiastic editing, a device that would work as a purely cinematic sexual metaphor, and one with a provocative topical resonance.[123] John D'Emilio and Estelle Freedman argue that World War II brought unprecedented opportunities for premarital experience, and *Phantom Lady*, rather than condemning or sidestepping this issue, embraces the new sexual liberalism.[124] Even the promotional campaign exploited these connotations of sexual experimentation, with the main poster tagline promising the story of "a night he could not forget . . . with a WOMAN he could not remember!" (See figure 13.) Another declared, "She gave him the six most reckless hours of her life . . . then vanished!"

Phantom Lady was released at a moment of charged media discourse regarding women's increasing presence in Times Square and other urban nightspots. In his "Times Square Diary" Meyer Berger recounts the round-the-clock revelry of this "Mecca of pleasure-seekers" in mid-1944. As the nighttime crowd arrives at 8:00 P.M., he notes that "women in limp summer prints outnumber five to one the sailors in whites." He charts the interactions of women and servicemen as the "square is given over pretty much to alcoholic and amorous atmosphere. . . . American, British and

FIGURE 13 *Phantom Lady*'s poster exploits connotations of wartime sexual freedoms.

French service men are forming the nightly stag lines along the curbs and in front of shop windows, ogling girls and women surging towards Forty-Second Street subway stations." However, the gaze is also reversed, as at 1:00 A.M. "in front of the Paramount two drunken civilians and two tipsy tars change shirts and hats to the shrill enjoyment of the girls." At 4:00 A.M., as a "very unsteady wench in startling green silk, but not much of it, lurches by twirling a red handbag . . . two middle-aged women with hair dyed raven black stop at the all-night out-of-town newsstand."[125] The Times Square of 1944, as characterized by Berger, is one in which women outnumber men. Embracing the contradictions and unlikely juxtapositions of the square, the women who frequent it are simultaneously spectacle and spectator, sexually desirable and sexually desiring, lurching reveler and out-of-town war worker. What's more, discourses of bodily discipline, adornment, and transformation are central to Berger's account of the hybrid femininity on display in Times Square: the "shrill" voices of the female "oglers"; the "unsteady wench in startling green silk"; the "limp summer prints"; and the "hair dyed raven black" of the women workers.

As we have seen, many women's social lives changed as a result of wartime employment. Hundreds of thousands of working women relocated to the urban centers where most of the war work in factories was situated, and resultantly had greater disposable income and less direct influence from family. Women increasingly went out in groups rather than with male partners, partially due to husbands, boyfriends, and potential dates being overseas, and partially as a result of women meeting in factories and new friendships springing up. Shift work meant that bars, dance clubs, restaurants, and even cinemas in areas such as Times Square stayed open almost around the clock to meet demand. In his "Times Square Diary" Berger continues that as night blurred into day the "jitterbug line for the first morning show" formed outside the Paramount, while "the Rialto, which closed less than five hours ago, [was] open for customers with a new horror show."[126] And more of those customers than ever before would be women.[127] Women's transgression of conventional gender roles in cinema auditoriums, urban leisure districts, and wartime workplaces, perhaps unsurprisingly, encouraged media, government, and social scientific discourse that condemned the young women who sought "sexual adventure in the dingy amusement sections of the community."[128]

Despite sensational outbreaks of male youth violence from mid-1942 onward, most significantly the 1943 "Zoot Suit Riots," female delinquency—and particularly sexual delinquency—provoked the greatest anxiety for the media, legislators, and social scientists, particularly in the urban centers of war industry.[129] Combating female delinquency was a personal mission for FBI director J. Edgar Hoover, who sensitized the media and the public to what was in his view the home front's central moral concern through his extensively reported, hyperbolic speeches. For example, in March 1943 Hoover attacked "the alarming upswing in crime among women and girls"—including a 104.7 percent increase in female sex offenses—and called for Americans "to keep the home front clean, wholesome, and strong."[130] *Newsweek* identified this "moral breakdown amongst teenage girls" as "the gravest tragedy of the war," highlighting a 100 percent increase in "delinquent girl cases" in New York in the last year and noting that the teenage bobby-sox brigade and older victory girls' courting of servicemen in and around Times Square was the major problem for police and juvenile courts.[131]

The female delinquency problem was also debated in a concurrent cycle of Hollywood "juvenile delinquency pictures," causing further concerns for the media, censors, and government agencies. These low-budget B features—including *Where Are Your Children?* (1943), *Youth Runs Wild* (1944), *Are These Our Parents?* (1944), *Delinquent Daughters* (1944), *I Accuse My Parents* (1944), and *Youth Aflame* (1944)—were mostly evaluated in the middlebrow press in relation to the local contexts of the behavior and policing of youth in their respective cities. They judged them not for their aesthetic merits but for their potential positive or negative influences on both female delinquency and the policies and strategies to police it within their localities.[132] Fearing a more far-reaching negative influence, the Office of War Information, the Office of Censorship, and the Federal Security Agency attempted to stifle this cycle of production on the grounds that these films might be used as ammunition for Nazi propaganda against "decadent democracies."[133] Alternately, insiders attributed Hollywood's "self-imposed censorship regarding girl delinquency" to a general "squeamishness" within the industry rather than to federal intervention on political grounds.[134] The bigger studios mostly sidestepped this timely issue, "allaying fears with reassuring comic convention" in a concurrent cycle of juvenile comedies, most starring Shirley Temple.[135] Val Lewton—whose RKO production unit made its only explicit intervention into wartime issues with *Youth Runs Wild*—protested against this government intervention and RKO's subsequent sabotaging of his film. He maintained that it was "more important to produce worthwhile films to combat a tangible danger on the home front [than] to neglect this because of an intangible fear that some of the pictures might possibly be used as propaganda in Europe."[136]

Within such a climate, producers like Lewton and Harrison were able to address women's experiences in Times Square and other urban centers far more effectively and evocatively in horror and mystery films such as *The Seventh Victim* and *Phantom Lady* than in narratives that dealt directly with wartime concerns. Through Kansas's successful mastery of the bars and dance clubs of Times Square (and downtown New York's even seamier underbelly of underground jazz clubs and run-down apartment buildings), *Phantom Lady* evokes the potential liberations and excitement engendered by women's more colorful and contradictory social and, perhaps, sexual experiences, in ways that the juvenile delinquency films and the bobby-soxer comedies could not. Although Harrison was afforded the opportunity to foreground these contradictions and complexities in class-A form in her first film for Universal, this freedom was curtailed as the war came to a close in 1945.

"Getting Away with Murder": The Strange Treatment of Harry and Harrison

Universal was happy to exploit Harrison's dual perspective for a woman's mystery story in late 1943, but, perhaps unsurprisingly, her more ambitious proposed follow-up of a film to be made entirely by women was not sanctioned.[137] Instead, following her reasonable critical and box-office success for Universal with *Phantom Lady*, her second assignment as producer was the adaptation of Thomas Job's successful and sensational play that "shocked Broadway," *Uncle Harry*. In the Broadway version that opened on May 20, 1942, a sympathetic male character who is dominated by his two sisters gets away with murdering one of them by framing the other for the crime.[138] For this project, initially retitled *The Strange Affair of Uncle Harry* (1945), Harrison chose to team up again with *Phantom Lady*'s director, Robert Siodmak, and leading lady, Ella Raines. Like their previous collaboration, the film follows the female monster film's triangular structure of two women—one a resourceful career woman, the other pathologically tied to the domestic realm—competing for the same man. As the pressbook revealed, however, *Uncle Harry* was "a new type of triangle story, involving a brother, sister, and girlfriend."[139] Perhaps surprisingly, it was the film's murder plot rather than its incest angle that most troubled the Hays

Office, holding up its release and initiating a battle between Harrison and Universal over the film's ending that would ultimately end her association with the studio. The film, particularly its much-maligned "tacked-on ending," indicates the postwar direction of industry policy in relation to women and horror production that helped motivate the end of the female monster cycle.

In the version of *Uncle Harry* released in 1945, the meek bachelor Harry Quincey (George Sanders), head clothes designer in a small-town factory, lives with his domineering sisters—the glamorous hypochondriac Lettie (Geraldine Fitzgerald) and the pernickety widow Hester (Moyna MacGill). Harry gains newfound confidence when the New York fashion expert Deborah Brown (Ella Raines) arrives in the quaint New Hampshire town of Corinth. His developing romance with this new work colleague promises happiness, but it is thwarted by passive, then increasingly active opposition from his sister Lettie, particularly after Harry and Deborah become engaged. Lettie feigns illness on the eve of the wedding, and Deborah, realizing this is a trick, leaves town alone, calling off the engagement and then marrying someone else. When Lettie reveals her manipulations Harry attempts to poison her, but his other sister, Hester, drinks the lethal concoction. Because of Harry's popularity and high standing in the community, the malevolent Lettie is blamed and sentenced to death, even after Harry, overcome with guilt, attempts to confess. In the tacked-on ending, Harry wakes from a dream in time to discard the poison and leave town with Deborah, who has called off her marriage and returned just as he awakes. As Harry somewhat ironically exclaims, "I can hardly believe you're here."

The original ending penned by Stephen Longstreet, under guidance from Siodmak and Harrison, stressed the irony of the perfect crime by making Harry have to live with his guilt, while implying the possible salvation of a romantic future with Deborah. This was achieved by framing the film with a prologue and epilogue. In the prologue Harry is at the station waiting for a train that will take him to an insane asylum. In the epilogue Deborah arrives at the station and says she still wants to leave with him, but Harry's doctor stops her, and Harry leaves on the train alone. Siodmak filmed this prologue and epilogue on June 15, 1945, but Universal's production manager, Martin Murphy, fearing the "morally dubious" ending might stall the film's release, insisted on filming the alternate dream ending. The veteran Universal director Roy William Neill was called in after Siodmak refused to participate (as did Fitzgerald), and Harrison resultantly ended her contract over the decision to release this version.[140]

The film certainly embraces tropes of the female monster cycle both textually and extratextually, employing the triangular structure of two women competing for the same man, though now, particularly through the incestuous link between Harry and Lettie, diminishing the sympathy afforded to the monstrous rival. On the other hand, the working woman Deborah is unambiguously positioned as the solution to Harry's emasculation problem. Harry, said the *Time* reviewer, is "the kind of man everybody likes and nobody quite respects" until Raines's character "wakes him up and threatens to make a man of him."[141] As the *Time* review asserts, this is Harry's story, not "a girls' quest" like *Phantom Lady*, and Raines's role is chiefly the restoration of Harry's masculinity.

Although Raines's career woman character is less central to the narrative, and is displaced from her native New York to naïve New Hampshire, the film unequivocally celebrates "the pluck and drive of [the] city girl" over the "boudoir femininity" of small-town Lettie.[142] Deborah's positive assertiveness is clearly tied to shifts in women's relationship to work and leisure. Lettie advises Harry to take Deborah to see the house where George Washington once stayed, but instead they attend a women's baseball game, where Deborah cheers on the local Women's Tigers team. Deborah is clearly linked to wider wartime progress and social change, in this case in opposition to the inconsequential official history of the town. The war gave women their first serious professional team sport in the form of the All-American Girls Professional Baseball League, set up in 1943. Although the league never expanded beyond the Midwest, and therefore never reached New Hampshire, the rules were almost identical to the game played by men, and the league became very popular, drawing large crowds and providing these sportswomen with public attention, admiration, and a reasonable wage ($40 to $100 per week plus expenses). Significantly, as with other female shifts into male occupations (as Joan Harrison might well have attested), publicity and outfits stressed the player's feminine features and demeanor, and the league demanded behavior appropriate to the "highest ideals of womanhood."[143] In the context of the film, though, women's baseball is clearly invoked as an agent of positive social change. It is the past and tradition that are characterized as the problem, through the declining wealth and status of the Quinceys. Lettie warns Deborah that "the modern world will ruin" Harry, but it is clearly his link to his familial past (albeit admittedly in its incumbent matriarchal form) that is destroying him.

The decision to attend a women's baseball game also intimates shifts in traditional gender relations in respect to dating and sexual practice. When Deborah thanks Harry for taking her on the date he responds, "At times I wondered who was taking who." Furthermore, when small-town Harry says, "It's late . . . almost ten," Deborah responds, "In New York life is just beginning." The introduction of Harry to this assertive "city girl," far from emasculating him, brings about the process of his revitalization or sexual awakening. In a moment of unabashed double entendre, Harry proposes she come back to his room to see his "nine-inch telescope," while proffering the warning, "We might have to wait a while before it rises high enough." The spirited and optimistic Deborah responds, "We could try." Deborah is not characterized as chaste and innocent; in fact, it is her assertive and assured sexuality that is juxtaposed to Lettie's unhealthy sexual dysfunction. Later when Lettie, wearing an inappropriately oversized hat, visits Deborah in her cramped hotel room to warn her that her late-night trysts with Harry might be "misinterpreted," she responds, "If Harry wishes to stop by my hotel at any time I'll always be glad to see him." Sexually vital and self-assured, Deborah is in marked contrast to the narcissistic Lettie, who is too lethargic and infantilized to be the diva she aspires to be. As in the Siodmak-directed *Son of Dracula*, it is the "monstrous" female's pathological attachment to the family home and her petulant refusal to leave that are the corrupting influence in the narrative, not hypersexuality or independence. The same can be said, in fact, of most the era's classic femmes fatales, who are villainized not for entering the public sphere but for their pathological attachment to the domestic and dependence upon men.[144]

The film's promotion embraced the female monster film's iconography, simultaneously connecting and distancing *Uncle Harry* from conventional horror. As with *Phantom Lady*, the promotional material extols Harrison's unique woman's slant on the "murder drama" genre, as well as her training with Hitchcock. The poster tagline alludes to the film's incest theme, asking, "What kind of love can make a woman become a monster . . . a man a murderer?" Another key tagline reads "One Hungry Moment Together . . . And another woman he had loved became a monster, a creature he must KILL!" (See figure 14.) Fitzgerald's far-from-supernatural character Lettie is characterized as a horror "monster" or "creature," drawing on the intertextual links to the female monster films. Other poster images show Lettie

FIGURE 14 The poster for *The Strange Affair of Uncle Harry* evinces the film's generic links to the female monster film.

reclining in the typical femme fatale pose, with Deborah either fearfully holding on to Harry's arm or in a romantic embrace with him. Much like the female monster publicity, the posters emphasize the film's triangular romantic structure, reducing the female leads to monster and victim while expanding the narrative's necessarily muted sexual angle.

In the pressbook articles *Uncle Harry* is sold as a "genuine shocker," significantly stressing Universal as a master in this field, but it is differentiated from conventional horror pictures. An article entitled "Studio Gives Definition of Movie Murder Drama" reports that "although Universal is 'home of horror pictures' at the studio they say 'a murder drama is a horror story without Boris Karloff.'"[145] The press material is again at pains to highlight Harrison as central to the authoring of this new kind of horror drama. The pressbook claims that "Joan Harrison, one of Hollywood's few feminine producers, was chosen to pilot the production because of her women's slant, and because of her skill in dramatizing crime stories for the screen."[146] It even asserts that she has "elevated herself to a pinnacle where she can be said to rival the great Alfred Hitchcock as the producer of suspenseful film fare." Even while acknowledging the atypical nature of Harrison's role, the publicity material does little to challenge gendered power relations in regard to systems of looking. It notes, "Instead of the producer examining the actress' legs to see if she gets the part, the actor now takes a peek at the producer's gams to see whether he wants the part."[147]

This negotiation of Harrison's seemingly irreconcilable masculine and feminine selves, and their relationship to the bifurcated female identities represented in the film, are taken up again in an article entitled "Crime Study, Hobby of Feminine Producer." It reads, "A girl with wavy blonde hair, dimples and a 24-inch waistline could entertain people with something more than crime stories. But not Joan Harrison. She lives and breathes crime." It continues to detail her training with Hitchcock but also states that "long before she ever heard of the noted melodrama director, she was secretly reading horror and mystery books, against the wishes of her parents who wanted their little Joan Harrison to grow into a demure, small town gentlewoman."[148] The publicity also links the "self assured," "ambitious" Harrison to Raines's role as the "New York fashion authority" with her "brisk modern day girl appearance" and "library of detective stories." It continues that Raines chose the role because it was "her idea of a shiny faced American babe. She wears clever clothes, shows aggressiveness and initiative in dealing with a man and does appear completely honest and straightforward."[149] In the film, Raines's character, Deborah, distinguishes herself from stereotypical media representations of women, refusing to be called Miss Brown because it "sounds like a boss's secretary in a magazine serial." Like her character, whose field of employment has shifted from construction to fashion, however, Raines's star persona is increasingly linked to her "clever" fashion choices; a number of pressbook articles showcase the original suit designs by Travis Banton for Ella Raines.[150]

Released on August 17, 1945, just a couple of days after V-J Day, the film received disappointing and disappointed reviews, particularly in relation to its "tacked-on ending which the audience is requested not to tell—presumably on the assumption that everybody has the right to feel sold out." *Time* continued that *Uncle Harry*'s "hints of psychological incest, which are so arranged that you can take them or leave them, are even more interesting in their Hays Office aspects than as drama."[151] Bosley Crowther's review for the *New York Times* concurred, complaining that "the business—compelled by the Hays Office—of having murderers dream their crimes is becoming extremely aggravating."[152] The following day Crowther was inspired to write a further piece, entitled "Getting Away with Murder," which raged that the Hays Office should be embarrassed for the "silly boner that it pulled on Uncle Harry." He mocked, "The Hays Code, although it forced the 'murderer' to dream his crime, did not proscribe him from dreaming a very questionable attachment to his sister at the same time." He continued that having Harry subconsciously dream an "amoral love" had "permitted a situation that any student of Freud could tell, from a moment's observation, is loaded with impropriety." Crowther concluded that "it's just such deflections in enforcement that make the Code appear futile and absurd."[153]

Like Crowther, other critics centered the strange treatment of *Uncle Harry* as a clear example of the hypocrisy and stupidity of the Hays Code and the timidity of the industry.[154] In the aforementioned "Glamour Galvanic," Hopper praises the strength and integrity Harrison showed in her heated battle with and subsequent resignation from Universal over the ending of the film. She explains that although Harrison pushed to retain the film's "stark, staring realism . . . the studio got cold feet and let the Hays

Office have its way. Why, they shot five different endings, and at the end of each Joan grew madder and madder, until they finally decided to call the whole thing a dream." She concludes, "You've got to take your hat off to the little gal—she's got plenty of nerve."[155] *Time* also commended Harrison for defying a conservative and impersonal industry by offering her friend Geraldine Fitzgerald an "artist's salvation" through her role in *Uncle Harry*. The article suggests that Fitzgerald had been barred from realizing her potential, following her success with *Dark Victory* (1939) and *Wuthering Heights* (1939), because of her refusal to kowtow to a patriarchal industry. It explained, "David Selznick wanted her for the title role in Hitchcock's smash *Rebecca*, but she turned it down. . . . That sort of independence is neither admired nor understood in Hollywood."[156]

Following the war, however, the female producer's assertiveness and independent spirit were seen as less attractive. In January 1946 a *Citizen-News* article revealed that Harrison, "after some months of comparative idleness," had signed a contract with RKO after quitting Universal over "that much-disputed picture." In opposition to Hopper's article, this one, somewhat sarcastically titled "Joan Harrison Worrying about Butter," goes on to tame her reputation as "something of the stormy petrel" by pointing out that "the funny thing about Joan, despite her preoccupation with a film career, is that the housewifely instinct will come to the fore." It emphasizes her proclivity for entertaining at home, where she can make sure she has enough butter for the guests, and underlines that while she provides "an example of industry and ambition that would be hard to excel," she would "be glad of the right kind" of marriage, and if she were to have a baby, she would "regard it as the greatest production of [her] career."[157]

This article therefore works to reconcile the contradictions that arise between the feminine and masculine realms of private and public labor that are celebrated in the earlier Hopper article. Like her films, which celebrate wartime career women's abilities to synthesize the twin demands of desirability and productivity, the appeal of the "galvanic" Harrison was seen as increasingly redundant following the war, as men returned to reclaim their roles and restore women's central productive roles of housekeeping and childbirth. Tellingly, the "Showmanship" section of the *Uncle Harry* pressbook encourages male theater owners to send "'Direct Mail Plugs' to prominent women in your community or members of women's clubs . . . written in a feminine hand or typed on a good grade of ladies' stationery" explaining that the film is the "greatest thrill in screen entertainment." This minor deception intimates the increasing shift away from genuinely attempting to address the wartime woman's point of view and toward restoring a male perspective and authority to Hollywood's strategies as the war came to a close. The evolution of the cycle of "women's mystery dramas" heralded the impending secularization and psychologization of horror that would bring about the demise of the female monster following the war.

4

From Whatdunit to Whodunit

The Postwar Psychologization of Horror, 1945–1946

I went to see *The Spider Woman Strikes Back* feeling absolutely sure that the sleek brunette would be metamorphosed into a fat, furry Black Widow. . . . Actually, the best she can do is indulge in a little amateur horticulture and kill off a few cows.

–Bert McCord, *New York Herald Tribune* (March 23, 1946)

The *New York Herald Tribune*'s disappointment at *The Spider Woman Strikes Back*'s undercutting of generic expectations exposes the ubiquity of the female monster by 1946, but also her postwar secularization.[1] As Rick Altman explains, "Once a genre is recognized and practised throughout the industry, individual studios have no further economic interest in practising it as such (especially in their prestige productions) . . . When a genre reaches saturation point, studios must either abandon it, restrict it to 'B' productions, or handle it in a new way."[2] Following its unsuccessful attempt to handle them in a new way—as the quote above attests—Universal did indeed decide to abandon its female monster franchises altogether. Although the female monster character took temporary refuge in Poverty Row, shifts in audience tastes and pressure from the critics and censors made even these impoverished offerings untenable.

A cycle of "psychiatric pictures" emerged in mid-1946 that provided a scientific corrective to the problems raised by the horror genre, transferring the otherworldly anxieties of the female monster cycle into the secular world of psychological drama. Following its 1946 merger with William Goetz's International Pictures, Universal abandoned production of B films and vowed to produce only quality product. The newly formed

Universal-International's first release, *The Dark Mirror* (1946), answered postwar calls for both a reconversion to prewar gender roles and more positive depictions of the psychiatric profession in horror films.[3] This chapter will explore how discourses regarding gender, science, and the role of cinema became intimately conjoined in this period, as postwar America attempted to lay to rest the psychological tensions and contradictions unearthed by the war.

"Beauty or Beast . . . Woman or Monster . . . ?": Secularizing the Female Monster

Dana Polan proposes a fundamental shift in horror cinema in the early forties, as monstrosity is brought into the secular and psychological realm of the human subject, making it accessible as an object of science and opening up the "possibility of horror's cure."[4] As earlier chapters have demonstrated, however, this process was later arriving than Polan states within these female-centered horror texts. Throughout the war years the nonsynthesizable bodies of female monster characters stood in for the old country as the last "exotic repository of a non-scientific knowledge, a battery of beliefs and institutions" previously embodied in the classical horror mise-en-scène of a temporally and topographically indistinct Europe.[5] By 1946 this secularizing impulse had infiltrated the female monster film.

In March 1946, *Variety* criticized the secularization of Universal's recent horror films, bemoaning that *The Spider Woman Strikes Back*'s "title gives little hint of the yarn."[6] It also complained about the "fence-sitting attitude" and "constant underplaying of the horror motif" in Universal's subsequent *She-Wolf of London* (1946), which "never quite makes up its mind whether it's to be a straight whodunit or a horror film."[7] This retreat from the supernatural is in congruence with Polan's proposed secularization of the genre in the 1940s, with both films representing "composite forms, mixing horror with a rationalized view of the world."[8] Unlike some of the female monster films discussed in previous chapters, particularly RKO's, *She-Wolf of London* was given a tagline poser with very little narrative ambiguity: "beauty or beast . . . woman or monster?" The answer was easy; as the *New York Post* scoffed, "Hep Rialto audiences don't believe for one minute that cute June Lockhart is a killer."[9] The narrative predictably reveals the orphaned Phyllis as the victim of an unscrupulous but secular plot to drive her insane by playing on her fears of a family werewolf curse.

Despite this shift from whatdunit to whodunit narratives, contemporary reviewers did place *She-Wolf of London* within the female monster cycle, albeit pointing out recent horror cinema's (perhaps resultant) anodyne nature. In her review of the film Rose Pelswick identifies the extension, yet limitation, of women's changing roles in Universal horror films, linking them specifically to wartime shifts in women's employment. She comments that, "apparently working on the theory that if the girls could step into such previously man-held jobs as riveters and train conductors they could also handle movie monster chores," Universal had added the Spider Woman and the She-Wolf to its monstrous canon. She continues, however, by saying that these "lady fiends" posed little threat to the ratings of "veteran boogiemen" such as Boris Karloff and Bela Lugosi.[10] This sense of women being temporary, inferior stand-ins for more experienced, qualified male performers has clear parallels in the wider postwar employment field. Before moving on to discuss these wider social implications, however, this chapter will focus in more detail on the contradictory discourses that designate these horror texts as banal and anachronistic yet, simultaneously, morally reprehensible and historically pertinent. This irreconcilability can be linked to wider pseudo-scientific debates regarding gender roles and horror cinema, which became inextricably linked in discussions around seemingly inconsequential films such as *She-Wolf of London*.

Promoted provocatively as "The Greatest Double-Shock Show in History," *She-Wolf of London* was twinned with *The Cat Creeps* (1946), a murder mystery that received equally bemused reaction regarding its incongruous title and *Cat People*–inspired marketing campaign.[11] Like most reviewers, *Motion Picture Daily* expressed disappointment that "the cat of the title is a regular representative of the feline species, nothing more occult or mysterious."[12] Rather than a secularization of horror, *Cue* feared that *The Cat Creeps* represented an extension of Hollywood's recent obsession with the "occult arts" and "phoney sciences." The review links this trend to the wider popularity of "screwball sects and cults all throughout Los Angeles," including black magic, spiritualism, clairvoyance, hypnotism, and other "assorted pseudo-scientific idiocies." The reviewer continues, "When this kind of witch-doctor infantilism is tossed into a reasonable—if thoroughly third rate—murder mystery it seems time to call a halt. *The Cat Creeps* is a case in point."[13]

Thus *Cue* sees the film as a symptom of a contemporary antiscientific impulse that was discursively feminized in much mainstream media, as discussed in relation to *The Uninvited.* Though *The Cat Creeps* is construed as merely a third-rate murder mystery, it appears to be precisely the infiltration of these irrational principles into this inconsequential, generic form that the reviewer believes should inspire such trepidation in responsible readers. A politics of taste regarding murder mystery audiences imbued with certain connotations of class and gender is at play here, and again we see this paradoxically dismissive yet anxious tone. As the *Hollywood Reporter* explains of *Jungle Captive* (1945) (Universal's third and final ape-woman film), this "Jekyll-Hyde transformation stuff is too old to be of much interest, but is still horrible."[14] More fervently a representative of Zeta Phi Eta, a politically minded female sorority at Howard University in Washington, D.C., attacked the film as "a hideous horror picture, evidently designed to break down our humanitarian tendencies and to make war and its atrocities easier to take."[15] Recently perceived as the escapist pastime of wartime audiences, the horror film became increasingly the serious subject of psychological study and scientific speculation following the war.

In a striking circularity, a number of postwar articles discuss the infiltration of psychology into horror and crime films, while proffering psychology as the answer to the genre's peculiar popularity. Prefiguring a number of later arguments regarding the dangers of horror, psychologists rationalized the genre's appeal through recourse to discourses of vicarious pleasure and desensitization. A lengthy *New York Times* article, reporting the responses of a number of psychologists and film practitioners to the question of crime and horror cinema's contemporary popularity, summarizes: "These learned men, in mumbo-jumbo all their own, assert that because of the war the average moviegoer has become calloused to death, hardened to homicide and more capable of understanding a murderer's motives. . . . In short the war has made us psychologically and emotionally ripe for motion pictures of this sort."[16] Alternatively, the article goes on to propose, the number of horror and crime films could be explained away as purely a case of the "time-honored Hollywood formula of follow-the-leader." The popularity of *Double Indemnity* (1944) in particular is centered as the catalyst for a subsequent cycle of similar "rough, tough murder yarns," with Raymond Chandler proffering the more liberal attitude of the Hays Office, and consequently the greater realism of the films themselves, as a key reason for their contemporary popularity.[17]

While censorship loosened up on urban crime drama, the policy on horror became increasingly tight, largely in response to its perceived reckless approach to scientific and psychological issues. The disparity between the responses of the Hays Office and contemporary reviewers to *The Spider Woman Strikes Back* reveals the growing impossibility of producing plausible and engaging horror narratives. Following the presumption of the psychological resonance of horrific images following the war, the *Hollywood Reporter* condemned *The Spider Woman Strikes Back* for being out of touch with the modern audience's capacity for horror and death—"it might have occurred to those responsible for the plot that the public has gained a familiarity with wartime blood banks that removes a large share of the horror of such mild blood-letting."[18] Despite the perceived restraint and ineffectuality of the film, it had great difficulty gaining approval from the MPPDA, which deemed the original script unacceptable under the Production Code. It was refused due to the "extremely gruesome angles" of transfusion scenes, shots of spiders feeding on flies and moths, and the intimation that girls' bodies were being fed to carnivorous plants, which would "undoubtedly prove objectionable to audiences generally."[19]

The Spider Woman Strikes Back was intended as the first in a series of Spider Woman horror films featuring Gale Sondergaard's "female Moriarty" character from the 1944 Sherlock Holmes film. The Universal press department claimed that the studio had decided to launch the series due to the realization that the character "really caught on with the public" and had brought in Arthur Lubin to direct after he proved his box-office clout with the prestige shocker *Phantom of the Opera* (1943).[20] This "Mistress of Menace"—who has almost no correspondence with the original character and only a loose connection to her arachnid moniker—did not inspire a sequel, however, and in fact marked the end of the producer Howard Welsh's Universal career (see figure 15).

Blaming a large backlog of low-budget films, the studio also announced in July 1946 that it had given notice to the head of horror production, Ben

FIGURE 15 *The Spider Woman Strikes Back* doesn't deliver the female "menace" its poster promises.

Pivar, responsible for *She-Wolf of London*, and the executive producer of *Jungle Captive*, Morgan Cox.[21] Following a halfhearted attempt to adapt its generic formula, Universal decided to abandon production of these unsuccessful female monster franchises, therefore fulfilling the first of Altman's assertions in regard to the conclusion of film cycles and subgenres. It is within such an untenable climate for horror production that the supernatural female monster was overtaken by the secular femme fatale of film noir, who seemingly gave the Hays Office far less concern.

With Universal disbanding its horror production units, and transferring the skills, style, and thematic concerns of talent such as Robert Siodmak and Edward Dmytryk to the urban crime milieu, it was left to the Poverty Row studios to extend the ill-fated life of the female monster. In his cultural history of horror Andrew Tudor suggests that "the war period is *the* period of American B-pictures," when the dominant forces in horror production, Universal, Columbia, and RKO, were joined by Poverty Row studios like Republic, Monogram, and PRC—testament to the genre's great wartime popularity.[22] For example, the tropes, themes, and style of RKO's and Universal's female monster films were imitated by Republic in *The Woman Who Came Back* (1945), *The Vampire's Ghost* (1945), and *Catman of Paris* (1946).

As this book has revealed, the female monster cycle had begun in the realm of B or B+ productions at RKO, but the major studios' heavier investment in A-class films such as Paramount's *The Uninvited* and MGM's *Bewitched* (1945) had encouraged an expansion of RKO's and even Universal's budgets for their female monster films after 1944. With RKO also dissolving its horror unit following Lewton's only moderate box-office success with *The Body Snatcher* (1945) and *Bedlam* (1946)—both historical horror pieces with secular narratives and lavish period settings—Poverty Row became the final haunt of the female monster character. Furthermore, even these low-budget quickies exhibited the shift toward secular narratives as evinced in Universal and RKO's final outputs.

Perhaps more than any of these, PRC's *Devil Bat's Daughter* (1946), an intended sequel to the studio's Bela Lugosi vehicle *The Devil Bat* (1940), provides a useful microcosm of the dissolution of the female monster cycle. The title's shift in emphasis from *Daughter of the Devil Bat* to *Devil Bat's Daughter* is telling of the female character's relegation from subject to object of her own narrative—a postwar shift representative of the cycle as a whole. In a synopsis submitted to the Hays Office dated August 20, 1945, titled "*Daughter of the Devil Bat*—A Horror Story," the plot revolves around a supernatural "Mystery Woman" who is driven by the "spell of Dr. Caruthers"—the crazed scientist turned Devil Bat of the earlier film. This script employs the female monster cycle's distinctive tropes of a supernatural narrative, a tragic and ambiguous female monster character, and a heroic heroine with whom she is doubled.[23]

The film passed by the Hays Office on February 28, 1946, titled *Devil Bat's Daughter* and classified generically on the analysis sheet as "melodrama/psychological-murder," removes all the supernatural elements from the earlier treatment, as well as the ambiguity and autonomy surrounding the female characters.[24] In the finished film Nina (played by Rosemary La Planche, a former Miss America) is discovered facedown in the road in a small town in upstate New York, the result of the shock of discovering that her dead father was arrested for murder and accused of being the vampiric Devil Bat of the earlier film. She comes to believe that she also turns into a giant bat at night and kills people, a fear that is understandably exacerbated when the dog and wife of the psychiatrist who has taken her in, Dr. Morris, are murdered. The psychiatrist's stepson, Ted, a returning World War II veteran who has taken a shine to Nina, uncovers that the psychiatrist has made her psychotic and framed her in order to murder his wealthy wife, however.

Thus, in keeping with Universal's postwar films (including *The Spider Woman Strikes Back* and *She-Wolf of London*), the narrative shifts from a supernatural to natural explanation, clearing the female protagonist from accusations of monstrosity and revealing, as *Motion Picture Herald* proposes, that "despite its title, the picture is not a horror film. . . . It is rather a melodrama of the mind, and its villain is a psychiatrist. (The psychiatrist has apparently replaced the town banker as the source of all evil.)"[25] There was, as suggested, an increasing concern about the representation of the psychiatric profession in a number of 1940s horror films, in which, as Polan explains, "at the extreme, the psychiatrist and the mad scientist become interchangeable figures, equal violators of the rules of normality" in their unbridled, and often explicitly sexualized, desire for power.[26] Correspondingly the *Hollywood Reporter* complained that "psychiatry on the screen reaches a new low estate with the PRC picture called *Devil Bat's Daughter*."[27]

"Bad Medicine": The Aggressive Fem Hero and the Mad Psychiatrist

William Graebner argues that with the moral certainties of wartime diminished, society increasingly looked to scientists, and particularly psychologists, as cultural and moral authorities to "ground and anchor values, or at least to function more effectively within the milieu of contingency."[28] The overarching teleology of scientific progress can be seen in the immediate postwar conflation of discourses of psychology, cinema, and gender. This is demonstrated in a *Variety* article from August 29, 1945, titled "Chicago Psychiatrist Traces Aggressive Girls to Pix' Not-So-He-Men" and reporting the findings of a University of Chicago psychology professor. "If anyone needs proof that American women have become more aggressive during World War II," the article insisted, that proof was in the professor's statistics, which showed the cause to be "changes in types of fem heroes" and "not-so-he-men" onscreen. The professor complained, "Aggressive is the only word that can be used to describe the modern American female."[29]

Although *Devil Bat's Daughter* exploits the subversive threat of one such "fem hero" in its epiphenomena, the narrative neutralizes this threat through the reconversion to a patriarchal household led by a postwar "he-man." The film's poster, with the tagline "By Night . . . A Screeching Devil Bat . . . By Day . . . A Beautiful Girl," gives the impression that Nina, like *Cat People*'s Irena, has a "second self that emerges at night in purely sexual terms."[30] As suggested, however, the dark side of her psyche turns out to be the construction of the male psychoanalyst Dr. Morris, who instructs Nina: "I have forbidden you to read anything other than what I prescribe." Though it appears, as in *Cat People*, that psychoanalysis is indicted as a disciplinary mechanism directed at women, this potentially critical dimension is fatally undermined in *Devil Bat's Daughter*.

Dr. Morris is coded as problematic not through his potentially manipulative profession but through his status as a kept man—he is branded by his mistress as a man who has "married for money and position" and told that he "should stand on [his] own two feet." This "not-so-he-man" refuses to fight when the war veteran Ted strikes him, instead fleeing with the exclamation "It's no use following me. I won't fight back." Rather than free Nina to rediscover who she really is, however, the psychiatrist's demise allows the supposed hero Ted to eradicate her identity all together. Equilibrium is restored in the final moments when Nina agrees to marry the returning veteran, who, as his mother's heir, has taken over as head of the (recently suburban) household.[31] Before the customary final embrace Ted effaces Nina's desire for her own subjectivity, a search that has been characterized as misguided and destructive, with this dialogue:

NINA: Will I ever really believe in myself again?

TED: What does it matter, as long as you believe in me?

NINA: You're right, it doesn't matter at all.

Therefore, while the publicity material centers Nina (and of course "Miss America" La Planche) as the primary draw, the film is increasingly revealed as a narrative about restoring a (real) man to the center of the postwar family.[32]

Furthermore, Nina's "neurosis" is specifically linked to her bad experiences during World War II. It is when she is questioned about her role "in England working in a government office" during the war that Nina hallucinates a bat attack, exclaiming "bats, bats, my father." Dr. Morris concludes, "You went through a very trying and emotional time during the war. Instinctively, unconsciously you were looking for help. You looked to your father as a last resort." Although Dr. Morris is revealed as manipulating his position of power, his diagnosis of a female Oedipal dilemma brought on by the pressures of wartime is confirmed by her need for Ted to take on this patriarchal role. As the final scene reveals, her independent status may forever be tainted by wartime neurosis, her happiness can only be attained through her reliance upon and subordination to her future husband. The final message of the film is that passivity and dependence is the formula for female contentment.

Susan Hartmann suggests that "as men returned home from the war, box-office—and social—demands changed. Slowly heroines moved into the background, becoming less aggressive or incapable of working out their own fates."[33] Although this is a somewhat reductive analysis of postwar film (the imposing figure of the femme fatale can hardly be accused of shrinking into the background, even if she is accused of everything else), it is an apt description of the plot of *Devil Bat's Daughter*, which mutates into a male-centered text during its sixty-seven-minute duration. This is largely achieved through the "delegation of the detecting gaze to another male figure who is on the side of the law."[34] As in the final Universal films, it is a male suitor, Ted, who solves the enigma that frees Nina from the neurosis that precludes her rational perspective to solve it herself. Ted even manages to reinscribe the meaning of the original *Devil Bat* film by absolving Nina's father from any wrongdoing, thus clearing her bloodline for a future mothering role.

Just as Nina's wartime role is linked to her neurosis in *Devil Bat's Daughter*, in *The Spider Woman Strikes Back* the female protagonist Jean's career is diagnosed as untenable in the long term. When Hal asks her, "What happened to the career you wanted?" she responds: "I had it for a little while. I got to be merchandise manager for a woman's shop in San Francisco. I loved it but it was too hectic. My doctor ordered me to take a rest." This expert intervention encourages her to return to small-town

Domingo and resultantly to her first love, Hal, with whom she had broken up to pursue her career.[35] These female-centered horror films could be seen to have incorporated elements of what Betty Freidan characterizes as the "exorcising of the forbidden career drama," a specifically postwar type of feminine morality story, drawing upon wider media and scientific discourse that advocated women were able to "find fulfillment only in sexual passivity, male domination, and nurturing maternal love."[36] Historians have questioned whether the overarching ideology of the "feminine mystique" was as univocal as Friedan states, but it certainly represented a key part of the postwar cultural puzzle.[37]

Although the tail end of the female monster cycle exorcised wartime horror cinema's "aggressive fem" and "not-so-he-man," it maintained its somewhat paranoid view of Freudian science.[38] As the trade press reviews for *Devil Bat's Daughter* suggest, the media became increasingly concerned about Hollywood horror's potentially socially damaging representation of the psychiatric profession and psychological themes. As this chapter will move on to discuss, psychiatric pictures such as *The Dark Mirror* would ultimately address these concerns, but MGM's *Bewitched* (1945)—based upon a popular radio play by Arch Oboler—provides an interesting comparison piece, as it brings a more traditional horror approach to the female split-personality theme. In *Bewitched* the bifurcated female monster (tagged in the film's promotion as "one moment a loving sweetheart . . . the next, a tigress") is suffering from "schizophrenia," but her psychiatric condition is the result of supernatural possession by a recently executed murderess.

The film proved especially problematic for New York reviewers, because it was deemed to blur generic boundaries between horror and psychological drama. For example, Wanda Hale of the *Daily News*, who saw this picture as "a sort of feminine counterpart of Jekyll and Hyde," and thus as a straight horror film, dismissed it as "morbid and unpleasant, and, to me a little ridiculous."[39] By contrast, other reviewers saw *Bewitched* as a problem precisely because they believed that its makers were aspiring to fashion something more than just a straight horror film, due to their apparent efforts seriously to engage with psychological issues. "There ought to be a law about movies like [this]," a reviewer writing for *PM* advised. "If you saw *Bewitched* at your local creep house, with Dr. Karloff skulking around . . . , you could just file it and forget it along with the year's crop of Draculas and stuff." This reviewer concluded, however, by lamenting that "in full top-budget regalia . . . you have a right to expect a certain clinical validity."[40]

The backlash against the type of representation on show in *Bewitched* reached an apotheosis during the outcry over Twentieth Century–Fox's *Shock* (1946). In this film, a psychiatrist, Dr. Cross (Vincent Price), murders his wife and then attempts to use hypnotic suggestion to drive insane the only witness: Janet, the nervous wife of a recently returned prisoner of war. Dr. Cross tries to kill Janet by administering a lethal dose of insulin as he gives her shock treatment. The scene plays out in such a way as to encourage audience horror, using superimposition to juxtapose a close-up of Janet's pained, distressed face and a rapid montage of injections, surgical apparatus, records of increasing doses, and calendar pages. The intense disorientation that the scene is clearly designed to induce is enhanced by the eerie musical score, which is built around the swelling drone of a theremin—a musical instrument that was used regularly at this time on the soundtracks of psychological horror films. In the final minutes of *Shock*, Dr. Cross sees the error of his ways. He strangles his nurse-cum-lover, who had intended to proceed with the plan, and saves Janet by injecting her with adrenaline. He then quite literally hangs up his doctor's coat and gives himself up to the police. This conciliatory gesture was seen by film critics and psychological scientists as having failed to offset the material that had gone before it.

In New York more than anywhere else, the middlebrow press was quick to condemn the film as causing damage to the psychiatric profession. In a *New York Times* review entitled "Bad Medicine," Bosley Crowther opined that, although horror films could usually be "quietly dismissed," *Shock* amounted to nothing short of a "social disservice at this time," adding that the film "should excite the critical observer to protest in no uncertain terms." Crowther feared that a film like *Shock* could induce a distrust of the psychiatric profession among potential patients and their relatives, a concern that he felt was compounded by the fact that the "treatment of nervous disorders is being practiced today upon thousands of men who suffered shock of one sort or another in the war." Crowther went on to attack both the film's producer, Aubrey Schenck, and its distributor, Twentieth Century–Fox, using the term "deplorable" to lambast the decision to make and release such a picture.[41] John McManus of *PM* went even further than his colleague at the *New York Times* when, the day after Crowther's review was published, he complained that *Shock* had made him "not only physically ill, but almost tearfully angry and deeply ashamed for the studio." McManus supported his four-column polemic with statistics on the number of soldiers that had been discharged or rejected from the army on the grounds that they were suffering from mental and emotional disorders. He called for a team of medics to assess *Shock* and, if it turned out that they shared his views on its harmfulness, to appeal to Darryl F. Zanuck to "yank it off the screen and burn it." If Zanuck refused, the medical experts should "go after it in the courts, as a menace to public health and welfare."[42]

The New York press continually denounced *Shock* as emblematic of Hollywood's generally irresponsible handling of psychological themes. One week after his first attack on the film, Crowther wrote a much longer polemic. He argued that *Shock* was representative of a cycle of what he called psychological pictures, all of which fostered among an already skeptical public a phobia of psychology generally and of insulin shock therapy in particular, by making standard treatments appear to be "deliberately evil practices." Crowther cited a contemporaneous article from the *Hollywood Quarterly*, in which a Professor Franklin Fearing of the University of California had bemoaned Hollywood's representation of the psychological sciences, as well as its overuse of amnesia as a plot device, which, explained Fearing, "occurs about as often as toothache, according to these films."[43] In that article, Fearing suggested that psychological conditions were ideal plot devices for melodramas and mystery thrillers, because "the layman," as he called the general public, already viewed such conditions with a "curious mixture of fascination and horror."[44] Fearing nevertheless encouraged Hollywood to complement its need to entertain audiences with a greater degree of discrimination when it came to mobilizing material related to psychopathology, which he stressed ought best serve "justifiable aesthetic, social or educational ends."[45]

Less generous than Fearing, Crowther derided horror pictures as simultaneously standardized and sensationalized, while also attacking their producers—in particular Twentieth Century–Fox—for their commercial exploitation of a "witless" public.[46] He went on to suggest that a series of documentaries that had been recently produced by the U.S. Army promised to offer a much-needed riposte that would showcase the benefits of this new and misunderstood science. Singled out for praise was John Huston's *Let There Be Light* (1946), a documentary about servicemen undergoing successful psychological treatment that had been screened at New York City's Museum of Modern Art. Here, Crowther invoked a politics of taste by contrasting the passive consumers of supposedly standardized horror against what he saw as the refined tastes and social engagement of the connoisseurs who visited this prestigious location.

Following Crowther's campaign against *Shock*, the *New York Times* persuaded Dr. Manfred Sakel—an internationally renowned neurophysiologist and psychiatrist, and the pioneer of insulin shock therapy—to attend a screening of the film at New York's notorious grind-house, the Rialto. Sakel concluded that the film did indeed do damage to psychiatry. "Having the psychiatrist attempt to hypnotize a patient," he lamented, "puts the science into the realm of demonology." Sakel asserted that Hollywood could exert a positive influence on the "more than 600,000 mental cases in institutions in America today by studying the problem as it really is."[47] Perhaps in response to Sakel's objections, as well as to the protests of medical bodies such as the New York Society for Clinical Psychiatry, the New York Academy of Medicine, and the American Psychiatric Association, censors in Canada deleted all references to insulin shock treatment from the prints of the film that were set to be circulated in their country.[48]

The following week, the *New York Times* reported that Dr. Lawrence Kubie, a practicing psychiatrist and neurologist at the New York Neurological Institute, had called for a commission of qualified psychiatrists to study the effects on mass audiences of such films as "horror pictures with strong neurotic impact." This report also called for producers to seek advice from qualified independent psychiatrists when making films that tackled psychiatric subjects. Kubie stressed the screen industry's responsibility to the six million Americans who would need psychiatric treatment in the future, calling for Hollywood to fund research into the psychological effects of its products and to pay fees to the psychiatrists whom they would employ as consultants during the production of their films.[49] Social psychologists, including Professor Fearing, would go on to challenge Kubie's assertions that psychiatrists should conduct research for, and serve as consultants to, Hollywood, claiming that social psychology was better suited to shedding new light on the influence of the media.[50]

While the furor over *Shock* had begun to subside by late April 1946, the American media continued to alert the public and the medical profession to the dangers of Hollywood's representations of psychiatry. For example, in an October issue of the *New York Times*, Dr. Carl Binger, an assistant professor of clinical psychology at Cornell University, warned against scientific misinformation being spread by what he described as "the sensation seekers in Hollywood." He homed in on a spate of "far-fetched psychiatric films," which he argued effectively laid down the gauntlet to psychiatrists to push for more accurate cinematic representations of their profession and its practices.[51] Perhaps surprisingly, Universal looked to "Hollywood's top horror man," Robert Siodmak, to provide a corrective to these previous representations that psychiatrists, censors and the middlebrow press had identified as being so problematic.[52]

"Untangling the Twin Sisters Puzzle": Psychiatric Solutions in *The Dark Mirror*

On October 18, 1946, some seven months after *Shock* had prompted calls for positive representations of the psychiatric profession, Universal-International opened *The Dark Mirror* in New York City. Although it went into production before the aforementioned controversy broke, the promotional strategies and critical reception of *The Dark Mirror* were certainly influenced by the debates surrounding *Shock*.[53] It was both framed and received as a serious portrayal of psychiatry, in which a psychologist and his psychological procedures are presented as redemptive. The film showcased an innovative split-screen technique to allow Olivia de Havilland to play identical twin sisters, Ruth and Terry, one of whom is a murderer. Although eyewitness accounts place one of the twins at a murder scene, the pair refuse to reveal the identity of the guilty party, thereby obstructing police efforts to apprehend and prosecute the culprit. The psychiatrist Dr. Scott Elliott (Lew Ayers) ultimately reveals that Terry is guilty, thanks to his use of psychiatric and scientific methods including Rorschach tests, a polygraph machine, and exercises in free association. In separating the sisters' conjoined identities, the renowned psychiatrist frees Ruth from suspicion, and thus the domination of her dark double. Dr. Elliott is rewarded with the possibility of pursuing his romantic interest in Ruth, the "much more beautiful" of the identical twins.

The Universal-International publicity department differentiated *The Dark Mirror* from "orthodox murder mysteries" in that it "derives all its tensely developed dramatic values solely from the brain, and by a scientifically tested method of procedure." Correspondingly the pressbook sold the film as an "accurate, as well as entertaining picture" in which "the scientific aspects of the drama were checked and double checked for accuracy." It went on to say that its writer-producer, Nunnally Johnson, "kept a psychology expert at his elbow all the while he was producing the screenplay" and visited the Federal Bureau of Investigation in Washington to "okay all the scientific data."[54] Resultantly contemporary reception positioned *The Dark Mirror* as both part of and a corrective to a proposed psychiatric film cycle. The *New York Times* explicitly linked the film to the recent debates regarding Hollywood's postwar role in representing science and medicine responsibly, celebrating that "luckily Lew Ayres has returned from the Army Service to rescue medical practice, this time as a psychiatrist."[55] The pressbook clarified that Ayres chose this as his first role after his four-year Hollywood hiatus because he believed that the psychiatrist "has a meaning which can be a help to struggling humanity." He had returned from the horrors of war with an "entirely new set of values," it continued, and a reaffirmed faith that "his life work of entertainment is eminently worthwhile."[56] He thus put into action the postwar perception that psychiatry held the answers to an increasingly contingent and uncertain world, and that Hollywood had a responsibility to reflect this onscreen.

The press praised the film for its scientific accuracy and resultant cinematic realism. The *Los Angeles Times* stressed that the film was "closer to being psychological than most pictures thus labeled," commending that the "psychoanalysis it goes in for . . . makes credible the premise of the film, which on analysis, must be regarded as fantastic."[57] In addition to stressing the link between realism and the proper use of psychology, the review also situated the film as part of a burgeoning cycle of psychiatric films or, as *Time* magazine characterized it, "the current crop of movies that mix homicide with psychiatry."[58] The trade press also positioned the film as part of a "cycle of psychiatric pictures," even identifying the specific generic tropes that distinguished it.[59] *Variety* emphasized, "*The Dark*

Mirror runs the full gamut of themes currently in vogue—from psychiatry to romance back again, to the double identity gimmick and murder mystery."[60] The film's publicity explained, "Intelligent scientific deduction and the sure fire emotion of love make equal contributions to the solution of the tangled identities."[61]

Early in the film Dr. Elliott, the renowned author of *Twins: A Clinical Study*, flirts with the sisters, saying, "I'd like to add you two to my collection . . . of twins." The poster's tagline embraces this conflation of the medical and romantic gaze, posing the question: "Can his lips tell which is which?" The film is certainly in keeping with the genre of the woman's film, in which, Mary Ann Doane explains, the "erotic gaze becomes the medical gaze. The female body is located not so much as spectacle but as an element in the discourse of medicine, a manuscript to be read for the symptoms which betray her story, her identity."[62] The despecularization of the female body in *The Dark Mirror*—its shift from the corporeal to the cerebral—corresponds with Polan's proposed secularization and psychologization of horror in the forties. Referencing the work of Robin Wood, Polan argues that "psychoanalysis displaces the source of the menace from physically traditional monster to the id as *initially* uncontrollable force, or, in many cases, as in film noir, to a femininity or urban condition (or to a confluence of the two) figured as the repository of a-social or antisocial forces."[63] *The Dark Mirror* utilizes these methods of containment, employing popularized psychology as the metanarrative to neutralize the mysteries of the modern world. This included the complexities and contradictions that had arisen around the female body following women's wartime shift into perceived male roles as detailed in earlier female monster films such as *Cat People*.

As with the final female monster films, *The Dark Mirror*'s sustained psychological investigation of women by a male authority figure is in stark contrast to the wartime films in which female investigators help clear neurotic men falsely accused of murder. These include Universal's *Phantom Lady* (1944) and Hitchcock's *Spellbound* (1945), which goes even further in casting a female psychiatrist (Ingrid Bergman) in its central role. The postwar drive to stabilize gender binaries can be seen in *The Dark Mirror*'s narrative shift toward bifurcating the good and bad sisters along strict gender lines, and consequently pathologizing the masculine traits previously deemed an advantage for women converting to wartime roles. Lucy Fischer concurs that in *The Dark Mirror* "the split is between 'feminine' and 'masculine' attributes, in the guise of good and evil sisters." She continues that this split reflects a "rupture in the social conception of woman," but she goes on to focus on the psychological, specifically Freudian, dimensions of this characterization rather than the historical or social implications.[64]

The end of the war saw a barrage of conservative discourse attacking the collapse of stable gender binaries that specifically identified the disciplining of the female body as central to the problem of postwar reconversion. A March 1946 article in the *New York Times* by Victor Dallaire titled "The American Woman? Not for This GI" attacked the wartime development of the "business Amazon," arguing that "being nice is almost a lost art among American women. They elbow their way through crowds, swipe your seat at bars and bump and push their way around regardless."[65] Admittedly a male former *Stars and Stripes* reporter wrote the article, but his argument was replicated by women writers in publications aimed specifically at a female readership. In *Harper's* magazine Anne Leighton lamented that "many American war veterans are . . . coming home to what used to be a pleasantly pliable and even appealingly incompetent little woman and finding a quietly masterful creature recognizing no limitations to her own endurance."[66] Furthering the monstrous imagery of Leighton's "masterful creature" metaphor (albeit in an attempt to argue for women's unique competencies in the employment field), another *New York Times* article from March 1946 bemoaned the misconception that the only way to succeed was to be a "pseudo-man—a monster of feminine gender who talks, walks, thinks, acts, reacts like a man." In this article Edith Efron attacked the media "hullabaloo about women having divided interests" and those who advocated the "hermaphroditic solution" suggesting that women must "defeminize" in order to succeed in the public sphere.[67]

The postwar backlash against the collapse of stable gender boundaries that Efron is challenging went pseudo-scientific in 1947 with the release of Ferdinand Lundberg and Marynia Farnham's *Modern Woman: The Lost Sex*, which was reprinted in part and paraphrased in numerous magazines. The book used a simplified version of Freudian psychoanalysis to urge a return to prewar gender roles. Its authors argued that during World War II feminists had prompted women to suppress their "true instincts" in favor of adopting flawed versions of male traits, a process that involved the repression of their nurturing roles. Lundberg and Farnham bemoaned the loss of the "old-time concepts of the 'good' and the 'bad' woman," which, they insisted, "had the merit of resting at least on generally factual physical, psychological and social differentiation of sexual function."[68] Polarizing women into two opposing camps—well-adjusted homemakers or neurotic career women—these writers advocated a government-backed program designed to restore prestige to the sexually ordained roles of the wife and the mother.

While wartime films such as *Phantom Lady* or *Cat People* complicated or even subverted these binaries by portraying an unnatural attachment to home and traditional notions of femininity as a form of neurosis, *The Dark Mirror* violently reinstates the physical, psychological, and social differentiation of sexual function that Lundberg and Farnham hoped for. This drive to naturalize and neutralize the threat of strong female characters is reflected in the press material for *The Dark Mirror*. The pressbook went into great detail about ambivalent psychoneurosis, the condition from which Terry suffered. It attributed theories about this condition to Carl Jung, who, it went on to explain, had learned psychoanalysis from Sigmund Freud. Invoking the authority of the most venerated experts in the field, *The Dark Mirror* transplants the categorizable, and potentially synthesizable, mind of the psychoneurotic as a substitute for the unsynthesizable body of the classic horror monster.[69]

As Polan explains, "In opposition to the fantastic, forties science itself takes on marvelous qualities: a resilient ability to find a place for any phenomenon no matter how aberrant it may initially appear."[70] In *The Dark Mirror* the ambivalence arising from the wartime bifurcation of the female body—manifested in monstrous hybrid imagery in the aforementioned horror films and media discourse—is resolved through recourse to modern psychoanalytic techniques. By employing the panoptic gaze of scientific reason, Dr. Elliott is able to reinstate the "old-time concepts of the 'good' and the 'bad" woman,' thus resolving the corporeal confusion engendered by the film's split-screen technique. The desire to penetrate this surface illusion by differentiating between the identical twins is the narrative drive for Dr. Elliott and, ultimately, the spectator. Lutz Koepnick explains that in the first half of *The Dark Mirror* the director, Robert Siodmak, employs a "formal rule of symmetry" that "provides the audience virtually no clues at all that could help distinguish the twins"—they are encouraged to embrace the "illogic" of "diegetic doubling" that the split-screen technique allows. The sisters are regularly shot within the same frame, making full use of the split-screen technology. They share reassuring glances and finish each other's sentences, attesting to their close and symbiotic relationship. In the second half of the film, however, the spectator is encouraged to adopt the psychiatrist's gaze as he diagnoses Terry's pathology, thus encouraging him/her to disidentify with the double and differentiate between the twins. Koepnick explains, "Refraction takes the place of reflection; discriminating perceptions and judgments triumph over Terry's cinema of doubling."[71] As the twins' relationship becomes more antagonistic, the film's earlier formal symmetry, particularly the framing of shots, becomes more fragmented. In the second half of the film the twins are positioned far less frequently within the same frame, and when they are onscreen together, one is often shown reflected in a mirror.

Koepnick overlooks the gendered implications of the pivotal shift of identification from ambiguous female doubles to omniscient male psychiatrist—a key shift from woman as subject to woman as object, as discussed in relation to the film's divergence from the wartime *Phantom Lady* and *Spellbound*. The traits celebrated in the female protagonist of *Phantom Lady*, such as intelligence, assuredness, and mastery of the public sphere, are deemed symptoms of Terry's pathology in *The Dark Mirror*. Dr. Elliott makes this link explicit when he says, "One of our young ladies is insane. Very clever, very intelligent, but insane." Ruth later explains that Terry is more intelligent, or, as Terry herself insists, "the smart one," thus hinting at the identity of the evil twin. In contrast, Ruth's intellectual and emotional dependence are marked as key to her being "natural and normal" and therefore more attractive to Dr. Elliott. The film's publicity material embraced the increasing nostalgia for essentialist gender roles, or the return of the perceived "pleasantly pliable and even appealingly incompetent little woman" of the prewar years.[72] Like the posters, the pressbook stories juxtaposed the characterization of the androgynously named Terry to that of Ruth, "an honest girl, full of the best instincts, including the normal search for romance" (see figure 16). The publicity material's recourse

FIGURE 16 The poster for *The Dark Mirror* promotes women's healthy desire for heterosexual romance.

to the idea of an eternal femininity is certainly representative of the film's narrative. As Dr. Elliott explains to Ruth (albeit Terry pretending to be Ruth, as the doctor knows all too well), on the surface there is "so little to choose between you," but "men are attracted to something inherent" in Ruth. Later, Dr. Elliott explains to Terry, "It was Ruth [whom Dr. Peralta, the murder victim] really loved without even knowing she existed. It was you he courted, took to dinner, to movies, to dances, and he asked to marry him. He didn't know there were twins. All he knew was that the girl at the counter brought him warmth he missed at other times." Although Terry is the girl he dated, even asked to marry him, it is the "warmth" of home-loving Ruth that attracted him, not her gregarious sister.

Thus the hybrid nature of the wartime woman—shop and office workers by day and sexual adventurers by night—is reconverted into two separate entities in *The Dark Mirror*, one good and one bad, or one "natural" and one "insane." Likewise, embracing the pervasive theory of "momism," the overprotective Terry is characterized by Ruth as "like a mother too, because we've been orphaned since we were ten." As in the monstrous matriarchal households of *The Spider Woman Strikes Back* and *She-Wolf of London*—in which surrogate mother figures attempt to kill off young women with poisoned milk—Terry's vampiric momism is "rooted in her insatiable appetite for devouring her young and preventing them from developing into independent adults."[73] Terry's parasitic connection to her twin encouraged her to sabotage all Ruth's previous romances, not just the one with Dr. Peralta. This increasing denigration of female relationships, including within the stronghold of the family unit, is revealed in Dr. Elliott's conclusion that "all women are rivals fundamentally," particularly sisters, who "can hate each other with such terrifying intensity." This female sibling rivalry might have been interpreted by contemporary spectators as a commentary on the well-publicized rivalry between de Havilland and her own sister, Joan Fontaine. A 1946 *New York Times* article declared, "A curious switch took place last week involving two sisters, both leading lights of the screen between whom jealousy has frequently been reported by gossip columnists." It continued that de Havilland had pulled out of *Ivy* (1947) because the role of the "selfish, homicidal woman too closely resembled her last film, *The Dark Mirror*," but Fontaine had signed up four days later.[74]

This intertextual dimension supports, therefore, the psychologist's extraordinary outburst regarding women's, and particularly sisters', inherent rivalry. The empathetic bonds between women and the positive characterization of intelligent and resourceful female leads in the wartime films are replaced by the mode of psychologically reinforced bifurcation that Lundberg and Farnham deemed necessary in order to correct the "American Woman's Dilemma," born of first-wave feminism and the recent upheavals of war.[75] As discussed, the film achieves this through the pivotal shift in identification as the mystery of the split-screen technique is unraveled through scientific means. In congruence with Koepnick's reading of the film, the *Los Angeles Times* reviewer noted that the identities of the twins was "more confused in the earlier scenes than the latter, but then, they are supposed to register as confusing." He went on to say that once the "psychiatric processes" were introduced, "you find yourself competing with Miss de Havilland in observing the blotting cards, for instance, and deciding what they illustrate."[76]

The "Showmanship" section embraces this key spectatorial pleasure, offering the audience a template newspaper article that encourages them to turn their own panoptic gaze upon Terry and asking, "What conclusions would you reach after studying her analysis of the ink blots?" This stunt offers the amateur psychoanalysts in the audience only Terry's ink blots as evidence in detecting her true personality, but in the film itself, shifts in form, mise-en-scène, and genre conspire against Terry and the duplicitous split-screen technique that has been concealing her true self. During the ink-blots scene the spectator is encouraged to concur with Dr. Elliott's diagnosis that one of the sisters is "very intelligent, but insane." In these Rorschach tests the feminine and leisured Ruth sees a drum majorette, two old ladies in a streetcar, and an ice show. The cloaked and defensive Terry, on the other hand, sees a mask with a fixed expression, a woman dancing with a puppet, and a lamb with two men under its paws, which "all seems symbolic of something. [Perhaps] the lamb is death." The psychologist instructs the police, and the spectator, that there should be little doubt, as this technology "reflect[s] the true secret patterns of their minds." In a subsequent free association test Ruth discloses her suspicions about her sister when she responds to Dr. Elliott's prompt "mirror" with the association "death." Following this, Terry is furious with Ruth for yielding to the psychiatrist's panoptic probing, exclaiming, "How could you have said it?"

Although overlooked in Koepnick's authorial account, de Havilland's much-praised performance is equally important to the resolving of the split-screen puzzle; as *Film Daily* explained, "Paralleling the technical accomplishments is Olivia de Havilland's intriguing dual role portrayal."[77] In the first half of the film de Havilland's performance gives little away as to the identity of the evil twin; Terry's more assertive and self-assured approach appears initially to be a benevolent act to protect and reassure her understandably nervous sister. Ruth's fidgeting and inability to maintain eye contact evince her anxiety about the investigation but do not necessarily indicate either a guilty conscience or her suspicion of her sister. De Havilland initiates the pivotal shift in spectator identification, however, by intensifying the sister's distinctive traits as Terry becomes the monster to Ruth's victim. Precisely halfway into the film, Terry's protectiveness toward her sister is suddenly revealed as "poison and jealousy" when she delivers the line "If you ever suspected me, I don't know what I'd do." Standing in the shadows of their shared bedroom, de Havilland intensifies her expression into a fixed and cavernous stare, revealing her earlier strength and assuredness as a symptom of her psychotic desire to dominate. Terry's jealousy escalates when she oversees Dr. Elliott kissing Ruth. When confronted later that night, Ruth lies about the kiss. Subsequently Terry convinces her that she has been "talking and dreaming and sobbing" in her sleep. Ruth believes that she is recovering from her nervous episodes, but Terry's deception instantly restores her earlier restlessness and fidgety behavior, much to the pleasure of the maniacally grinning Terry.

In this scene the transformation of the twins' relationship, or more accurately the spectator's realization of it, is emphasized through framing. Though earlier the symbiosis of the twins is highlighted in their being framed together, taking full advantage of the split-screen technology, in this scene Terry's image is reflected in a mirror behind Ruth as they talk. Symmetry is replaced by opposition, or, as Dr. Elliott says of twins, "everything in reverse." Although framing, dialogue, and performance in these scenes have begun to intimate the twins' opposing personalities, and specifically Terry's ingrained rivalry, in the subsequent lie detector sequence the spectator's shift in positioning is fully realized.

While Dr. Elliott is questioning Terry, the spectator is afforded his view of the polygraph machine as the needle begins to move erratically when she mentions Ruth's failed romances. The spectator is now explicitly positioned on the side of the male psychiatrist in his competition with Terry, who has disparaged his psychiatric techniques as "kindergarten games." Terry's suggestion that she can "beat [Dr. Elliott] every time" is increasingly undermined by the spectator's privileged view of the successful operation of his psychological methods, as well as by Terry's increasingly strange and erratic behavior. In this scene cinematography, editing, and performance are employed to guide the spectator in adopting the psychiatrist's perspective. From this point on the twins are increasingly differentiated through iconography, particularly in their different-colored costumes (stereotypically light and dark), as the deception of the split-screen breaks down. Dr. Elliott's scientific technologies thus increasingly side with the cinematic ones in revealing Terry's pathology. This is a clear power reversal from the first half of the film, in which the inseparable twins' deception of the helpless authorities is facilitated by the split-screen technology.

Following this decisive spectatorial shift, Terry exploits the techniques of horror cinema in a desperate bid to prevent Dr. Elliott's division of the identical twins. In a sequence that evokes the aesthetics and tone of the female Gothic or paranoid woman's film but reverses its typically male antagonist, Terry uses a flashgun to simulate paranoid hallucinations in the mind of her sleeping sister.[78] By exploiting horror special effects Terry attempts to replicate the psychological rupture experienced in her own mind, driving her inherently good sister insane, thus irrevocably eradicating their fundamental difference. The scene employs the chiaroscuro lighting and obtuse angles that have come to be associated with film noir, but its tone and imagery invoke more the silent horror texts from which noir is often claimed to derive. Drawing on the imagery of F. W. Murnau's *Nosferatu* (1922), Terry's gruesome expression and clawed arm are spotlighted through a natural iris effect as she rises from the bed to terrorize her sister with the flashgun. Ruth screams herself awake, exclaiming, "I'm so scared I don't know what to do."[79] As Terry "comforts" her distraught sister, the spectator, unlike Ruth, is privy to the twisted grin on her face; Terry is now fully transformed into the vampiric predator to Ruth's helpless victim.

In this macabre act of psychological torture, horror cinema techniques, female spectatorship, and the misuse of psychiatric methods become intimately conjoined. Mirroring the fears of the censors, the mainstream media, and the psychiatric professions, *The Dark Mirror* provides a metacommentary on the dangers of horror cinema to impressionable spectators—namely, its ability to produce the very psychological ruptures that it depicts. The psychologically frail Ruth is now fully dependent on the skills of the psychiatrist (and spectator) to see through Terry's ultimate deception. In the final scenes, Terry pretends to be Ruth in order to first murder the meddling Dr. Elliott, then claim herself to be the innocent twin when a phone call reveals that the other has "killed herself." Neither doctor nor spectator is fooled by Terry's increasingly erratic and manic performance, however. Back at their apartment Terry pretends to be Ruth, so she can claim that the body in the bedroom is that of guilt-ridden Terry, thus clearing "herself." However, the real Ruth appears from the bedroom, revealing Terry's masquerade and incriminating her for the murder to which she has just inadvertently confessed. Terry, incensed, throws an ashtray, smashing a mirror in which her sister's image is reflected. With this symbolic act Ruth is freed from the domination of her dark double. She is now able to commit to a purely personal relationship with Dr. Elliott. Terry strived to beat the psychiatrist at his own game, but Ruth is content in the knowledge that Dr. Elliott thinks her "so much more beautiful than [her] sister." With this conjoined professional and personal triumph, the psychiatrist restores the film's heterosexual equilibrium and commits the dark and mysterious side of the female psyche to an asylum where it can be further examined, categorized, and contained.

From psychological horror to the psychiatric picture and conflicted female (inter)subjectivity to the disciplinary male gaze, *The Dark Mirror* provides a corrective to the unruly elements of the female monster cycle. Through the heroic psychiatrist's untangling of the film's central twin-sisters puzzle, the audience is encouraged to experience the resolution of the gendered and generic confusion the war had unearthed. Reversing Hollywood horror's damaging representations of the psychiatric profession, psychology becomes the all-encompassing teleology of *The Dark Mirror*, and even the explanation for its attractiveness to spectators. As Siodmak explained in the pressbook, "Audiences love a picture like *The*

Dark Mirror because it affords what psychoanalysts call a psychic renovating."[80] This unwavering belief in the curative powers of psychoanalysis is even extended to the site of exhibition. Sutured into the role of amateur psychoanalyst, the spectator is charged with the occupation of penetrating the screen, seeing beyond the surface similarities of the identical twins and synthesizing the irreconcilable contradictions at the very heart of postwar American society.

Conclusion

Only for the Duration

Shifting the analytic focus from movie genres to film cycles, *Phantom Ladies* has demonstrated how the conflicting and shifting demands of industries and audiences might be resituated within their wider cultural contexts. In his growing body of research into the relationship between the serial production of movies and the public sphere they participate in, Peter Stanfield has developed and empirically tested an increasingly nuanced theory of cyclical change. Drawing upon the theories of historians, literary theorists, and business scholars, he has analyzed a range of Hollywood film cycles across a number of essays, identifying the often conflicting textual impulses of repetition and innovation, and the multiple ways in which films relate to their historical contexts. He explains:

> In each study, the causal relationship behind the formation of a cycle and its association with the topical is complex and often indirect. In some cases, the connection between the film and the social is filtered through synergies with other media forms, or via changes in leisure activities; in others, it is tied to modifications in censorship and industry self-regulation, or to shifts in audience demographics and sites of exhibition, as well as to the more direct exploitation of contemporary events such as wars and moral panics.[1]

If we add to this list the critical intervention of psychiatrists and social psychologists, as well as popular film critics and social commentators, we come some way to explaining the complex evolution, development, and diffusion of this single cycle of female monster films, and its overlaps with and transformations into adjacent cycles of horror and crime films.

Phantom Ladies has argued that it was indeed shifts in audience demographics and exhibition practices, influenced directly by the war, that were the key factors in the evolution and consolidation of this cycle. This was evinced in trade press and newspaper reports and resultant marketing exploitation of the popularity of horror, and particularly in an emergent market for horror among women, whose attendance and behavior at previously male-oriented exhibition sites was interpreted as a specifically wartime phenomenon. It moved on to explain how these developments were linked to cultural shifts in other leisure realms and practices—particularly working women's round-the-clock revelry at urban dance halls and bars, and a wartime revival of the occult that was manifested in adjacent film cycles and in other media forms including ghost stories, supernatural radio plays, and newspaper astrology. This realization that the female monster film was tapping into both an expanding market and wider cultural trends encouraged an escalation of the cycle through investment in prestige productions featuring big stars, some produced by studios not typically associated with horror. The increasing press coverage that these films received resulted in an exacerbation of media and social scientific discourse—if not full-scale moral panic—around what women were getting up to in cinemas and other entertainment venues. This encouraged both industry and critical intervention into these horror cycles, resulting in a tightening of censorship policy on these films, which, following direct intervention from psychological professionals, would ultimately bring about the transformation of the wartime female monster film into the postwar psychiatric picture.

Through its focus on the cultural and institutional history of these horror and crime cycles, *Phantom Ladies* has demonstrated that the relationship between gender, genre, and taste is critically contested, historically contingent, and socially pertinent. As a result, it has challenged long-held views in film history, genre studies, and feminist media scholarship about women's relationships to horror texts while offering a compelling model for a new cinema history.[2] In rejecting general histories of wartime cinema as too broad in their reach and individual genre histories as too limited, this book has argued that film cycles provide an alternative area of investigation that is complex yet manageable enough to explore the interrelationship between processes of cultural production and consumption in necessary depth. Groups of films must be understood in relation to, rather than as a reflection of, divergent discourses circulating in society during the moments of production, mediation, and consumption. As I have demonstrated, cycles of cross-media production—which includes the newspaper discourses that helped shape production and reception contexts—must be mapped in relation to shifting discursive struggles, converging and clashing across different national, local, and institutional contexts.

In shifting the analytic focus to film cycles, we can not only illuminate the divergent interpretative strategies that audiences brought to bear on films during their circulation within a range of exhibition contexts but also begin to account for the popularity and resonances of certain groupings of films at particular historical moments. Though, for some, Hollywood's mystifying female monsters may well have intersected with the types of official, patriarchal discourses John Berks identifies—as the male commanding officer of the WAC Training Center complained of wartime women in 1944, "They don't wear armbands. They are not branded on the forehead. They all look alike, the decent ones and the bad ones. You can't tell them apart, until you catch them in an overt act"—they also tapped into female experiences of lingering tragedy and temporary liberation on the home front.[3] As a result of this methodological intervention, *Phantom Ladies* has afforded a more nuanced understanding of the cultural landscape of this much-debated but often misunderstood period of social and media history.

But what is the relevance of *Phantom Ladies* for understanding the relationship between cultural producers and consumers today? Seventy years on from *Cat People*, the release of Pixar's animated film *Monsters University* (2013)—the sequel to its 2001 hit *Monsters, Inc.*—inspired a surprising critical uproar about the lack of female monsters onscreen. From the *New York Times* to mothering blogs, it was felt that keeping monstrosity a "largely male domain" meant that the range of identities and opportunities open to women was being restricted from an early age.[4] Female horror fans, feminist bloggers, and women writers continue to express their frustration that the type of psychologically and emotionally complex female characters in forties horror and crime cinema are absent from screens today.[5] As the novelist Sophia McDougall complains of 2013's media landscape:

"Sherlock Holmes gets to be brilliant, solitary, abrasive, Bohemian, whimsical, brave, sad, manipulative, neurotic, vain, untidy, fastidious, artistic, courteous, rude, a polymath genius. Female characters get to be Strong."[6]

Every decade in Hollywood's history throws up one or two interesting female monsters—from the genetically mutated cosmetics manufacturer of *Wasp Woman* (1959) to the tragic baby boomer of *Carrie* (1976)—but no other period has invested so heavily, both financially and philosophically, in female monstrousness as the early to mid-1940s.[7] As this book has shown, some of these representations were clearly problematic, but they offered women possibilities for thinking about themselves and their bodies in new and invigorating ways. Wartime contingency provided women with temporary liberation from ascribed gender roles and expectations that did not so much change as supplement the range of femininities and social experiences open to them. This included in the cinema auditorium, where they encountered the type of complex and contradictory female characters that horror fans yearn for today. The fact that women still look back to these tragic female shape-shifters and resilient lady detectives as intriguing and empowering representations of femininity is testament to both their uniqueness and continuing resonance. Blurring the boundaries between tragedy and excitement, escapism and engagement, femininity and masculinity, vulnerability and strength, the female monster films resonate not only with the confusions and contestations of home-front life but also with the frustrations and desires of contemporary women. Although these phantom ladies supplanted men in Hollywood horror's keystone roles only for the duration of the war, their legacies endure in the succession of surprise encounters and transformative experiences they continue to provoke.

NOTES

INTRODUCTION: HORROR ON THE HOME FRONT

1. "Entertainment News," *Sheboygan Press* (WI), August 10, 1943, 3; "Entertainment News," *Herald Press* (Joseph, MI), August 10, 1943, 11.
2. Tim Snelson and Mark Jancovich, "'No Hits, No Runs, Just Terrors': Exhibition, Cultural Distinctions, and Cult Audiences at the Rialto Cinema in the 1930s," in *Explorations in New Cinema History: Approaches and Case Studies*, ed. Richard Maltby, Daniel Biltereyst, and Philippe Meers (Malden, MA: Wiley-Blackwell, 2011), 199–211; Tim Snelson and Mark Jancovich, "Horror at the Crossroads: Class, Gender, and Taste at the Rialto," in *From the Arthouse to the Grindhouse: Highbrow and Lowbrow Transgression in Cinema's First Century*, ed. John Cline and Robert G. Weiner (Lanham, MD: Scarecrow Press, 2010), 109–125.
3. Arthur Mayer, *Merely Colossal: The Story of the Movies from the Long Chase to the Chaise Longue* (New York: Simon and Schuster, 1953), 179–180.
4. Universal, "Movie Doors Now Open to Taller Actresses," *Son of Dracula* pressbook, 1943, Margaret Herrick Library, Beverly Hills, California.
5. The only anomaly previous to the wartime period reported by Mayer was the billing of *Dracula's Daughter* in 1936. Mayer asserted that "we have not been able to keep women out of the theatre since the picture opened. They are keen on seeing a member of their sex destroy vaunted male prestige in cold-blooded villainy." According to Mayer, there was nothing masochistic about the female audience's identification with *Dracula's Daughter*. They were flocking to see the film out of a purely sadistic desire to see men terrorized onscreen. Nor was this female monster considered to be inferior to her male predecessor, he continued: "Old man Dracula used to make needles run up and down our spines, but his little gal makes them run all over us." This gendered power inversion on and off screen was therefore perceived, at least according to Mayer, as a significant attraction for women who might not typically frequent his downtown "chamber of horrors." However, women would have to wait until 1942 for more of this type of film fare. "Cup Bearer to the Bloodthirsty," *New York Times*, May 17, 1936, X3.
6. Fred Stanley, "The Year in Hollywood," *New York Times*, December 26, 1943, X3.
7. Barbara Klinger uses the term "local genre" to designate the transitory but recognized means of classifying films used for short historical periods. Barbara

Klinger, *Melodrama and Meaning: History, Culture, and the Films of Douglas Sirk* (Bloomington: Indiana University Press, 1994), 56. Between 1942 and 1946, only 17 percent of Hollywood's total output represented what Russell Earl Shain refers to as "WWII-related Hollywood features." Russell Earl Shain, *An Analysis of Motion Pictures about War Released by the American Film Industry, 1939–1970* (New York: Arno, 1976), 31. It is these films, and typically their role as propaganda vehicles, however, that provide the focus of most accounts of wartime Hollywood production. The 83 percent of "escapist" films seen by the majority of audiences tend to be relegated to a supporting role in studies of wartime Hollywood and its audiences. See, for example, Michael S. Shull and David Edward Wilt, *Hollywood War Films, 1937–1945: An Exhaustive Filmography of American Feature-length Motion Pictures Relating to World War II* (Jefferson, NC: McFarland, 1996); Lewis Jacobs, "World War II and the American Film," *Cinema Journal* 7 (Winter 1967–1968): 1–21; Jeanine Basinger, *The World War II Combat Film: Anatomy of a Genre* (New York: Columbia University Press, 1986); Thomas Doherty, *Projections of War: Hollywood, American Culture, and World War II* (New York: Columbia University Press, 1993); Clayton Koppes and Gregory Black, *Hollywood Goes to War: How Politics, Profits, and Propaganda Shaped World War II Movies* (New York: Free Press, 1987); Wheeler Winston Dixon, ed., *American Cinema of the 1940s* (Oxford: Berg, 2006); Colin Shindler, *Hollywood Goes to War: Films and American Society, 1939–1952* (London: Routledge, 1979); Robert McLaughlin and Sally Parry, *We'll Always Have the Movies: American Cinema during World War II* (Lexington: University Press of Kentucky, 2006); Bernard Dick, *The Star-Spangled Screen: The American World War II Film* (Lexington: University Press of Kentucky, 1996); Edward F. Dolan, *Hollywood Goes to War* (Twickenham: Hamlyn, 1985); Robert Fyne, *The Hollywood Propaganda of World War II* (Metuchen, NJ: Scarecrow Press, 1994); Kathryn Kane, *Visions of War: Hollywood Combat Films of World War II* (Ann Arbor, MI: UMI Research Press, 1982); Roger Manvell, *Films and the Second World War* (South Brunswick, NJ: A. S. Barnes, 1974); Terry Christensen, "The 1940s: Hollywood Goes to War," in Terry Christensen and Peter J. Haas, *Projecting Politics: Political Messages in American Film* (Armonk, NY: M. E. Sharpe, 2005); Robert Beverley Ray, "Classic Hollywood's Holding Pattern: The Combat Films of World War II," in *A Certain Tendency of the Hollywood Cinema, 1930–1980* (Princeton, NJ: Princeton University Press, 1985), 113–127; Arthur McClure, "Hollywood at War: The American Motion Picture and World War II, 1939–1945," *Journal of Popular Film* 1, no. 2 (Spring 1972): 123–135.

8. Steve Neale, *Genre* (London: BFI Publishing, 1980), 61; Tania Modleski, "The Terror of Pleasure: The Contemporary Horror Film and Postmodern Theory," in *Studies in Entertainment: Critical Approaches to Mass Culture*, ed. Tania Modleski (Bloomington: Indiana University Press, 1986), 163–164.
9. Barbara Creed, "Horror and the Monstrous-Feminine: An Imaginary Abjection," *Screen* 27, no. 1 (January–February 1986): 70; see also Barbara Creed, *The Monstrous Feminine: Film, Feminism, Psychoanalysis* (New York: Routledge, 1993).
10. Linda Williams complicates these accounts by arguing that classic horror is exceptional in that it *does* allow women a position from which to "look" that

can be potentially empowering. She contends that there is a "surprising (and at times subversive affinity) between monster and woman," who through their exchange of looks recognize "their similar status, as potent threats to a vulnerable male power." However, Williams explains that although this identification can give expression to female transgression, the female spectator—like the diegetic heroine—is ultimately punished for looking; she is forced to witness the "vindictive destruction" of the monster with whom she identifies. This is why, Williams suggests, women "refuse to look," covering their eyes or averting them from the screen. Linda Williams, "When the Woman Looks," in *Re-Vision: Essays in Feminist Film Criticism*, ed. Mary Ann Doane, Patricia Mellencamp, and Linda Williams (Washington, DC: American Film Institute, 1984), 90.

11. Brigid Cherry, "Refusing to Refuse to Look: Female Viewers of the Horror Film," in *Identifying Hollywood's Audiences*, ed. Melvyn Stokes and Richard Maltby (London: BFI, 1999), 205, 228.
12. Cheryl Christina Crane, "Hollywood's Newest Pin-Up," *Photoplay*, December 1943, 33.
13. See, for example, "Women in War Jobs Still Find Time to Have Fun and Run Households," *New York Times*, March 3, 1943, 16.
14. Klinger, *Melodrama and Meaning*, 122.
15. Even recent revisionist film histories that aim to convince readers of the primacy of cycles, rather than genres or individual films, as the key object of historical inquiry re-create such problems, extolling "film cycles as a mould placed over the zeitgeist, which when pulled away reveals the contours, fissures, and complicated patterns of the contemporary moment." Amanda Ann Klein, *American Film Cycles: Reframing Genres, Screening Social Problems, and Defining Subcultures* (Austin: University of Texas Press, 2011), 20.
16. Rhona Berenstein, *Attack of the Leading Ladies: Gender, Sexuality, and Spectatorship in Classic Horror Cinema* (New York: Columbia University Press, 1996); Richard Nowell, *Blood Money: A Study of the First Teen Slasher Film Cycle* (New York: Continuum, 2010).
17. William H. Chafe, *The American Woman: Her Changing Social, Economic, and Political Roles, 1920–1970* (New York: Oxford University Press, 1972). Susan Hartman, for example, concurs with Chafe's assertion that the female labor force grew by more than 50 percent during the war, with women's employment growing in every field except domestic service; these six million new female employees increased the percentage of women in the American labor force to 36 percent by 1944. She further finds that the most spectacular gains in terms of both higher income and higher numbers (a 460 percent increase, in fact) were in war manufacturing, where women worked in formerly almost solely male domains. However, Hartman asserts that these wartime gains in employment, and more generally in the reorientation of gendered roles, were largely temporary. Furthermore, twelve million women were already working outside the home before the war started; the biggest changes were in the number of married women and mothers entering the labor force and in the opening of female positions in certain "skilled jobs" that had been considered as predominantly or solely

male jobs. Susan Hartman, *The Home Front and Beyond: American Women in the 1940s* (Boston: Twayne, 1982), 21. For more on American women's experience of work and leisure on the home front, see Karen Anderson, *Wartime Women: Sex Roles, Family Relations, and the Status of Women during World War II* (Westport, CT: Greenwood Press, 1981); D'Ann Campbell, *Women at War with America: Private Lives in a Patriotic Era* (Cambridge, MA: Harvard University Press, 1984); Leila J. Rupp, *Mobilizing Women for War: German and American Propaganda, 1939–1945* (Princeton, NJ: Princeton University Press, 1978); Miriam Frank, Marilyn Ziebarth, and Connie Field, *The Life and Times of Rosie the Riveter: The Story of Three Million Working Women during World War II* (Emeryville, CA: Clarity Educational Productions, 1982); Sherna Berger Gluck, *Rosie the Riveter Revisited: Women, the War, and Social Change* (Boston: Twayne, 1987); John Costello, *Love, Sex and War: Changing Values, 1939–1945* (London: Pan, 1986); John W. Jeffries, *Wartime America: The World War II Home Front* (Chicago: I. R. Dee, 1996); Richard R. Lingeman, *Don't You Know There's a War On? The American Home Front, 1941–1945* (New York: Putnam's, 1970); Paul Fussell, *Wartime: Understanding and Behavior in the Second World War* (New York: Oxford University Press, 1989); Penny Colman, *Rosie the Riveter: Women Working on the Home Front in World War II* (New York: Crown Publishers, 1995); J. E. Trey, "Women in the War Economy—World War II," *Review of Radical Political Economics* 4, no. 3 (July 1972): 40–57; Kenneth O'Brien and Hudson Parsons Lynn, eds., *The Home-Front War: World War II and American Society* (London: Greenwood, 1995); William M. Tuttle Jr., *"Daddy's Gone to War": The Second World War in the Lives of America's Children* (New York: Oxford University Press, 1995); Susan B. Anthony, *Out of the Kitchen—Into the War* (New York: Stephen Daye, 1943); Margaret Mead, *"And Keep Your Powder Dry": An Anthropologist Looks at America* (New York: William Morrow, 1942).

18. Max Lerner, *Public Journal: Marginal Notes on Wartime America* (New York: Viking Press, 1945), 19.
19. Max Lerner, 1943, quoted in Emily Yellin, *Our Mothers' War: American Women at Home and at the Front during World War II* (New York: Simon and Schuster, 2004), 305.
20. On the contradictory representation of women in wartime media and propaganda, see Maureen Honey, "Maternal Welders: Women's Sexuality and Propaganda on the Home Front during World War II," in *The American Experience in World War II*, ed. Walter L. Hixson (New York: Routledge, 2003), 31–71; Phil Goodman, "'Patriotic Femininity': Women's Morals and Men's Morale during the Second World War," *Gender & History* 10, no. 2 (August 1998): 278–293; Robert Westbrook, "'I Want a Girl, Just Like the Girl That Married Harry James': American Women and the Problem of Political Obligation in World War II," *American Quarterly* 42, no. 4 (1990): 587–614; Jane Gaines, "The Showgirl and the Wolf," *Cinema Journal* 20, no. 1 (Fall 1980): 53–67; Susan Gubar, "'This Is My Rifle, This Is My Gun': World War II and the Blitz on Women," in *Behind the Lines: Gender and the Two World Wars*, ed. Margaret Randolph Higonnet et al. (New Haven, CT: Yale University Press, 1987), 227–259; Susan Ohmer, "Female Spectatorship

and Women's Magazines: Hollywood, *Good Housekeeping*, and World War II," *Velvet Light Trap* 25 (Spring 1990): 53–68.

21. Melissa Dabakis, "Gendered Labour: Norman Rockwell's *Rosie the Riveter* and the Discourse of Wartime Womanhood," in *Gender and American History since 1890*, ed. Barbara Melosh (London: Routledge, 1993), 190.
22. Gluck, *Rosie the Riveter Revisited*, 13.
23. Rupp, *Mobilizing Women for War*, 156, 97.
24. Ibid., 146.
25. Westbrook, "'I Want a Girl,'" 603.
26. Robert Westbrook, "'I Want a Girl, Just Like the Girl That Married Harry James': American Women and the Problem of Political Obligation in World War II," *American Quarterly* 42, no. 4 (1990): 603; Maria Elena Buszek, *Pin-Up Grrrls: Feminism, Sexuality, Popular Culture* (Durham, NC: Duke University Press, 2006), 186.
27. Francis Merrill, *Social Problems on the Home Front: A Study of War-time Influences* (New York: Harper and Brothers, 1948), 100. In early 1944 an article in *Newsweek* revealed that "the greatest tragedy of the war is the moral break-down among American girls." It explained that the police had been forced to impose a curfew for under-sixteens in Times Square, because of the number of "the victory girls or the bobby sox brigade" hanging around dance halls, bars, restrooms, and bus terminals. "Combating the Victory Girls," *Newsweek*, March 6, 1944, 88.
28. "American Social Hygiene Report," quoted in Costello, *Love, Sex and War*, 281–282.
29. Ibid., 281.
30. See Sonya Michel, "American Women and the Discourse of the Democratic Family in World War I," in Higonnet et al., *Behind the Lines*, 154–167.
31. Dr. Cooper Booth, quoted in *Daily Telegraph*, June 29, 1943, in Marilyn Lake, "Female Desires: The Meaning of World War II," in *Feminism and History*, ed. Joan Wallach Scott (New York: Oxford University Press, 1996), 438.
32. Rick Altman, *Film/Genre* (London: BFI Publishing, 2004), 60–62.
33. See Peter Stanfield, *The Lost Trail: Hollywood, Westerns and the 1930s* (Exeter: University of Exeter Press, 2001); *Horse Opera: The Strange History of the 1930s Singing Cowboy* (Urbana: University of Illinois Press, 2002); "Crossover: Sam Katzman's *Switchblade Calypso Bop Reefer Madness Swamp Girl* or 'Bad Jazz,' Calypso, Beatniks and Rock 'n' Roll in 1950s Teenpix," *Popular Music* 29, no. 3 (Autumn 2010): 437–456; "Intent to Speed: Cyclical Production, Topicality, and the 1950s Hot Rod Movie," *New Review of Film and Television Studies* 11, no. 1 (2013): 34–55.
34. Peter Stanfield, "'Pix Biz Spurts with War Fever': Film and the Public Sphere—Cycles and Topicality," *Film History: An International Journal* 25, nos. 1–2 (2013): 218.
35. Robin Wood, "An Introduction to the American Horror Film," in *Planks of Reason: Essays on the Horror Film*, ed. Barry Keith Grant (Metuchen, NJ: Scarecrow Press, 1984), 183; Andrew Tudor, *Monsters and Mad Scientists: A Cultural History of the Horror Movies* (Oxford: Basil Blackwell, 1989), 33–38. See also Carlos Clarens, *An Illustrated History of the Horror Film* (New York: Paragon Books, 1967); S. S. Prawer,

Caligari's Children: The Film as Tale of Terror (London: Oxford University Press, 1980); David J. Skal, *The Monster Show: A Cultural History of Horror* (London: Plexus, 1993); Jonathan Lake Crane, *Terror and Everyday Life: Singular Moments in the History of the Horror Film* (London: Sage, 1994).

36. Donald Kirkley, "Film Notes," *Baltimore Sun*, May 2, 1943, 7.
37. Dellie Hahne, quoted in Studs Terkel, *"The Good War": An Oral History of World War II* (London: Hamish Hamilton, 1984), 117.

CHAPTER 1 *REBECCA* MEETS *THE WOLFMAN* AT RKO

1. See, for example, Douglas Gomery, "The Rise of National Theatre Chains," in *Shared Pleasures: A History of Movie Presentation in the United States* (Madison: University of Wisconsin Press, 1992), 34–56.
2. Barbara Berch, "Gold in Them Chills," *Collier's*, January 29, 1944, 66.
3. Rick Atman, *Film/Genre* (London: BFI Publishing, 2004), 60.
4. Val Lewton quoted in Joel Siegel, *Val Lewton: The Reality of Terror* (Secker and Walberg: London, 1972), 41. An internal memo to Sid Kramer, following a test screening for RKO promotions and sales staff, refers to the film as "*Rebecca* in the West Indies." "Internal Reports to Sid Kramer," *I Walked with a Zombie* (1943), No. 396, RKO Radio Production Files, Charles E. Young Research Library, University of California at Los Angeles.
5. J.T.M., "See the Pretty Panther Woman," *PM*, December 7, 1942. *Cat People* shared not only the elegant staircase set from *The Magnificent Ambersons* (1942)—a piece of resourceful recycling inspired partially by budgetary limitations and partially by War Production Board restrictions on set construction—but also Welles's regular editor, Mark Robson, also "booted downstairs" following the film's poor box-office run.
6. Kim Newman, *Cat People* (London: BFI Publishing, 1999), 7.
7. See Siegel, *Val Lewton*, 21–27. In fact, Edmund Bansak suggests that the "two men had an appreciation for one another" and that Koerner backed Lewton's ideas for *Cat People* when he faced opposition from the B-pictures supervisor, Lou Ostrow, who thought them too "pretentious." Edmund Bansak, *Fearing the Dark: The Val Lewton Career* (Jefferson, NC: McFarland, 1995), 125.
8. See, for example, Robbin Coons, "Hollywood Sights and Sounds," *Salamanca Republican Press* (NY), October 9, 1942; Robbin Coons, "Gentleman with Sense of Humor Is Assigned RKO Task," *Port Arthur News* (TX), October 11, 1942.
9. A 1947 Columbia University report explains that while advertising in newspapers and magazines is the principal source by which respondents learn about pictures, hearsay and reviews (taken as independent sources) are both more influential than any advertising source. Leo A. Handel, *Hollywood Looks at Its Audience: A Report of Film Audience Research* (Urbana: University of Illinois Press, 1950), 89.
10. Susan Ohmer, "Measuring Desire: George Gallup and Audience Research in Hollywood," *Journal of Film and Video* 43, no. 1 (1991): 13.

11. Alfred Hitchcock quoted in François Truffaut, *Hitchcock* (New York: Simon and Schuster, 1983), 127.
12. David O. Selznick memo in Tania Modleski, *The Women Who Knew Too Much: Hitchcock and Feminist Theory* (New York: Methuen, 1988), 43.
13. *Rebecca* was followed closely by *Pride and Prejudice* (1940) in terms of female preferences, while Hitchcock's other Gothic *Suspicion* (1941) and Welles's *Citizen Kane* (1941) also attracted more women than men. ARI, "Audience Research Institute Report 165: Princeton, July 14, 1942," in George Gallup et al., *Gallup Looks at the Movies: Audience Research Reports, 1940–1950* (Wilmington, DE: Scholarly Resources, 1979).
14. ARI, "Audience Research Institute Report 163, Princeton, July 25, 1942."
15. Val Lewton quoted in Siegel, *Val Lewton*, 41.
16. Bansak, *Fearing the Dark*, 79.
17. David O. Selznick memo quoted in Bansak, *Fearing the Dark*, 121.
18. Siegel, *Val Lewton*, 12–13.
19. Lucy Lewton (sister) quoted in Bansak, *Fearing the Dark*, 122.
20. Siegel, *Val Lewton*, 21.
21. Walt, "The Wolf Man," *Variety*, December 17, 1941, 8.
22. Although *The Wolf Man* is, probably rightly, not held in such high esteem as *Cat People*, this might have been different if its writer, Curt Siodmak, had had the freedom Lewton seemingly enjoyed at RKO. Siodmak revealed, "I also didn't want to show the Wolf Man's face except when Lon Chaney looked at his own image in a mirror or in a pool of water. But George [Waggner, the producer-director] changed all that, maybe rightly." Curt Siodmak quoted in P. Riley, comp. and ed., *MagicImage Filmbooks Presents "The Wolf Man,"* Universal FilmscriptsSeries, Classic Horror Films, vol. 12 (Absecon, NJ: MagicImage Filmbooks, 1993), 14. In addition to this more subtle, psychological approach, Siodmak clearly intended the film to have a sociocultural resonance beyond its supernatural theme. In his autobiography he says he "saw in it the fight of good and evil in man's soul, and the inescapable working of fate, which also had shaped my life." As a German Jew who had fled Nazi Germany for America in 1937, he would have found special resonance in the story of a man's stable existence turned to chaos, and his choice of a people marked for death by the sign of the star seems deliberate. Curt Siodmak, *Wolf Man's Maker: Memoir of a Hollywood Writer* (Lanham, MD: Scarecrow Press, 2001), 261.
23. Newman, *Cat People*, 12; Altman, *Film/Genre*, 60.
24. E. A. Cunningham, "*Cat People*," *Motion Picture Herald*, November 14, 1942; "*Cat People*," *Daily Variety*, November 13, 1942; Walt, "Film Reviews," *Variety*, November 18, 1942.
25. J.T.M., "See the Pretty Panther Woman."
26. Ohmer, "Measuring Desire," 17.
27. ARI, "Audience Research Institute Report 165, Princeton, July 14, 1942."
28. John Costello, *Love, Sex and War: Changing Values, 1939–1949* (London: Collins, 1985), 223–224.

29. "Sex Up the Beautiful Hunks of Men in Film Ads to Lure Unescorted Fems," *Variety*, March 11, 1942, 1, 53.
30. "Shudder Films Popular; Studios Have 24 Lined Up," *Hollywood Reporter*, May 10, 1943, 4.
31. Universal, "Showmanship," *Wolf Man* pressbook, 1941, University of Southern California Library, Los Angeles.
32. RKO Radio, "Exploitation," *Cat People* pressbook, 1942, University of Southern California Library, Los Angeles, 16.
33. "Showmandiser," *Boxoffice*, October 27, 1943, 5.
34. "Who Said a Cat Only Has Nine Lives?" (*Cat People* advertisement), *Hollywood Reporter*, April 12, 1943, 5. The Hawaii's proprietor, Albert Gaston, explained to the *Los Angeles Times* in 1943 that when he saw *Cat People* he said, "Here's a picture that has exploitation value. We converted our box office into the head of an immense cat and sold tickets through its mouth. We had cat's heads floating around the audience. It really got them in the mood. The picture cost RKO $140,000; we ran it for two months and our film rental paid 10% of the whole cost." Albert Gaston quoted in *The Val Lewton Screenplay Collection*, http://www.whiskeyloosetongue.com/hawaii_theater.html (accessed July 21, 2009).
35. RKO Radio, "*Cat People* New Kind of Thriller," *Cat People* pressbook.
36. Gerard Lenne, "Monster and Victim: Women in the Horror Film," in *Sexual Stratagems: The World of Women in Film*, ed. Patricia Erens (New York: Horizon Press, 1979), 35, 32.
37. RKO Radio, *Cat People* pressbook, 13–14.
38. Diane Waldman, "'At Last I Can Tell It to Someone!': Female Point of View and Subjectivity in the Gothic Romance Film of the 1940s," *Cinema Journal* 23, no. 2 (1984): 31.
39. Mary Ann Doane, *The Desire to Desire: The Woman's Film of the 1940s* (Bloomington: Indiana University Press, 1987), 96, 125.
40. Val Lewton quoted in George Turner, "A Retrospective of the 'Original' Val Lewton's *Cat People*," *Cinefantastique* 12, no. 4 (1982): 25. Jacques Tourneur went even further, suggesting that Randolph was "built like a wrestler." Newman, *Cat People*, 51.
41. Bosley Crowther, "Purrrr," *New York Times*, December 7, 1942. The *Dallas Morning News* concurred that "for the most part she's more the cuddly, purry tabby type." F.N., "Simone Comes Up to Scratch Again," *Dallas Morning News*, January 15, 1943.
42. Robert Westbrook, "'I Want a Girl, Just Like the Girl That Married Harry James': American Women and the Problem of Political Obligation in World War II," *American Quarterly* 42, no. 4 (1990): 603; Maria Elena Buszek, *Pin-Up Grrrls: Feminism, Sexuality, Popular Culture* (Durham, NC: Duke University Press, 2006), 186. Mary Beth Haralovich has widely discussed the infusion of pinup photography into film advertising in the war years. The popularity of unregulated candid-camera magazines and, particularly, the perception of their role in the war effort put pressure upon the MPPDA to relax its mandates on "good taste" in movie advertising. The poster campaign for *Cat People* is clearly in keeping with

this trend of featuring women with "significant cleavage in frontal poses" and provocative taglines, such as selling the unusual dream girl Irena as the key attraction of "the strangest story you ever tried to get out of your dreams!" Mary Beth Haralovich, "Advertising Heterosexuality," *Screen* 23, no. 2 (1982): 56.

43. Westbrook, "'I Want a Girl,'" 605.
44. Jeanine Basinger, *A Woman's View: How Hollywood Spoke to Women, 1930–1960* (Hanover, NH: Wesleyan University Press, 1993), 87.
45. "Displays—Inside, Outside," *Motion Picture Herald*, January 23, 1943, 64. After just one week at the Rialto the *Hollywood Reporter* was reporting that the cinema was "coming within a few dollars of breaking the house record" with *Cat People*, which was running from 8:30 a.m. to 5:00 a.m. to meet demand. "Cat People Audience," *Hollywood Reporter*, December 9, 1942, 8.
46. Dana Polan, "Knowledge and Human Interests: Science, Cinema, and the Secularization of Horror," in *Power and Paranoia: History, Narrative, and the American Cinema, 1940–1950* (New York: Columbia University Press, 1986), 173, 186.
47. See, for example, Susan Gubar, "'This Is My Rifle, This Is My Gun': World War II and the Blitz on Women," in *Behind the Lines: Gender and the Two World Wars*, ed. Margaret Randolph Higonnet et al. (New Haven, CT: Yale University Press, 1987), 227–259. Significantly, as with French actress Simone Simon in *Cat People*, European or other ethnically "exotic" actresses were typically cast in the female monster parts, as later chapters will discuss in more detail.
48. Joy Davidman, "Screen Spookery: Supernatural Horrors in *The Cat People* and Elsewhere," *New Masses*, December 22, 1943, 31.
49. John Berks, "What Alice Does: Looking Otherwise at *The Cat People*," *Cinema Journal* 32, no. 1 (1992): 33.
50. Robin Wood, "An Introduction to the American Horror Film," in *Planks of Reason: Essays on the Horror Film*, ed. Barry Keith Grant (Metuchen, NJ: Scarecrow Press, 1984), 146–192.
51. Karen Hollinger, "The Monster as Woman: Two Generations of *Cat People*," *Film Criticism* 13, no. 2 (1989): 39.
52. Berks, "What Alice Does," 38, 39.
53. Karen Hollinger, "Dialogue: *Cat People*," *Cinema Journal* 33, no. 1 (1993): 55.
54. "The Woman's Angle," *Variety*, January 17, 1933, 15. Paramount's mad scientist narrative based on H. G. Wells's novel *The Island of Dr. Moreau* relies largely on the type of "transformations to grotesque and marauding characters" against which *Cat People* was set up in opposition. "Cat People," *Daily Variety*, November 13, 1942. In a memo regarding casting for *Cat People* Lewton informed his executive producer, Lou Ostrow, "I took a look at the Paramount picture *The Island of Lost Souls* and after seeing their much-publicized 'panther woman,' I feel that any attempt to secure a cat-like quality in our girl's physical appearance would be disastrous." Turner, "A Retrospective of the 'Original' Val Lewton's *Cat People*," 25.
55. Linda Williams, "When the Woman Looks," in *Re-Vision: Essays in Feminist Film Criticism*, ed. Mary Ann Doane, Patricia Mellencamp, and Linda Williams (Frederick, MD: AFI Publishing, 1984), 83–89.

56. See, for example, Ethel Gorman, *So Your Husband's Gone to War!* (New York: Doubleday, Doran, 1942).
57. Maxine Davis, "Women without Men," *Good Housekeeping*, March 1942, 181.
58. Karen Anderson, *Wartime Women: Sex Roles, Family Relations, and the Status of Women during World War II* (Westport, CT: Greenwood Press, 1981), 111.
59. "Women, Women Everywhere," *Time*, October 19, 1942.
60. Berks, "What Alice Does," 38.
61. Anderson, *Wartime Women*, 111.
62. Letter from Will Hays to William Gordon, July 13, 1942, MPPDA Files, Margaret Herrick Library, Beverly Hills, California.
63. Gregory William Mank, *Hollywood Cauldron: Thirteen Horror Films from the Genre's Golden Age* (Jefferson, NC: McFarland, 1994), 215.
64. William H. Chafe, "World War II as a Pivotal Experience for American Women," in *Women and War: The Changing Status of American Women from the 1930s to the 1940s*, ed. Maria Diedrich and Dorothea Fischer-Hornung (New York: Berg, 1990), 22.
65. Mary Brewster quoted in "Unruffled," *Time*, June 21, 1943. Hollywood responded to the call for utilitarian costuming. As Edith Head, chief designer at Paramount, asserted, "Luxury costumes are not only old fashioned, they're unpatriotic and in bad taste." However, Hollywood was able to exploit unpatriotic connotations of excessive pleats, ruffles, and accoutrements to characterize certain female characters as "transgressive," most blatantly the noir femme fatale. Edith Head quoted in Thomas Doherty, *Projections of War: Hollywood, America Culture, and World War II* (New York: Columbia University Press, 1993), 159.
66. *Seattle Times*, March 15, 1942, quoted in Anderson, *Wartime Women*, 87; Sherna Berger Gluck, *Rosie the Riveter Revisited: Women, the War, and Social Change* (Boston: Twayne, 1987), 13.
67. Julie Wosk, *Women and the Machine: Representations from the Spinning Wheel to the Electronic Age* (Baltimore: John Hopkins University Press, 2003), 28.
68. Anderson explains that "nationally, there were 1,118,000 more marriages between 1940 and 1943 than would be expected pre-war rates." Anderson, *Wartime Women*, 76.
69. See Betty Friedan, *The Feminine Mystique* (New York: W. W. Norton, 1963).
70. Edwin Schallert, "*Cat People* Lukewarm Film Thriller at Hawaii," *Los Angeles Times*, January 15, 1943, 23; "The New Pictures," *Time*, January 4, 1943; E. A. Cunningham, "*Cat People*," *Motion Picture Herald*, November 14, 1942.
71. Ernest L. Schier, "Simone Simon and Tom Conway Star in First-Runs at the Pix," *Washington Post*, January 11, 1943, B5.
72. DeWitt Bodeen, "*The Cat People*: Original Screenplay," in *The Val Lewton Screenplay Collection*, 36.
73. Doane, *The Desire to Desire*, 48.
74. Bodeen, "*The Cat People*: Original Screenplay," 1.
75. Anderson, *Wartime Women*, 111.
76. Hayes to Gordon, July 13, 1942; Hayes to Gordon, July 18, 1942, MPPDA Files, Margaret Herrick Library, Beverly Hills, California. As the review in the literary film

journal *Rob Wagner's Script* suggested, "Sex (the Hays Office insists it be kiss) is the lever which prongs the animal in the lady to destroy." Herb Sterne, "*The Cat People*," *Rob Wagner's Script* 27, no. 42 (November 21, 1942): 18.

77. See Grace Palladino, "Andy Hardy Goes to War: Soldiers, Defense Workers, 'V-Girls,' and Zoot Suiters," in *Teenagers: An American History* (New York: Basic Books, 1996), 63–79.
78. Although Lewton chose Simon for her cute "kitten" features, it is also possible that he wished to bring the "ever provocative Simone Simon back to the screen" in order to exploit the intertextual connotations of her sexual double life. The *Los Angeles Times* is referring to her Hollywood hiatus following unwanted publicity surrounding a sex scandal that arose after she accused her secretary of stealing money from her. The secretary eventually revealed details of Simon's "private life," most sensationally that she showered a number of male lovers, including George Gershwin, with expensive gifts including gold keys to her house engraved with her initials. Schallert, "*Cat People* Lukewarm"; "Girl Stole $16,000 from Miss Simon," *New York Times*, April 24, 1938; "Simone Simon's Life Must Be Kept Secret," *New York Times*, July 20, 1938.
79. Philip Scheuer, "Trio Gives Horror Picture New Dress," *Los Angeles Times*, March 28, 1943, C3.
80. Ibid.
81. F.N., "Voodoo Lifts Its Weird Head," *Dallas Morning News*, July 12, 1943, 8.
82. Val Lewton quoted in DeWitt Bodeen, "Val Lewton," *Films in Review* 14, no. 4 (1963): 218.
83. James Agee, *Agee on Film*, vol. 1 (New York: Universal Library, 1969), 76.
84. Sylvie Pierre, "The Beauty of the Sea," in *Jacques Tourneur*, ed. Claire Johnston and Paul Willemen (Edinburgh: Edinburgh Film Festival, 1975), 46.
85. The original script concluded with the now happily married Betsy and Paul living in Ottawa and a reassuring return to Betsy's voice-over narration. This ending was clearly cut in favor of the polyvalent image of Ti-Misery and a more tragic voice-over by an unknown but seemingly black narrator. Curt Siodmak and Ardel Wray, "*I Walked with a Zombie* Original Screenplay," *The Val Lewton Screenplay Collection*, 72.
86. Waldman, "'At Last I Can Tell It to Someone!,'" 31.
87. RKO Radio, "Ancient Witchcraft" and "Horror and Romance in New Thrill Film," *I Walked with a Zombie* pressbook, 1943, British Film Institute Library, London, 2.
88. ARI, "Audience Research Institute Report 169: *I Walked With a Zombie.*"
89. RKO Radio, "Eerie Voodoo Rites Form Background for Strange Tale of Romance and Thrills," *I Walked with a Zombie* pressbook, 2.
90. Diane Waldman, "From Midnight Shows to Marriage Vows: Women, Exploitation and Exhibition," *Wide Angle* 6, no. 2 (1984): 48.
91. ARI, "Audience Research Institute Report 165: Princeton, July 14, 1942."
92. "RKO Launches Another Exploitation Special!" *Hollywood Reporter*, April 26, 1943.
93. "*I Walked with a Zombie* Hit," *Hollywood Reporter*, March 16, 1943.
94. "*I Walked with a Zombie*," *Variety Daily Trade Show*, March 16, 1943.

95. RKO Radio, "Frances Dee Plays a Nurse to a Zombie," *I Walked with a Zombie* pressbook. The same year saw the release of one of the most famous female-centered war films of the era, *So Proudly We Hail* (1943), which celebrated the participation and bravery of trained nurses in the "exotic location" of Bataan.
96. RKO Radio, "About a Real Zombie That Was Met by a Lady with Red Hair," *I Walked with a Zombie* pressbook.
97. Susan Hartmann, *The Home Front and Beyond: American Women in the 1940s* (Boston: Twayne, 1982), 201.
98. Basinger, *A Woman's View*, 83–113.
99. N.B.B., "Diverting Double Bill at Pix," *Washington Post*, May 17, 1943.
100. V.K., "*I Walked with a Zombie*," *Motion Picture Herald*, March 20, 1943.
101. Siegel, *Val Lewton*, 112.
102. An internal report to Sid Kramer praised the film as "more than just a horror-thriller; it's an entertaining, fascinating, suspenseful, first rate psychological melodrama. . . . In some respects it is *Rebecca* in the West Indies." Jay Sanford to Sid Kramer, "Internal Report," 1943, RKO Radio Production Files, Charles E. Young Research Library, University of California at Los Angeles.
103. Mark Robson on Universal horror in Newman, *Cat People*, 69.
104. Bansak, *Fearing the Dark*, 147.
105. Ardel Wray quoted in Siegel, *Val Lewton*, 42.
106. That said, the studio-sanctioned press material did attempt to reduce the complexities of the narrative by describing it as "a series of sequences which disclose that the wife really is a 'zombie.'" RKO Radio, "The Story," *I Walked with a Zombie* pressbook.
107. Seemingly referencing this review, Val Lewton explained in a letter to his sister that "you shouldn't get mad at the New York reviewers. Actually it's very difficult for a reviewer to give something called *I Walked with a Zombie* a good review." Siegel, *Val Lewton*, 48.
108. T.M.P., *New York Times*, April 22, 1943, 31. I have read dozens of horror reviews in the *New York Times* for the 1930s and 1940s in research for this project. Many are affectionately dismissive, but none express the feverous "disgust" leveled at *I Walked with a Zombie*. This is clearly not inspired by its generic status.
109. Dorothy Jones, "OWI Script Review—*Battle Hymn*," August 20, 1942, in Clayton Koppes and Gregory Black, *Hollywood Goes to War: Patriotism, Movies and the Second World War: From "Ninotchka" to "Mrs. Miniver"* (London: Tauris Park, 2000), 142. Following protests from the MPB, black characters were also written out of *Action in the North Atlantic* (1943) and *An American Romance* (1944), for example. Koppes and Black explain that membership in the black actors union fell by 50 percent during the war (180).
110. See Mary A. Renda, *Taking Haiti: Military Occupation and the Culture of U.S. Imperialism, 1915–1940* (Chapel Hill: University of North Carolina Press, 2001).
111. James Myers, *The Bureau of Motion Pictures and Its Influence on Film Content during World War II: The Reasons for Its Failure* (New York: Edwin Mellen Press, 1998), 100–101.

112. Clayton Koppes and Gregory Black, *Hollywood Goes to War: How Politics, Profits, and Propaganda Shaped World War II Movies* (Berkeley and Los Angeles: University of California Press, 1990), 127–128.
113. The MPPDA did in fact draw attention to the possible problems the film might face in the export market at preproduction stage. Although the synopsis submitted to the Hays Office stressed that the film was set on a "mythical island . . . in the West Indies," Breen still recommended a "switch from West Indies to Africa" to be safe, because of "possible reaction of the countries of the West Indies region." Letter from Joseph Breen to William Gordon, October 15, 1942, MPAA Files, Margaret Herrick Library, Beverly Hills, California.
114. Alexander Nemerov, *Icons of Grief: Val Lewton's Home Front Pictures* (Berkeley and Los Angeles: University of California Press, 2005), 112. "America Again at the Crossroads" was the title of chapter 45 of Gunnar Myrdal's *American Dilemma*; see below.
115. Carey McWilliams, "What We Did about Racial Minorities," in *While You Were Gone: A Report on Wartime Life in the United States*, ed. Jack Goodman (New York: Simon and Schuster, 1946), 70.
116. This race/sex analogy has been frequently evoked to discuss American women's rights. It dates back to abolitionist campaigns of the 1840s and 1850s when white women drew a parallel between their own condition and that of the African slaves they were trying to free. In the 1840s, when male abolitionists were attempting to subjugate women within the movement by telling them to discard issues of women's rights and to be less forthright about the abolitionist cause, the prominent activist Sarah Grimké responded, "What can woman do for slaves when she herself is under the feet of man and shamed into silence?" William Chafe, *Women and Equality: Changing Patterns in American Culture* (New York: Oxford University Press, 1977), 25.
117. Gunnar Myrdal, "A Parallel to the Negro Problem," in *An American Dilemma: The Negro Problem and Modern Democracy* (New York: Harper and Brothers, 1944). This appendix was a reprint of chapter 22, "One Sex a Social Problem," from Myrdal's popular 1941 book *Nation and Family*. In his aforementioned article in the 1946 report on wartime life in America *While You Were Gone*, Carey McWilliams describes Myrdal's book as "a major event in the history of race relations in America." McWilliams, "What We Did about Racial Minorities," 78.
118. Chafe, *Women and Equality*, 83.
119. J. P. Telotte, *Dreams of Darkness: Fantasy and the Films of Val Lewton* (Urbana: University of Illinois Press, 1985), 54.
120. Jacques Tourneur quoted in interview with Bernard Tavernier in Johnston and Willemen, *Jacques Tourneur*, ed., 56. Sir Lancelot's omniscient commentator could be seen as a trickster character, one who outwits and humiliates his more powerful enemies through cunning and wit. The trickster is perhaps best represented by the Brer Rabbit tales of the North American slaves, in which Rabbit overcomes more powerful adversaries—analogous to slave masters and plantation owners. Having given the illusion that he did not know Wesley was there when he sang his humiliating song, the cunning Sir Lancelot tellingly says

he will "creep in like a little fox and warm myself in his heart." James C. Scott suggests that "nothing illustrates the veiled cultural resistance of subordinate groups better than trickster tales." James C. Scott, *Domination and the Arts of Resistance: Hidden Transcripts* (New Haven, CT: Yale University Press, 1990), 163.

121. Valentin Voloshinov, *Marxism and the Philosophy of Language*, trans. Ladislav Matejka and I. R. Titunik (Cambridge, MA: Harvard University Press, 1986), 4.
122. Telotte, *Dreams of Darkness*, 17.
123. Tzvetan Todorov, *The Fantastic: A Structural Approach to a Literary Genre* (Ithaca, NY: Cornell University Press, 1975), 167.
124. Ferdinand Lundberg and Marynia Farnham, *Modern Woman: The Lost Sex* (New York: Universal Library, 1947), 203.
125. Gluck, *Rosie the Riveter Revisited*, 13.
126. Siodmak and Wray, "*I Walked with a Zombie* Original Screenplay," 40.
127. Siegel, *Val Lewton*, 111.
128. Maya Deren, *Divine Horsemen: The Living Gods of Haiti* (New York: McPherson, 1953), 6. Regina Barreca claims that "voodoo—if we see it as the reaction of the vanquished to the victor, the skill adopted by the marginalized figure, the figure closest to banishment and death—is the power held by women in women's text." Though the author here is citing Jean Rhys's *Wide Sargasso Sea* (1966) to explicate her theory of voodoo providing a compelling metaphor for women's writing, she could just as easily be analyzing the precursory Caribbean rewriting of *Jane Eyre* under discussion here. Regina Barreca, "Writing as Voodoo: Sorcery, Hysteria, and Art," in *Death and Representation*, ed. Sarah Webster Goodwin and Elisabeth Bronfen (Baltimore: John Hopkins University Press, 1993), 180. Judie Newman makes a compelling argument for *I Walked with a Zombie* being a big influence on Jean Rhys's highly regarded "prequel" to *Jane Eyre* through a comparison of narrative and thematic coherences. Judie Newman, "I Walked with a Zombie: Jean Rhys, *Wide Sargasso Sea*," in *The Ballistic Bard: Postcolonial Fictions* (London: Arnold, 1995), 19–20.
129. Polan, "Knowledge and Human Interest," 10–11.
130. Ibid., 11; Telotte, *Dreams of Darkness*, 91.
131. Bansak, *Fearing the Dark*, 183. This followed the promotion of Jacques Tourneur, the director of *Cat People* and *I Walked with a Zombie*, to A pictures again as a result of those films' successes at the box office. The presence of Kim Hunter, loaned out by Selznick, in her debut role perhaps attests to the film's conceived A status. The pressbook explains that "less than two months after reaching Hollywood" Kim Hunter "signed a joint contract with Selznick and RKO Radio and a few days later had been given the feminine lead in *The Seventh Victim*." RKO Radio, "Emotional Find in Brilliant Miss Kim Hunter," *The Seventh Victim* pressbook, 1943, British Film Institute Library, London, 2.
132. Siegel, *Val Lewton*, 52. Carlos Clarens also sees it as Lewton's masterwork; "rarely has a film succeeded so well in capturing the nocturnal menace of a big city, the terror of the everyday, the suggestion of hidden evil . . . a hauntingly oppressive work." Clarens quoted in Bansak, *Fearing the Dark*, 195.

133. Val Lewton, "Letter to Nina and Lucy Lewton," November 30, 1939, in Nemerov, *Icons of Grief*, 10.
134. Although Lewton is often credited as "auteur" of these works, Ardel Wray described the environment of the RKO unit as an inexplicable "kind of togetherness" that bred an artistic *communitas* "more like a theatre." Wray quoted in Siegel, *Val Lewton*, 41–42.
135. The presence of Conway's Dr. Judd character, who appears to die in *Cat People*, would insinuate that the film is a prequel to that film. However, at one point in *The Seventh Victim* Judd tells a poet that he once knew a beautiful and mysterious woman who became a raving lunatic. This appears to reference Irena, therefore suggesting that he was only injured by her and thus that the film is a sequel to *Cat People*. Conway's character was not called Dr. Judd in treatments and memos before mid-April 1943 (he is Mr. Siegfried), so this decision may have been made or imposed in light of *Cat People*'s success. *The Seventh Victim* (1943), No. 416, RKO Radio Production Files, Charles E. Young Research Library, University of California at Los Angeles.
136. "*Seventh Victim*," *Daily Variety*, August 19, 1943; "Chiller in Best RKO Tradition," *Hollywood Reporter*, August 19, 1943.
137. Telotte, *Dreams of Darkness*, 20; Kalin, "*The Seventh Victim*," *Variety*, August 18, 1943.
138. Bosley Crowther, "Who's Looney Again," *New York Times*, September 18, 1943.
139. See Mark Jancovich, "Relocating Lewton: Cultural Distinctions and Generic Negotiations in the Critical Reception of the Val Lewton Horror Films," *Journal of Film and Video* 64, no. 3 (2012): 21–37.
140. Bansak, *Fearing the Dark*, 196.
141. Telotte, *Dreams of Darkness*, 85, 88.
142. Bansak, *Fearing the Dark*, 199.
143. Ibid., 157.
144. RKO Radio, "Folks Most Fear the Unseen Says Chiller-diller Producer," *The Seventh Victim* pressbook, 3.
145. Nemerov, *Icons of Grief*, 1.
146. Charles O'Neal and DeWitt Bodeen, "*The Seventh Victim* Screenplay," 1943, *The Daily Script*, http://www.dailyscript.com/scripts/SeventhVictim.htm (accessed April 24, 2007).
147. Costello, *Love, Sex and War*, 232–233; Sara Evans, *Born for Liberty: A History of Women in America* (New York: Free Press, 1997), 228.
148. Dellie Hahne quoted in Jean Bethke Elshtain, *Women and War* (New York: Basic Books, 1987), 180.
149. "Downtown Areas Boom," *Variety*, April 5, 1942, 7.
150. "War Workers Night Out," *Variety*, September 17, 1941, 1.
151. Voloshinov quoted in *The Bakhtin Reader: Selected Writings of Bakhtin, Medvedev, Voloshinov*, ed. Pam Morris (New York: Edward Arnold, 1994), 95.
152. Manny Farber, *Negative Space* (New York: Da Capo Press, 1998), 47–48. In congruence with Farber, Boris Karloff recollected that "Val used to say that the audience is the best actor in the theatre, if you give it a chance. Let the audience fill

in the details, Val said." Karloff quoted in Mark A. Vieira, *Hollywood Horror: From Gothic to Cosmic* (New York: Harry N. Abrams, 2003), 128.

153. F.N., "Voodoo Lifts Its Weird Head," *Dallas Morning News*, July 12, 1943, 8.
154. "Shudder Films Popular; Studios Have 24 Lined Up," *Hollywood Reporter*, May 21, 1943, 4.

CHAPTER 2 SERIES, SEQUELS, AND DOUBLE BILLS

1. Dee Lowrance, "Shebas of Shudders: Zombies, Werewolves, Bats and Ghouls—They're All in the Day's Work for These Heroines of Horror Films," *Oakland Tribune*, March 19, 1944, 69.
2. Rick Altman, *Film/Genre* (London: BFI Publishing, 2004), 60–61.
3. Steve Neale explains that the term "subgenre" is used to "refer to specific traditions or groupings within genres" divided along lines of plots, subject matter, character types. Steve Neale, *Genre and Hollywood* (London: Routledge, 2000), 7.
4. Jim Cunningham, "Creepy Pix Cleaning Up: Studios Cash In on Cycle," *Variety*, March 31, 1943, 7.
5. Ibid., 46. Correspondingly the columnist Sheilah Graham advised her readers, "You can look for an increase in horror pictures. Nearly every studio has one or more in preparation . . . And you can also look for an increase in movies with a strong female angle." Sheilah Graham, "Hollywood in Person," *Dallas Morning News*, February 28, 1943, 8.
6. F.N., "And Now a Lady Joins the Boo Clan," *Dallas Morning News*, July 7, 1943, 65. See Justin Wyatt, "Marketing the Image: High Concept and the Development of Marketing," in *High Concept: Movies and Marketing in Hollywood* (Austin: University of Texas Press, 1994), 109–154.
7. The film has another classic horror intertext in Universal's loose Edgar Allan Poe adaptation *Murders in the Rue Morgue* (1932), in which a sideshow mountebank played by Bela Lugosi attempts to mix the blood of a prostitute (a part initially to be played by Bette Davis) with that of a murderous and lustful ape in order to prove an evolutionary link. By 1943, however, Lugosi was experimenting on himself in a Poverty Row lab for Monogram, where he became the eponymous *Ape Man* (1943). Earlier Universal had transplanted the mind of a man mistakenly electrocuted for murder into a vengeful ape in the gangster-horror hybrid *The Monster and the Girl* (1941), and Twentieth Century–Fox had preempted *Captive Wild Woman* by transforming an ape captured on a jungle expedition into human form with less than satisfactory results for both doctor and spectator in *Dr. Renault's Secret* (1942).
8. "The Woman's Angle," *Variety*, January 17, 1933, 15.
9. "Picture Grosses," *Variety*, January 17, 1933, 9.
10. "Dates from Now to New Year," *Hollywood Reporter*, July 29, 1941.
11. Paramount, *Island of Lost Souls* pressbook, 1933, quoted in Rhona Berenstein, *Attack of the Leading Ladies: Gender, Sexuality, and Spectatorship in Classic Horror Cinema* (New York: Columbia University Press, 1996), 75.
12. "Dates from Now to New Year."

13. Universal preproduction advertisement, *Variety*, July 13, 1941, 14.
14. The actor Milburn Stone was chosen for the role of the animal trainer, Fred Mason, because he resembled Clyde Beatty, who appears in *The Big Cage*, therefore making matching up scenes easier.
15. "*Captive Wild Woman*," *Daily Variety*, April 27, 1943; "U's Captive Wild Woman Robust Chiller-Diller," *Hollywood Reporter*, April 27, 1943, 3.
16. Bosley Crowther, "Old Black Magic," *New York Times*, June 13, 1943, X1; Wear, "Captive Wild Woman," *Variety*, April 28, 1943, 8. A week earlier another *Times* reviewer bemoaned the "decidedly poor taste" of the film. T.M.P., "At the Rialto—*Captive Wild Woman*," *New York Times*, June 7, 1943, 9.
17. Universal, *Captive Wild Woman* pressbook, 1943, Cinema-Television Library, University of Southern California, Los Angeles, 1.
18. "'B's Ballyhooed into 'A' BO: Benefit from Merchandizing," *Variety*, April 28, 1943, 7.
19. Universal, "Showmanship," *Captive Wild Woman* pressbook.
20. Elizabeth Hawes, "Woman War Worker: A Case History," *New York Times*, December 26, 1943, 9.
21. Dana Polan, *Power and Paranoia: History, Narrative, and the American Cinema, 1940–1950* (New York: Columbia University Press, 1986), 179.
22. Peter Stallybrass and Allon White, *The Politics and Poetics of Transgression* (Ithaca, NY: Cornell University Press, 1986), 184.
23. Ibid., 187, 190, 182.
24. Sigmund Freud, *Dora: An Analysis of a Case of Hysteria*, trans. D. Bryan (1909; New York: Macmillan, 1966), 103. Again the close similarities between Dora and Dorothy, like those between Sigmund Walters and Sigmund Freud, seem purposeful.
25. Walters has earlier admitted a link between the two seemingly distinct realms: "We have something in common. In your business you use animals for entertainment purposes. In mine we use them for scientific experiment."
26. Universal, *Captive Wild Woman* pressbook.
27. Noël Carroll, *The Philosophy of Horror; or, Paradoxes of the Heart* (New York: Routledge, 1990), 195. Carroll defines "art-horror" as the sudden conceptual realization of the joint threat and impurity of monstrous figures when experiencing representations of monstrosity. Ideally the coexistent sensation should be triggered and run parallel with that of a diegetic onlooker in the film/novel/picture. For a full definition see Carroll, 27–35.
28. Berenstein, *Attack of the Leading Ladies*, 183.
29. Sigmund Freud, *The Question of Lay Analysis* (1926; New York: W. W. Norton, 1990), 38.
30. Universal, *Captive Wild Woman* pressbook, 7.
31. "*Captive Wild Woman* Features Acquanetta," *Captive Wild Woman* pressbook, 3. She was born Burnu Acquanetta ("Burning Fire, Deep Water") on an Arapaho reservation in Wyoming and claims mostly Native American ancestry. She told Gregory Mank in a 1992 interview that "my mother was Arapaho, and my father was part Cherokee. Actually, my father had an interesting background: my

father's father was the illegitimate son of the King of England and a French Jewess." Mank suggests—with a little understandable cynicism himself—that she has been challenged by "cynics" for her recently revealed ancestral link to the British royal family. Gregory William Mank, *Women in Horror Films, 1940s* (Jefferson, NC: McFarland, 1999), 203. However, working as a model in New York in the early forties, she was encouraged to fabricate a story that she was from Venezuela by columnist Walter Winchell, who told her "nobody cares about Indians." Michael Brunas et al., *Universal Horrors: The Studio's Classic Films, 1931–1946* (Jefferson, NC: McFarland, 1990), 356. However, though Acquanetta was initially encouraged to associate herself with the interest in Latin identities encouraged by the "Good Neighbor" era, she allegedly became subject to rumors of a seemingly less assimilable "otherness" in Hollywood's eyes. The screenwriter Ed Hartmann claims that Universal dropped Acquanetta from the third gorilla-girl movie, *Jungle Captive* (1945), and subsequently from her contract because they found out that her mother was black. Hartmann continues, "I told this to an actress I knew who also knew Acquanetta, and she told me that her mother was black. She was at Acquanetta's house and Acquanetta introduced her mother as the cook to try to hide the fact." Mank, *Women in Horror Films, 1940s*, 216.

32. See Dale Adams, "Saludos Amigos: Hollywood and FDR's Good Neighbor Policy," *Quarterly Review of Film and Video* 24, no. 3 (2007): 289–295.
33. Ella Shohat and Robert Stam, *Unthinking Eurocentrism: Multiculturalism and the Media* (London: Routledge, 1994), 138.
34. In *PM*'s review of the sequel *Jungle Woman* (1944)—discussed in the next chapter—the reviewer remonstrates that the "1943 version was challenged at the time of its production but this had not stopped Universal producing a sequel using the same . . . Nazi race theories." John T. McManus, "*Jungle Woman*," *PM*, July 16, 1944.
35. Letter from Mellett to Mrs. M. M. Albach, April 9, 1943, quoted in James Myers, *The Bureau of Motion Pictures and Its Influence on Film Content during World War II: The Reasons for Its Failure* (New York: Edwin Mellen Press, 1998), 118.
36. Michel Foucault, *The Will to Knowledge*, vol. 1 of *The History of Sexuality* (London: Penguin, 1998), 119.
37. Crowther, "Old Black Magic," 3.
38. For more on the media's incorporation of popular pseudo-psychoanalysis and psychology in the 1940s, see William Graebner, "Turning Inward," in *The Age of Doubt: American Thought and Culture in the 1940s* (Prospect Heights, IL: Waveland Press, 1991), 101–120.
39. Lois Sager, "Dallas Teen-Age Girls in Home Front Battle That Their City Forgot," *Dallas Morning News*, July 1, 1943, 1. See also "Sharp Crime Rise Shown for Girls," *New York Times*, March 21, 1943, 6.
40. "Females in Factories," *Time*, July 17, 1944.
41. Universal, "Beauty Submits to Horror Treatment," *Captive Wild Woman* pressbook.
42. Universal, "Movie Doors Now Open to Taller Actresses," *Son of Dracula* pressbook, 1943, Margaret Herrick Library, Beverly Hills, California.

43. Ibid.
44. Universal, "Sensational Role Goes to Louise Allbritton," *Son of Dracula* pressbook.
45. Berenstein, *Attack of the Leading Ladies*, 72–73.
46. Universal, "S.R.O. for Horror at Fox, St. Louis," *Variety*, March 24, 1943, 22.
47. "Woman's Angle Attractions Are Paying Off Big," *Film Daily*, August 6, 1943, 1, 11, 12.
48. "Combine Terror, Music in Picture," *Phantom of the Opera* pressbook, 1943, British Film Institute Library, London; "Woman's Angle Attractions Are Paying Off Big," 12.
49. "Reviews," *Film Daily*, August 17, 1943, 9.
50. "Horror Plus at Pix," *Washington Post*, December 13, 1943, B6.
51. Utilizing ARI reports on audience preferences for nine proposed genre types, Bosley Crowther states that the musical is far and away the most popular with American women, but it is halfway down the list for men. Bosley Crowther, "It's the Fans Who Make the Films," *New York Times*, June 24, 1945, 14.
52. Edmund Bansak, *Fearing the Dark: The Val Lewton Career* (Jefferson, NC: McFarland, 1995), 351. Such retrospective comments are certainly influenced by the directorial presence of Robert Siodmak, who would become renowned as a key film noir auteur for films such as *Phantom Lady* (1944), *The Killers* (1946), and *Criss Cross* (1949). The trade press at the time did praise Siodmak's innovative direction and use of low-key lighting, a style that would later be defined as prototypically noir, but they mainly stress that it is "a top-line entry in the shocker horror field" that is guaranteed box-office success with horror fans. "Blood-sucker up to Coffinfull of Old Tricks," *Hollywood Reporter*, October 29, 1943, 3. See also *Motion Picture Herald*, November 13, 1943, 626; *Variety*, November 3, 1943, 16.
53. F.N., "Double Portion of Chiller Fare," *Dallas Morning News*, December 20, 1943, 5. The film does ultimately switch focus, eventually redeeming Frank's soul through his rejection of the irredeemable Kay's "morbid" plan.
54. Kay's infantile connection to the plantation has potentially wider implications in that it is also a refusal to move beyond the nation's dark formative years of colonial conquest and enslavement. She is unable to mature with the nation into the proposed era of selfless and noble interventionism. *Son of Dracula* could be seen to invoke the shift from a colonial to an interventionist ideology. As discussed in relation to *I Walked with a Zombie*, the Motion Picture Bureau wanted Hollywood to promote the successes of American democratic ideals and stress its distinction from Nazi ideologies, and was therefore very sensitive about the depiction of America's history of slavery and institutional racism. See Clayton R. Koppes and Gregory D. Black, "What to Show the World: The Office of War Information and Hollywood, 1942–1945," *Journal of American History* 64, no. 1 (1977): 87–105.
55. Jeanine Basinger, *A Woman's View: How Hollywood Spoke to Women, 1930–1960* (Hanover, NH: Wesleyan University Press, 1993), 87.
56. Larry Williams, "Feature Viewing," March 15, 1943, *Son of Dracula* OWI file, quoted in Rick Worland, "OWI Meets the Monsters: Hollywood Horror Films

and War Propaganda, 1942–1945," *Cinema Journal* 37, no. 1 (Fall 1997): 51. In this article Worland is only interested in the horror films that directly referenced the war through setting and characters, and therefore came under the Office of War Information's remit of films engaging with propaganda themes both at home and abroad. He therefore discounts the relevance of *Son of Dracula* to his discussion because the Bureau of Motion Pictures insisted that the film was "pure fantasy." *Son of Dracula* is usefully compared, however, to Columbia's *Return of the Vampire* (1943)—the main focus of Worland's article. This Bela Lugosi vehicle set in wartime London features the aristocratic Dr. Jane Ainsley (Frieda Inescort) in the traditionally male role of the Van Helsing character, which Worland suggests is a development that is "implicitly related to wartime necessity" (57).

57. Polan, *Power and Paranoia*, 186
58. For a discussion of the use of images of the endangered female body in American World War II propaganda, see Susan Gubar, "'This Is My Rifle, This Is My Gun': World War II and the Blitz on Women," in *Behind the Lines: Gender and the Two World Wars*, ed. Margaret Randolph Higonnet et al. (New Haven, CT: Yale University Press, 1987), 227–259.
59. Agnes E. Meyer, *Journey through Chaos: The American Home Front* (New York: Harcourt, 1944), 209–210.
60. Helen McNamara, "*Mummy's Curse*," *Motion Picture Daily*, December 22, 1944.
61. Lowrance, "Shebas of Shudders," 69.
62. All these characters appear in three films during the war, though this includes films in which they were recombined, namely *Frankenstein Meets the Wolfman* (1943), *House of Frankenstein* (1944), and *House of Dracula* (1945). The Mummy had three films in his own right, though.
63. Universal, "Audience Slant," *Jungle Woman* pressbook, 1944, Margaret Herrick Library, Beverly Hills, California; "*Jungle Woman* Follow-up in CWW Series," *Hollywood Reporter*, May 22, 1944. See also Jack Cartwright, "Jungle Woman—Horror with Sex," *Motion Picture Herald*, May 27, 1944.
64. Otis L. Guernsey Jr., "Jungle Woman," *New York Herald Tribune*, July 15, 1944. The *Dallas Morning News* concurred "she will probably come to the screen again, probably many times." E.H., "An Ape Girl," *Dallas Morning News*, August 25, 1944, 16.
65. John T. McManus, "Jungle Woman," *PM*, July 16, 1944. The film was also initially condemned as "unacceptable" by the Hays Office for its "flavor of bestiality." Joseph Breen to Ben Pivar, "Re: Jungle Queen," January 27, 1944, MPAA Files, Margaret Herrick Library, Beverly Hills, California.
66. Bosley Crowther, "One Less Spider," *New York Times*, January 15, 1944.
67. G. E. Blackfoot, "The Spider Woman New Rialto Thriller," *New York Journal-American*, January 15, 1944. The *Motion Picture Herald* review explains that the studio-suggested title was *The Spider Woman* but that *Sherlock Holmes and the Spider Woman* was offered as an "optional title available to exhibitors whose audiences have been following the series with enthusiasm." W.R.W., "Spider Woman," *Motion Picture Herald*, January 15, 1944, 1714.
68. "Entertainment," *Frederick News* (MD), May 19, 1944, 16.

69. Fred Stanley, "Hollywood Shivers," *New York Times*, May 28, 1944.
70. "*The Spider Woman*," *Daily Variety*, January 6, 1944.
71. Alton Cook, "*Spider Woman* Full of Horrors," *New York World Telegram*, January 15, 1944.
72. Archer Winsten, "*Spider Woman* at Work in Rialto Theatre," *New York Post*, January 15, 1944.
73. "*Spider Woman*," *Hollywood Reporter*, January 6, 1944. *PM* also thought that "the Spider Woman is for my money a much shiftier and certainly a much niftier trick than was Prof. Moriarty of other days." John T. McManus, "Sherlock Eludes the *Spider Woman*," *PM*, January 16, 1944.
74. For more on these mystery and horror radio serials, see Richard L. Hand, *Terror on the Air! Horror Radio in America, 1931–1952* (Jefferson, NC: McFarland, 2006).
75. "*Weird Woman* Bizarre Pic," *Hollywood Reporter*, March 31, 1944.
76. Kate Cameron, "Neurotics Rampant on Rialto Screen," *New York Daily News*, April 1, 1944; Jim O'Connor, "*The Weird Woman*," *New York Journal-American*, April 1, 1944.
77. Bosley Crowther, "A Woman Scorned," *New York Times*, April 1, 1944.
78. W.R.W., "*Cobra Woman*," *Motion Picture Herald*, April 29, 1944.
79. "*Cobra Woman*," *Hollywood Reporter*, April 21, 1944. Rick Altman identifies the "recombinant form" of the "Hollywood hybrid" as central to the industry's creative and financial logic from the silent era onward. Altman, *Film/Genre*, 43.
80. Archer Winsten, "Animal Kingdom Congregates in *Cobra Woman* at Criterion," *New York Post*, May 18, 1944. RKO would incorporate similar characters and themes into its Tarzan series with *Tarzan and the Amazons* (1945) and, particularly, *Tarzan and the Leopard Woman* (1946), in which Acquanetta starred as the titular "priestess of the Leopard Men" whose "eyes promise love, lips decree death!"
81. Lucy Fischer, "Two-Faced Women: The 'Double' in Women's Melodrama of the 1940s," *Cinema Journal* 23, no. 1 (1983): 38.
82. Universal, "Totalitarian Aims Are Well Paralleled in *Cobra Woman*," *Cobra Woman* pressbook, 1944, British Film Institute Library, London.
83. Stallybrass and White, *Politics and Poetics of Transgression*, 5.
84. "U Finds Ghouls Pay in Gold," *Variety*, July 27, 1944, 5.
85. Columbia, "Foch, Hubart Bring Icicles to Spine in New Horror Fare," *Cry of the Werewolf/The Soul of a Monster* pressbook, 1944, British Film Institute Library, London.
86. Brunas et al., *Universal Horrors*, 381.
87. However, though *The Soul of a Monster* certainly draws inspiration from *I Walked with a Zombie*, Monogram's *Voodoo Man* (1944)—staring Bela Lugosi following Columbia's decision to drop him—is an unapologetic rip-off. Although *Motion Picture Herald* expressed surprise that "the Zombies in this melodrama are feminine fair and attired in frills, which is a change of menu for followers of scare movies," this "bevy of lovely zombies" in their flowing white gowns is directly based upon the iconic image of Jessica in *I Walked with a Zombie*. *Voodoo Man* makes no secret of its derivative nature with the male lead, a studio scriptwriter,

commenting of the main Jessica look-alike—"that outfit she's wearing, where in the world did she get it? You know I've seen people act like that in pictures, what do they call them, zombies or something?" In a final self-reflexive twist the scriptwriter pitches his experiences to his boss for a film called *Voodoo Man*, concluding with the afterthought "Why don't you try to get that actor Bela Lugosi, it's right up his alley." W.R.W., "*Voodoo Man*," *Motion Picture Herald*, April 1944.

88. Archer Winsten, "*The Soul of a Monster* bared at Rialto Theatre, Where Else?" *New York Post*, September 9, 1944, 251. *Daily Variety*'s pitiful review went further: "Although not credited on the screen, stars of *The Soul of a Monster* are French, Shriner, and Urner, manufacturers of footwear. Seldom, if ever, have two pairs of feet been the exclusive target of a camera for so long a time as they pursue each other back and forth across the screen." "*The Soul of a Monster*," *Daily Variety*, September 5, 1944.
89. Andrew Tudor, *Monsters and Mad Scientists: A Cultural History of the Horror Movie* (Oxford: Basil Blackwell, 1989), 36.
90. David J. Skal, *The Monster Show: A Cultural History of Horror* (London: Plexus, 1994), 218.
91. Tudor, *Monsters and Mad Scientists*, 38.
92. Rose Pelswick, "Werewolf Rialto Film," *New York Journal-American*, August 12, 1944.
93. Archer Winsten, "*Cry of the Werewolf* Sounded at the Rialto," *New York Post*, August 12, 1944. The screenplay for *Cry of the Werewolf* was written by *Captive Wild Woman*'s scriptwriter, Griffin Jay, though *Soul of a Monster*, as explained, was penned by Edward Dein, who had recently completed the script for its sequel, *Jungle Woman*.
94. Columbia, "Publicity," *Cry of the Werewolf/The Soul of a Monster* pressbook.
95. Altman, *Film/Genre*, 57. This strategy, as Rhona Berenstein argues, encouraged Universal to market its 1930s cycle not as horror films but as both "thrillers" and "romances" to attract both male and female audiences. Berenstein, *Attack of the Leading Ladies*, 66–70.
96. Rick Altman insists that Hollywood "has no interest . . . in explicitly identifying a film with a single genre," instead striving to evoke multiple genres in order to stretch a film's demographic appeal. The generic marker "horror" is also used adjectively, however, as in "horror drama," and a few other classifications such as "murder mystery" are utilized, but the publicity material is far more confident about positioning the films individually as "horror stories" or "horror screenplays" in their publicity stories, and particularly marketing them together as a "double horror bill" and "supernatural double horror show" on its posters. Altman, *Film/Genre*, 57.
97. As the award-winning journalist May Craig stated in her speech at the 1944 Women's National Press Club, "The war has given women a chance to show what they can do in the news world, and they have done well." "Women Come to the Front: Journalist, Photographers, and Broadcasters during World War II,"

Library of Congress, http://www.loc.gov/exhibits/wcf/wcf0002.html (accessed June 9, 2006).

98. B.C., "Yooeeew! *The Cry of the Werewolf*," *New York Times*, August 14, 1944. *Motion Picture Herald* reiterated the novelty of a female werewolf, proclaiming, "This latest Columbia excursion into legendary horror differs from past ones in that this time it is a girl who transforms into a wolf." Mandel Herbstman, "*Cry of the Werewolf*," *Motion Picture Herald*, August 6, 1944, 2053. In fact, the first-ever werewolf film, the lost silent *Werewolf* (1913), centered on a female lycanthrope, the daughter of a Navajo woman abandoned by her husband, who seeks revenge on all white men while in wolf form.

99. Robin Wood, "An Introduction to the American Horror Film," in *Planks of Reason: Essays on the Horror Film*, ed. Barry Keith Grant (Metuchen: NJ: Scarecrow Press, 1984), 183.

100. Ibid., 192–193.

101. Winsten, "*Cry of the Werewolf* Sounded at the Rialto," 274.

102. In this case the narrative does correspond somewhat with Barbara Creed's psychoanalytically informed theory of the "monstrous feminine" through its displacement of monstrosity onto the "abject maternal figure." Following Julia Kristeva's *Powers of Horror* (1982), Creed asserts that the horror film's ideological project is "separating out maternal authority from paternal law" through confrontation with, and ultimately rejection of, the "abject." Paraphrasing Freud, Kristeva suggests that "in the child's attempt to break away, the mother becomes an abject," and the child must therefore confront and break away from all the mother has come to represent in order to embrace the father, or more accurately the symbolic order he represents. The child becomes a (sexual) subject by projecting its early experiences (including playing with the body and its waste) onto the mother, who is then rejected; however, the maternal threatens to resurface in abject form. Following this model, Creed argues that the "monstrous-feminine" in horror films signifies the "unwanted" return of these abject elements represented in the obvious symbolic form of an archaic mother figure. Barbara Creed, "Horror and the Monstrous-Feminine: An Imaginary Abjection," *Screen* 27, no. 1 (1986): 53.

103. Reflecting wartime sexual double standards, the term "wolf" had taken on more positive connotations for men by this time, but the female derivation was entirely negative, referring to a woman with unacceptably "loose morals," according to Gaines. She places the earliest citation of the term "wolf" around 1917, when it was applied to a "male homosexual who was particularly aggressive," but she explains that its use was extended to the dangerous ladies' man by the 1930s. By World War II, "wolf" was applied positively to soldiers who were merely successful with the ladies but was also used negatively to refer to "the guys back home ravaging the women." Jane Gaines, "The Showgirl and the Wolf," *Cinema Journal* 20, no. 1 (Fall 1980): 62.

104. The article characterized this generational shift as an "encouraging improvement." "Women Can Be Wolves Also, Police Aver," *Dallas Morning News*, April 3, 1944, 9.

105. American Social Hygiene Report, quoted in John Costello, *Love, Sex and War: Changing Values, 1939–1945* (London: Pan, 1986), 281–282.
106. Ibid., 284. See also "Young Girls Found Menace to Troops: Outnumber Prostitutes 4–1 in Spreading Disease, Health Officers Say," *New York Times*, February 4, 1943, 18. Correspondingly in July 1943 the *Dallas Morning News* lamented that "teen-age girls are losing the fight for the future in the camouflaged battlegrounds of juke joints, midnight streets, hotel rooms and highways." Sager, "Dallas Teen-Age Girls in Home Front Battle," 1. See also "Sharp Crime Rise Shown for Girls," 6.
107. Meyer, *Journey through Chaos*, 366. A *New York Times* article from December 1942 expressed the War Department's fear that "gypsy war wives [would] jam the war effort." Nancy MacLennan, "Gypsy Wives—Army Style," *New York Times*, December 27, 1942, 19.
108. "War Horror, Sorrow Turning People to Religion, Prayer," *Dallas Morning News*, June 19, 1943. This might explain why the *Hollywood Reporter* saw the film as a "minor masterpiece" that "will please more than mere shocker fans." "Soul of Monster Excellent; Werewolf's Cry Is Feeble," *Hollywood Reporter*, September 5, 1944.
109. Fred Stanley, "A New Spiritual Resurgence in Hollywood," *New York Times*, March 7, 1943, X3. See also Fred Stanley, "Hollywood Turns to Inspirational Films," *New York Times*, December 19, 1943, X5; Bosley Crowther, "Sacred and Profane: Comments on the Miraculous Nature of Two of the Current New Films," *New York Times*, June 30, 1944, X3.
110. Altman, *Film/Genre*, 62.

CHAPTER 3 A-CLASS MONSTERS

1. Fred Stanley, "Hollywood Shivers," *New York Times*, May 28, 1944, 3. An earlier Fred Stanley article from April had explained that studios were "scrapping war stories" in favor of horror. Stanley particularly stressed Universal's upgrading to "A-picture status" with *House of Frankenstein* (1944) "in order to invade key cities' first-run houses previously denied these eerie fantasies." Fred Stanley, "Hollywood Flash: Studios Scrap Many War Stories; The Horror Boys Convene," *New York Times*, April 16, 1944, X3.
2. Richard Maltby, *Hollywood Cinema* (Malden, MA: Blackwell, 2003), 132.
3. Rick Altman, *Film/Genre* (London: BFI Publishing, 2004), 62.
4. Stanley's article goes on to also identify t *Laura* (1944), *Guest in the House* (1944), *Woman in the Window* (1944), and the horrific imagery and escalated budget invested in the Sherlock Holmes film *Spider Woman* (1944) as examples of this new prestige "horror cycle." Stanley, "Hollywood Shivers," 3.
5. The *New York Times* celebrated the female Hollywood producer—specifically Joan Harrison, Virginia Van Upp, and Harriet Parsons—as a new and specifically wartime innovation. The writer explained: "The ladies, no longer content with being just glamorous, are invading in increasing numbers the production

sphere, hitherto almost entirely masculine." Fred Stanley, "Hollywood Bows to the Ladies," *New York Times*, January 7, 1945, 1.

6. Norman Matson, "Gooseflesh Special," *New York Times*, May 28, 1944, 7.
7. Fairfax Nisbet, "Public Loves a Peep into the Future," *Dallas Morning News*, July 11, 1943, 1.
8. Gertrude Berger, "The Ouija Board Comes Back," *New York Times*, September 10, 1944, 46.
9. W.K., "Anxiety and Spiritualism Related," *New York Times*, October 29, 1944, E9. Owen Davies cites evidence from prosecution records of fortune-tellers and mediums to highlight a parallel occurrence of women (and to a lesser extent soldiers on leave) regularly visiting practitioners in Britain during World War I. Owen Davies, *Witchcraft, Magic, and Culture, 1736–1951* (Manchester: Manchester University Press, 1999), 266–267. See also Michael Hammond, *The Big Show: British Cinema Culture in the Great War, 1914–1918* (Exeter: Exeter University Press, 2006).
10. Arlene Wolf, "Ouija Board, Ouija Board, Where's My Soldier Boy?" *Dallas Morning News*, November 12, 1944, 10. An article from the *Baltimore Sun*—Baltimore being the city in which the patented William Fuld board was produced—also noted that the "most eager purchasers of Ouija boards are WACs, schoolgirls, and office workers." "Ouija Boards Mum in Three Languages on Invasion Day," *Baltimore Sun*, May 18, 1944, 24.
11. "First It Was Women's Panties, Now It Is Ouija Boards That Are in Demand," *Valley Morning News* (Harlington, TX), April 16, 1944, 2. This article goes on to report that "government girls" in Washington have been consulting Ouija boards in order to find out "when their particular Elmer will be back."
12. As the war came to a close the *New York Times* reported that two female secretaries at the U.S. War Production Board had consulted their Ouija board regarding the possible date of V-J Day while the chairman and other male board members were away at lunch. It continued, "After much concentration and positively no shoving the Ouija finally spelled it out: 'Wednesday.'" Although this ambiguous story dismisses the lunchtime séance held by these "government girls" as outside serious business, its choice to report the Ouija's response on page 2 of the paper indicates a significant symbolic investment in this "feminine" belief system. "Ouija Consulted at WPB: Asked about V-J Day It Spells Out Wednesday," *New York Times*, August 12, 1945, 2.
13. Theodor Adorno, "Theses against Occultism," in *The Stars Down to Earth* (London: Routledge, 1994), 177, 174.
14. Elmer Davis to Byron Price, January 1943, box 3, Office of War Information Files, in Thomas Schatz, *Boom and Bust: American Cinema in the 1940s* (New York: Charles Scribner's Sons, 1997), 269.
15. Manny Farber, "Earth on Heaven," *New Republic*, January 17, 1944, 84. Though Farber saw some merit in *A Guy Named Joe*'s patriotic comingling of supernatural and war themes, he attacked the similar generic hybrid *Happy Land* (1943) as "made to satisfy the most suspicious, narrow-minded upholders of American

goodness." In the film, when a soldier is killed in the combat, the ghost of his great-grandfather returns to earth to tell the boy's father to stop mourning and be proud of his son's sacrifice.

16. Rose, "A Guy Named Joe," *Variety*, December 29, 1943, 8; Adorno, "Theses against Occultism," 175.
17. "Spooks Emerging from the Closet to Dance on the Screen," *Motion Picture Herald*, June 17, 1944, 31.
18. Ibid.; "Ghost Stories Newest Cycle in Movie Circles," *Hartford Courant* (CT), April 2, 1944, 14.
19. "Femmes Shying Away from War Pics," *Variety*, November 18, 1942, 1, 54. Writing in 1950, Leo Handel reported that the industry had long been under the impression that the majority of the American moviegoing audience was female, some estimating as high as 70 percent. He continued that this "erroneous assumption" had led the industry to cater, largely, to "the tastes of female patrons both in their productions and in the promotional campaigns." Leo Handel, *Hollywood Looks at Its Audience: A Report of Film Audience Research* (Urbana: University of Illinois Press, 1950), 99. For example, a 1942 report by the Women's Institute of Audience Reaction, reported in *Film Daily*, concluded that "women compose 65% of picture audiences and that more than 99% of men who attend have been influenced by women." "Ask Operating Improvements," *Film Daily*, November 17, 1942, 1.
20. "War Films Cycle Now Over With," *Dallas Morning News*, August 17, 1943, 10. See also Jimmie Fiddler, "Hollywood in Clutches of New Horror Cycle," *Dallas Morning News*, September 23, 1943, 18; Nelson B. Bell, "But Not This Week at Least, For Non-War Theme Prevails," *Washington Post*, August 1, 1943, L3; Stanley, "Hollywood Flash: Studios Scrap Many War Stories."
21. "Shudder Films Popular; Studios Have 24 Lined Up," *Hollywood Reporter*, May 10, 1943, 4.
22. Phillip Scheuer, "Hollywood's Hellbent for Heaven," *Los Angeles Times*, January 9, 1944, C1.
23. Bosley Crowther, "*Between Two Worlds*," *New York Times*, May 6, 1944.
24. John T. McManus, "*Between Two Worlds*," *PM*, May 7, 1944.
25. Ibid.
26. Eileen Creelman, "*Between Two Worlds*," *New York Sun*, May 6, 1944.
27. Significantly *Between Two Worlds*, *A Guy Named Joe*, and *The Uninvited* are all set in Britain. Britain is seen as a place closer to the reality and mortality of wartime but also—perhaps partly due to the European roots of this type of supernatural storytelling tradition—a place where belief in the spirit-world is somehow more possible. *The Uninvited*'s opening voice-over explains that the coastline is known as "the haunted shore . . . not because there are more ghosts than in other places, mind you, it's just that the people who live hereabouts are strangely aware of them." Britain had comparable ghost narratives in films such as *The Halfway House* (1944), *Blithe Spirit* (1945), and *Dead of Night* (1945).

28. Crowther, "*Between Two Worlds.*"
29. "Exploitips," *Boxoffice: Showmandiser*, May 13, 1944, 16,
30. Tania Modleski, "Femininity as Mas(s)querade: A Feminist Approach to Mass Culture," in *High Theory/Low Culture*, ed. Colin McCabe (Manchester: Manchester University Press, 1986), 37–52.
31. Paramount, *Uninvited* pressbook, 1944, BFI Library, London.
32. A 1943 national survey of women conducted by the Women's Institute of Audience Reactions into the choice of books they wished to see adapted for the screen overwhelmingly "revealed that their tastes trend is towards spiritual themes. Stories with a war angle received practically no votes." "Poll Shows Women Want Spiritual Pix Theme," *Film Daily*, April 19, 1943, 1.
33. Miss Holloway says of Mary Meredith, "She was a goddess. Her skin was radiant. . . . The nights we sat here planning our whole lives. It wasn't flirtations and dresses we discussed. We weren't silly giggling girls. We intended to conquer life." Rhona Berenstein makes a convincing case for the "spectre" of lesbianism underlying the other relationships in the film rather than solely the one between Miss Holloway and Mary Meredith. Rhona Berenstein, "Adaptation, Censorship, and Audiences of Questionable Type: Lesbian Sightings in *Rebecca* (1940) and *The Uninvited* (1944)," *Cinema Journal* 37, no. 3 (Spring 1998): 16–37. Patricia White goes further, positioning the film generically as a "lesbian oedipal drama" in her book on lesbian representation in classical Hollywood cinema named after the film. Patricia White, "Female Spectator, Lesbian Specter," in *unInvited: Classical Hollywood Cinema and Lesbian Representability* (Bloomington: Indianan University Press, 1999), 73.
34. "The Playbill: Ghosts Attend Miss Skinner's Film Debut," *New York Herald Tribune*, 23 January 1944. The influence of Lewton's films on *The Uninvited* was also highlighted in the Hollywood gossip columnist Jimmie Fidler's insider report from Paramount Studios. Fidler, "Hollywood in Clutches of New Horror Cycle," 18.
35. William Weaver, "Review," *Motion Picture Daily*, April 3, 1944. As in *Cry of the Werewolf*, this generational shift displaces the female Oedipal struggle onto the daughter, though with a more successful outcome in Stella's case.
36. For example, Robin Wood argues that Lewton's approach "had little direct influence on [the] evolution" of the horror film, except "certain occasional haunted house movies" like *The Uninvited.* Robin Wood, *Hollywood: From Vietnam to Reagan* (New York: Columbia University Press, 1986), 85.
37. Harriet Parsons, "Keyhole Portrait," *Los Angeles Examiner*, May 24, 1944.
38. Paramount took out a double-page advertisement for the film in *Motion Picture Herald* featuring only pictures of Russell in various guises and poses, promoting her their "greatest find in years." "Screenland Salutes Gail Russell," *Motion Picture Herald*, April 1944, 66–67.
39. Manny Farber, "Personnel Department," *New Republic*, March 15, 1944, 681.
40. Paramount, "Cinderella Comes to Hollywood," *Uninvited* pressbook. However, Russell's particular "Cinderella myth" did not have a fairy-tale ending. She was dropped from her Paramount contract in 1950 due to a reported drinking problem and died of an alcohol-induced heart attack at just thirty-six.

41. Lowell E. Redelings, "*Uninvited* a Weird Ghost Film," *Hollywood Citizen News*, April 14, 1944; "The New Pictures," *Time*, February 21, 1944.
42. Edwin Schallert, "Classy Spooks Spread Shivers at Paramount," *Los Angeles Times*, April 14, 1944. As with Lewton's earlier films, this combination of "literary Gothic" and "movie chiller" aesthetics (despite horror cinema's literary origins) confounded critics somewhat. For example, the *Los Angeles Examiner* advised it "is so superior to the run-of-the-mill 'chiller' that it is almost a shame to refer to it in that category. Yet a thriller and a chiller it is." "*Uninvited* Excellent 'Chiller,'" *Los Angeles Examiner*, April 14, 1944.
43. Otis L. Guernsey, "*The Uninvited*," *New York Herald Tribune*, February 21, 1944.
44. Alton Cook, "*The Uninvited* Makes Adult Ghost Story," *New York World Telegram*, February 21, 1944. Other reviews agreed: "This is no simple horror film, with a hurried realistic explanation at the end. *The Uninvited* believes in ghosts. So, before the yarn is unwound, does most of the audience." Eileen Creelman, "The Uninvited, a Ghost Story with Humor and Chills, at the Globe," *New York Sun*, February 21, 1944.
45. Nelson B. Bell, "Goblins Get You on Screen at Capitol," *Washington Post*, February 11, 1944, 11.
46. Paramount, *Uninvited* pressbook.
47. John McManus, "The Ghost Goes Backwards," *PM*, February 21, 1944.
48. William R. Weaver, "*The Uninvited*—Ghost Story, Adult," *Motion Picture Herald*, January 8, 1944, 1705.
49. "Spooks Emerging from the Closet to Dance on the Screen"; Paramount, "Lobby Séance," *Uninvited* pressbook.
50. "Fortune Tellers Help Tomorrow," *Box Office: Showmandiser*, July 15, 1944, 5.
51. Paramount, "Ruth Hussey Able to Hold Own Even with Professors," *Uninvited* pressbook.
52. Earlier in the film, when Stella explains her excitement about her mother's ghost, Rick somewhat petulantly interjects, "But what about me? I thought you cared about me?" Stella calmly explains, "This has nothing to do with you . . . I can't think about you while she's out there."
53. Diana Basham explains how the Victorian women's rights movement and Victorian women's literature drew on old notions of female occult power. She asserts that this "curious alliance" was at once liberating and limiting. Diana Basham, *The Trial of Women: Feminism and the Occult Sciences in Victorian Literature and Society* (London: Macmillan, 1992).
54. See, for example, Karen Anderson, *Wartime Women: Sex Roles, Family Representations, and the Status of Women during World War II* (Westport, CT: Greenwood Press, 1981); Susan Hartmann, *The Home Front and Beyond: American Women in the 1940s* (Boston: Twayne, 1982); D'Ann Campbell, *Women at War: Private Lives in a Patriotic Era* (Cambridge, MA: Harvard University Press, 1984); John Costello, *Love, Sex and War: Changing Values, 1939–1945* (London: Pan, 1986); Sherna Berger Gluck, *Rosie the Riveter Revisited: Women, the War, and Social Change* (Boston: Twayne, 1987); Penny Colman, *Rosie the Riveter: Women Working on the Home Front in World War II* (New York: Crown, 1995).

55. Letter from Reverend Brendan Larnen to Will Hays, May 10, 1944, PCA Files, Margaret Herrick Library, Beverly Hills, California.
56. Letter from Luigi Luraschi to Joseph Breen, June 5, 1944, PCA Files, Margaret Herrick Library, Beverly Hills, California. Breen conducted his own audience research into the matter and reported back to Hays on June 5, "I am able to tell you that in not one single instance—in discussion with more than 20 people—did anyone indicate, even the slightest way, a reaction that could be even remotely suggestive of the reaction set forth by the Legion of Decency." Letter from Joseph Breen to Will Hays, June 5, 1944, PCA Files, Margaret Herrick Library, Beverly Hills, California.
57. Letter from Daniel A. Lord to Joe Breen, June 1944, PCA Files, Margaret Herrick Library, Beverly Hills, California.
58. Arthur Eilenberg, "Psychic or Sickly?" *New York Times*, March 5, 1944.
59. John D'Emilio argues that "World War II created something of a nationwide coming out experience" for lesbians. John D'Emilio, *Sexual Politics, Sexual Communities: The Making of a Homosexual Minority in the United States, 1940–1970*, 2nd ed. (Chicago: University of Chicago Press, 1998), 24. See also the oral history accounts of wartime women in Madeline Davis and Elizabeth Lapovsky Kennedy, "Oral History and the Study of Sexuality in the Lesbian Community, Buffalo, New York, 1940–1960," *Feminist Studies* 12, no. 1 (Spring 1986): 7–28; Gluck, *Rosie the Riveter Revisited*.
60. Crowther, "So Much Fear and Trembling."
61. "*The Uninvited*," *Variety*, January 5, 1944, 16.
62. "Spooks Emerging from the Closet to Dance on the Screen," 31. See also "Ghost Stories Newest Cycle in Movie Circles," 14.
63. "Spooks Emerging from the Closet to Dance on the Screen," 31.
64. Ibid. Some of the other texts the *MPH* identifies as part of the cycle include MGM's *The Canterville Ghost* (1944), Universal's *The Mummy's Ghost* (1944), UA's *Dark Waters* (1944), and even Twentieth Century–Fox's much-celebrated "film noir" *Laura* (1944).
65. Archer Winsen, "*The Curse of the Cat People* Descends on Tarrytown at Rialto," *New York Post*, March 4, 1944.
66. Weaver, "*The Uninvited*: Ghost Story, Adult."
67. "*Curse of the Cat People*," *Showmen's Trade Review*, February 19, 1944, 17.
68. "Trade Showing: *Curse of the Cat People*," *Daily Variety*, February 17, 1944. *Motion Picture Daily* concurred that "RKO started out to capitalize on its exploitable title, *Cat People*, but somewhere along the line changed its mind." "*Curse of the Cat People*," *Motion Picture Daily*, February 17, 1944.
69. Philip K. Scheuer, "Study of Child," *Los Angeles Times*, April 28, 1944.
70. Wear, "*Curse of the Cat People*," *Variety*, February 23, 1944, 10. See also Alton Cook, "New Rialto Thriller Cure for Insomnia," *New York World-Telegram*, March 4, 1944; Harold Barnes, "*The Curse of the Cat People*," *New York Herald Tribune*, March 4, 1944; "*Curse of the Cat People*: Sequel without Horror," *Motion Picture Herald*, February 19, 1944, 1769.
71. John T. McManus, "A Blessing in Disguise," *PM*, March 5, 1944, 14. Bosley Crowther of the *New York Times* was delighted to "find a quite wistful and

appealing" film at "that usually lurid place" the Rialto and was disappointed that "commercial considerations should have necessitated some horror in this film." Bosley Crowther, "A Child's Mind," *New York Times*, March 4, 1944, 11.

72. Scheuer, "Study of Child."
73. For an example of the imaginary-playmate interpretation, see Crowther, "A Child's Mind." Although most reviewers were decidedly underwhelmed by the film's "child psychology," it inspired the Hollywood Writers Mobilization and the Los Angeles Council of Social Agencies to hold a "special seminar on 'The Treatment of the Child in Film' . . . in order to exchange ideas between members of the industry and leading professionals in the field." Lewton and the film's director, Robert Wise, joined "leading child welfare officials, educators, child psychologists and writers," who commended the film's "presentation and treatment of the difficult problem of child psychology." Letter from Pauline Lauber of the Hollywood Writers Mobilization to Charles Koerner, September 20, 1944. RKO Production Files, USC Library, Los Angeles.
74. Kate Cameron, "Ghosts and Horror Stalk Rialto Screen," *New York Daily News*, March 4, 1944; Rose Pelswick, "*Cat People* on Rialto Screen," *New York Journal-American*, March 4, 1944.
75. Tzvetan Todorov, *The Fantastic: A Structural Approach to a Literary Genre* (Ithaca, NY: Cornell University Press, 1975), 167.
76. James Agee, "*The Curse of the Cat People*," *Nation*, April 1, 1944.
77. Manny Farber, "B Plus," *New Republic*, March 20, 1944.
78. Agee, "*The Curse of the Cat People*."
79. "Tilt Budgets for Horror Fare: Studios No Longer Stint on Chill-Thrill Pix," *Film Daily*, July 7, 1944, 11.
80. After 1944 Lewton produced two other "horror" films for RKO, in addition to *Isle of the Dead*. These were *The Body Snatcher* (1945), based on a Robert Louis Stevenson short story, and *Bedlam* (1946), a historical horror drama set in the infamous asylum and based upon Hogarth's *Rake's Progress* (1733); both featured Karloff in a central role. In these films Lewton's high cultural influences and background in prestige period dramas with Selznick came to the fore, a development that was simultaneously praised and derided for diverging from conventional horror tropes. For a detailed discussion of the cultural politics underlying the critical reception of the Lewton films, see Mark Jancovich, "Relocating Lewton: Cultural Distinctions and Generic Negotiations in the Critical Reception of the Val Lewton Horror Films," *Journal of Film and Video* 64, no. 3 (2012): 21–37.
81. However, Lewton's key inspiration for the film was Arnold Böcklin's painting (1880) from which the title was derived, and which appeared on the wall in *I Walked with a Zombie*.
82. "Review," *Hollywood Reporter*, September 7, 1945.
83. J. P. Telotte, "The Horror Mythos and Val Lewton's *Isle of the Dead*," *Journal of Popular Film and Television* 10, no. 3 (1982): 126
84. In August 2007 *Hollywood Reporter* revealed RKO's plans for a remake of *Isle of the Dead* in which the location would be shifted from Greece to war-torn

Afghanistan. Emphasizing Lewton's ability in the 1940s to take the "horror genre to a new place", RKO's chairman in 2007 suggested that the new version would likewise be a "perfect blend of contemporary themes and timeless scares." "RKO Reawakening with the Dead," *Hollywood Reporter*, August 15, 2007.

85. Wanda Hale, "Boris Karloff at Rialto in Spine Chiller," *New York Daily News*, September 8, 1945.
86. Wear, "*Curse of the Cat People*."
87. John L Scott, "Master of Horror Films Reveals His Technique," *Los Angeles Times*, June 10, 1945, B1.
88. Manny Farber, "Movies in Wartime," *New Republic*, January 3, 1944.
89. Barbara Berch, "A Hitchcock Alumna: Introducing Joan Harrison, Hollywood's Only Full-fledged Woman Producer," *New York Times*, June 27, 1943, X3. In early 1945 Virginia Van Upp was appointed as executive producer at Columbia, most famously going on to produce *Gilda* (1946).
90. Universal, "*Phantom Lady* First Mystery for Lady Fans," *Phantom Lady* pressbook, 1944, BFI Library, London.
91. The films on which Harrison worked with Hitchcock, from *The Lady Vanishes* (1938) through *Shadow of a Doubt* (1943), almost exclusively placed women in investigative positions.
92. Similarly, at Twentieth Century–Fox the producer Darryl Zanuck envisioned the female lead in *Laura* (1944), adapted from the novel by Vera Caspary, as being expanded into the central narrative and emotional crux of this women's mystery story. In a memo on the first draft continuity script he complained her character "seems terribly naïve—a complete sucker. She does no thinking in the picture at all. She has no decisions to make. She doesn't try to solve anything or really think in any situation." Darryl Zanuck, "Notes on First Draft Continuity," October 30, 1943, 20th Century–Fox Collection, USC Library, California, 2. In a later memo he complained again that Laura was a "distinct let-down to me because she is neither bright nor witty, nor particularly smart." He stressed "all the other characters are either bastards or hard-boiled guys. . . . Laura should be everything that they are not." Darryl Zanuck, "Memo from D. Zanuck to Otto Preminger," March 20, 1944, 20th Century–Fox Collection, USC Library, California, 8.
93. Alton Cook, "Franchot Tone a Villain in Macabre *Phantom Lady*," *New York World Telegram*, February 18, 1944.
94. Manny Farber, "Two Phantoms," *New Republic*, March 1944, 346.
95. Robert Siodmak's biographer reports that the character was directly based on Harrison. Deborah Lazaroff Alpi, *Robert Siodmak: A Biography, with Critical Analysis of His Film Noirs and a Filmography* (Jefferson, NC: McFarland, 1998), 122.
96. Marcella is perhaps the nearest to a "femme fatale" figure, but she is never seen. We only see Scott's reaction to her dead body and her portrait, which dominates the scene when Scott returns to the apartment to find his wife dead and three policemen waiting to arrest him.
97. This offer is somewhat ambiguous; it is not a proposal of marriage. Harrison, who did not marry until in her forties, claimed, "I am not a great believer in

marriage as I see it now. Put it this way: I'm a believer in marriage as it might be." Gilbert Millstein, "Harrison Horror Story," *New York Times*, July 21, 1957, 44.

98. For discussions of *Phantom Lady* as seminal noir, see R. Borde and E. Chaumeton, *Panorama dufilm noir américain, 1941–1953* (Paris: Editions de Minuit, 1955); Robert Ottoson, *Reference Guide to the American Film Noir* (Metuchen, NJ: Scarecrow Press, 1981); J. P. Telotte, *Voices in the Dark: The Narrative Patterns of Film Noir* (Chicago: University of Illinois Press, 1988): Michael Walker, "Robert Siodmak," in *The Movie Book of Film Noir*, ed. Ian Cameron (London: Studio Vista, 1992), 110–115; Foster Hirsch, *The Dark Side of the Screen: Film Noir* (Cambridge, MA: Da Capo Press, 2001); Sheri Chinen Biesen, *Blackout: World War I and the Origins of Film Noir* (Baltimore: John Hopkins University Press, 2005).
99. Eileen Creelman, "*Phantom Lady*, a Horror Thriller about Some Murders and a Charming Maniac," *New York Sun*, February 18, 1944; "*Phantom Lady*," *Daily Variety*, January 21, 1944.
100. Milt Livingston, "*Phantom Lady*," *Motion Picture Daily*, January 21, 1944.
101. Floyd Elbert Stone, "*Phantom Lady*," *Motion Picture Herald*, January 29, 1944. *Film Daily* thought the film "would do credit to Hitchcock himself," while *Motion Picture Daily* suggested the film was in "best Alfred Hitchcock manner." *Phantom Lady* review advertisement, *Variety*, February 9, 1944, 22–23.
102. Bosley Crowther, "*Phantom Lady*," *New York Times*, February 18, 1944, 15. Far more positively, *PM* considered the film typical of the "middle period Hitchcock" on which Harrison had worked. James Agee insisted that "she gets from Hitchcock only some of the broad show-wise aspects of his style." John T. McManus, "*Phantom Lady* Kicks the Gong," *PM*, February 18, 1944.
103. This corresponds with Marc Vernet's analysis of the origins of film noir. Marc Vernet, "Film Noir on the Edge of Doom," in *Shades of Noir: A Reader*, ed. Joan Copjec (London: Verso, 1993), 1–31.
104. Janey Place, "Women in Film Noir," in *Women in Film Noir*, ed. E. Ann Kaplan (London: BFI Publishing, 2005), 47–68.
105. Mary Ann Doane, *The Desire to Desire: The Woman's Film of the 1940s* (Bloomington: Indiana University Press, 1987), 39–42. Similarly, in *Spellbound* (1945) Ingrid Bergman's psychiatrist decked out in spectacles, white coat, and plain coiffure is juxtaposed to her flamboyant patient (Rhonda Fleming), who uses her sexuality to entice then attack male staff members.
106. See, for example, Shari Roberts, "'The Lady in the Tutti-Frutti Hat': Carmen Miranda, a Spectacle of Ethnicity," *Cinema Journal* 32, no. 3 (Spring 1993): 3–23.
107. Antonia Lant, *Blackout: Reinventing Women for Wartime British Cinema* (Princeton, NJ: Princeton University Press, 1991), 66.
108. However, the displacement of narratives to the turn of the century allowed films such as *Gaslight* (1944) to retain some of this glamour and spectacle without characters appearing unpatriotic. These temporally displaced representations highlighted the expectation of an at least partial return to prewar modes of femininity. In the *Gaslight* pressbook the haircut Ingrid Bergman has in the film, dubbed "Reveille," is said to be designed to "wake up the women of America to the importance of being feminine." It is characterized as "a distinct departure

from the tailored, mannish trends of the moment, the coiffure will prove just as at home in a defense plant as in a ballroom." Although it is suggested that "Reveille" blurs the distinction between perceived male and female realms, it is perhaps an ominous sign for women in 1944 that the MGM publicity department should promote a haircut designed for a London parlor in 1870 as the future for women's postwar fashion. MGM, "New Hair Style Shown in Ingrid Bergman Picture," *Gaslight* pressbook, 1944, Margaret Herrick Library, Beverly Hills, California.

109. The femme fatale figure in *Phantom Lady* is actually Scott's wife, who is only seen in the form of her portrait. The portrait of the femme fatale, with its narcissistic connotations, is utilized in a number of contemporary noirs including *Laura* (1944) and *Woman in the Window* (1944).
110. Christina Lane, "Stepping out from behind the Grand Silhouette: Joan Harrison's Films of the 1940s," in *Authorship and Film*, ed. David Gerstner and Janet Staiger (New York: Routledge, 2003), 105. Lane explains that Joan Harrison was responsible for the intricate details of Rebecca's wardrobe and bedroom accessories so integral to the construction of her character. As in the mannerist mise-en-scène of the first Mrs. de Winter's room in *Rebecca*, Ann Terry's bedroom is filled with symbolically charged objects that reveal this mentally rather than physically absent character.
111. J. M. Sinclair, ed., *Collins Concise Dictionary* (Glasgow: HarperCollins, 2001), 1124.
112. "The New Pictures," *Time*, February 28, 1944.
113. Ibid. Likewise a pair of disconnected women's legs in stockings, which could be Kansas's or Ann Terry's, feature on many of the film's posters.
114. Hedda Hopper, "Glamour Galvanic!" *Chicago Daily Tribune*, October 14, 1945, F2.
115. Jerry D. Lewis, "'Murder,' She Says," *Collier's*, August 14, 1943, 55, 70.
116. Ann Daggett, "It's a Woman's World Too," *Modern Screen*, February 1945, 20–22.
117. Place, "Women in Film Noir," 53.
118. Crowther, "*Phantom Lady*," 15.
119. Farber, "Two Phantoms," 346. Likewise, studio publicity promoted it as "one of the wildest scenes recently put on the screen." Universal, *Phantom Lady* pressbook.
120. James Agee, "*Phantom Lady* review," *Nation*, February 26, 1944. Manny Farber agreed that the film achieved a "certain degree of lust and frenzy" out of the "jazz bit." Farber, "Two Phantoms," 346.
121. McManus, "*Phantom Lady* Kicks the Gong."
122. Letter from Joseph Breen to Maurice Pivar, September 3, 1943, "Re: screenplay dated August 24, 1943," MPAA Files, Margaret Herrick Library, Beverly Hills, California.
123. The Pennsylvania censors objected to Cliff's "drumming frenzy" in its edited form and insisted that it "must be eliminated." "Memo January 31, 1944," MPAA Files, Margaret Herrick Library, Beverly Hills, California.
124. John D'Emilio and Estelle B. Freedman, "Redrawing the Boundaries," in *Intimate Matters: A History of Sexuality in America*, 2nd ed. (Chicago: Chicago University Press, 1997), 260.

125. Meyer Berger, "Times Square Diary," *New York Times*, September 3, 1944, 16.
126. Ibid., 16. The Rialto closed at 4:00 A.M.
127. Arthur Mayer, *Merely Colossal* (New York: Simon and Schuster, 1953), 179–180. This development was not unique to the Rialto. In January 1945 *Variety* reported that "in the last three years audiences in motion picture and presentation houses have become more and more like they were in the days of the Old Bowery." George Jessel, "Unruly Audiences—And Why?" *Variety*, January 3, 1945, 24.
128. Francis Merrill, *Social Problems on the Home Front: A Study of War-time Influences* (New York: Harper and Brothers, 1948), 100.
129. Ralph Turner and Samuel Surace, "Zoot-Suiters and Mexicans: Symbols in Crowd Behavior," *American Journal of Sociology* 62, no. 1 (1956): 14–20; "Delinquency Rise among Girls Told," *New York Times*, October 28, 1942.
130. "Sharp Crime Rise Shown for Girls," *New York Times*, March 21, 1943, 16. For more on Hoover's role in the wartime juvenile delinquency moral panic, see James Gilbert, "Rehearsal for a Crime Wave," in *A Cycle of Outrage: America's Reaction to the Juvenile Delinquent in the 1950s* (New York: Oxford University Press, 1988), 24–41.
131. "Combating the Victory Girl," *Newsweek*, March 6, 1944, 88. For more on wartime debates in the New York press regarding female youth, see Tim Snelson, "From Juke Box Boys to Bobby Sox Brigade: Female Youth, Moral Panics and Subcultural Style in Wartime Times Square," *Cultural Studies* 26, no. 6 (2012): 889.
132. Tim Snelson, "Delinquent Daughters: Hollywood's War Effort and the 'Juvenile Delinquency Picture' Cycle," *New Review of Film and Television Studies* 11, no. 1 (2013), 56–72.
133. Otis Guernsey, "*Where Are Your Children?*" *New York Herald Tribune*, January 17, 1944.
134. Fred Stanley, "All Is Confusion: Hollywood Views Juvenile Delinquency Films through Haze of Censorship," *New York Times*, October 17, 1943, 3.
135. Ilana Nash, *American Sweethearts: Teenage Girls in Twentieth-Century Popular Culture* (Bloomington: Indiana University Press, 2006).
136. Stanley, "All Is Confusion," 3.
137. "The New Pictures," *Time Magazine*, February 28, 1944.
138. Universal, "Production Highlights," *Strange Affair of Uncle Harry* pressbook, 1945, Margaret Herrick Library, Beverly Hills, California.
139. Ibid.
140. For fuller production history and extracts of the original script, see Joseph Greco, *The File on Robert Siodmak in Hollywood, 1941–1951* (Boca Raton, FL: Universal, 1999), 59–63.
141. "The New Pictures," *Time*, August 27, 1945.
142. Greco, *The File on Robert Siodmak*, 66.
143. Hartmann, *The Home Front and Beyond*, 194–195. See also Merrie Fidler, *The Origins and History of the All-American Girls Professional Baseball League* (Jefferson, NC: McFarland, 2006).
144. Mark Jancovich challenges this reductive assumption in much scholarship in his article "Female Monsters: Horror, The 'Femme Fatale' and World War II," *European Journal of American Culture* 27, no. 2 (2009): 133–149.

145. Universal, "Studio Gives Definition of Movie Murder Drama," *Uncle Harry* pressbook.
146. Universal, "UH Declared Extraordinary Picture," *Uncle Harry* pressbook.
147. Universal, "Everyone a Potential Killer Says Producer," *Uncle Harry* pressbook.
148. Universal, "Crime Study, Hobby of Feminine Producer," *Uncle Harry* pressbook.
149. Universal, "Ella Raines, Quick to Attain Cinema Stardom," *Uncle Harry* pressbook.
150. Universal, "Hollywood Style Review," *Uncle Harry* pressbook.
151. "The New Pictures," *Time*, August 27, 1945.
152. Bosley Crowther, "Uncle Harry Taken from Stage Melodrama," *New York Times*, August 24, 1945.
153. Bosley Crowther, "Getting Away with Murder," *New York Times*, August 26, 1945.
154. See also James Agee, "Films," *Nation*, August 25, 1945.
155. Hopper, "Glamour Galvanic!" F2.
156. "The New Pictures," *Time*, August 27, 1945.
157. Florabel Muir, "Joan Harrison Worrying about Butter," *Hollywood Citizen-News*, January 16, 1946.

CHAPTER 4 FROM WHATDUNIT TO WHODUNIT

1. Bert McCord, "*The Spider Woman Strikes Back*—Rialto," *New York Herald Tribune*, March 23, 1946.
2. Rick Altman, *Film/Genre* (London: BFI Publishing, 2004), 62.
3. See Bernard Dick, *City of Dreams: The Making and Remaking of Universal Pictures* (Lexington: University Press of Kentucky, 1997).
4. Dana Polan, "Knowledge and Human Interests: Science, Cinema, and the Secularization of Horror," in *Power and Paranoia: History, Narrative and the American Cinema, 1940–1950* (New York: Columbia University Press, 1986), 170, 174.
5. Ibid., 173, 186.
6. *Daily Variety* stressed that "*The Spider Woman Strikes Back* is a crime thriller with horror touches. Title gives little hint of the yarn." "*The Spider Woman Strikes Back*," *Daily Variety*, March 13, 1946.
7. Stal., "*She-Wolf of London*," *Variety*, April 10, 1946, 16. *Harrison's Report* also complained that "unlike the title there is nothing about either the action or the characters that is horrifying or terrifying." "*She-Wolf of London*," *Harrison's Report*, April 13, 1946.
8. Polan, "Knowledge and Human Interest," 185.
9. Irene Thirer, "*The She-Wolf of London* Creepy Gaslight Rialtopus," *New York Post*, April 6, 1946.
10. Rose Pelswick, "At the Rialto," *New York Journal-American*, April 6, 1946.
11. Likewise, the *New York Herald Tribune* complained, "There is nothing either frightening or mysterious about the law-breaking in *The Cat Creeps*." Otis Guernsey Jr., "*The Cat Creeps*," *New York Herald Tribune*, May 18, 1946. For more information on the influence of *Cat People* on the narrative and marketing of *The Cat Creeps*, see Edmund Bansak, *Fearing the Dark: The Val Lewton Career* (Jefferson, NC: McFarland, 1995), 370–371.

12. William Weaver, "*The Cat Creeps*," *Motion Picture Daily*, April 10, 1946.
13. "Hollywood'll Haunt You," *Cue*, May 18, 1946, 20.
14. Significantly the review centers the "refreshingly real" detective character as the film's only saving grace. "Cowan Refreshing; Story Line Formula," *Hollywood Reporter*, June 12, 1945.
15. Tom Weaver, Michael Brunas, and John Brunas, *Universal Horrors: The Studio's Classic Films, 1931–1946* (Jefferson, NC: McFarland, 2007), 487.
16. Lloyd Shearer, "Crime Certainly Pays on the Screen," *New York Times*, August 5, 1946, 17.
17. Ibid., 37. In the article James M. Cain concurred: "It's got nothing to do with the war or how it's affected the public or any of that bunk. If Billy Wilder, for example, had made 'Double Indemnity' back in 1935 the picture would have done just as well as it has now."
18. "*The Spider Woman Strikes Back*," *Hollywood Reporter*, March 13, 1946. *Cue* went further: "The yawpy nonsense that has in recent years mushroomed into so-called 'horror' films descends into its nadir in this ridiculous mess of celluloid chicanery—a moronic tale of an evil woman who bleeds girls to death so she may use their blood to nourish a carnivorous plant." "At the Rialto," *Cue*, March 30, 1946.
19. Letter from Joseph L. Breen to Maurice Pivar, "Re: script dated May 8, 1945," May 14, 1945, MPAA Files, Margaret Herrick Library, Beverly Hills, California.
20. Universal, "Gale Sondergaard Gains Fame as Spider Woman," *The Spider Woman Strikes Back* pressbook, 1946, Margaret Herrick Library, Beverly Hills, California.
21. "Universal to Drop Four 'B' Film Units," *New York Times*, July 26, 1946.
22. Andrew Tudor, *Monsters and Mad Scientists: A Cultural History of the Horror Movie* (Oxford: Basil Blackwell, 1989), 32.
23. The script outline details that a young "foreign woman," Clare, who has come to Heathville to run the local cosmetic company, is blamed for recent murders, but the "Mystery Woman" responsible turns out to be a local "society dame," Mary Layton. Clare is integral to her capture and helps drive a stake into Dr. Caruthers. This action also kills Mary, who in fact "wishes to be released from the spell" through death. PRC, "Daughter of the Devil Bat—A Horror Story," August 20, 1945, MPAA Files, Margaret Herrick Library, Beverly Hills, California.
24. "*Devil Bat's Daughter*—Analysis Chart," February 28, 1946, MPAA Files, Margaret Herrick Library, Beverly Hills, California. The film's title change is acknowledged in a letter dated January 4, 1946, from Joseph Breen to Jack Jungmeyer. It also indicates the inclusion of the Dr. Morris character, the reoriented script's secular villain.
25. "*Devil Bat's Daughter*," *Motion Picture Herald*, April 13, 1946, 2938.
26. Polan, "Knowledge and Human Interests," 179.
27. J.D.G., "*Devil Bat's Daughter*," *Hollywood Reporter*, April 3, 1946.
28. William Graebner, *The Age of Doubt: American Thought and Culture in the 1940s* (Prospect Heights, IL: Waveland Press, 1998), 27.
29. "Chicago Psychiatrist Traces Aggressive Girls to Pix' Not-So-He-Men," *Variety*, August 29, 1945, 1, 16.

30. Jeanine Basinger, *A Woman's View: How Hollywood Spoke to Women, 1930–1960* (Hanover, NH: Wesleyan University Press, 1993), 100.
31. In keeping with the postwar program of "white flight," Ted's family has just relocated from New York City to the house they have "always dreamed of" in suburban Westchester County. Suburbanization obviously helped to redefine the distinction between the domestic and public sphere of work. For example, George Lipsitz argued that "during the decades following World War II, urban renewal helped construct a new 'white' identity in the suburbs" fueled by and consolidating conservative racial and gender politics. George Lipsitz, *The Possessive Investment in Whiteness: How White People Profit from Identity Politics* (Philadelphia: Temple University Press, 1998), 7.
32. The pressbook articles also channel La Planche's independent sexuality into a patriotic and collective purpose, with the justifications that in the capacity of Miss America she "travelled 20,000 miles during the war years performing before audiences at military camps." The suggestion is that as inspirational "pinup" she did her (women's) part in the war effort; one seemingly not necessary now the conflict is over. PRC, *Devil Bat's Daughter* pressbook, 1946, BFI Library, London.
33. Susan Hartmann, *The Home Front and Beyond: American Women in the 1940s* (Boston: Twayne, 1982), 201.
34. Mary Ann Doane, "The "Woman's Film": Possession and Address," in *Home Is Where the Heart Is: Studies in Melodrama and the Woman's Film*, ed. Christine Gledhill (London: BFI Publishing, 1987), 228.
35. In *She-Wolf of London* Phyllis explains, "I guess I'm just on edge, because there is no man in our house." As in *The Spider Woman Strikes Back*, the heroine would have avoided her "neurosis" if she had taken up a proposal of marriage when initially asked, rather than attempting to prolong her independence.
36. Betty Freidan, *The Feminine Mystique* (1963; New York: Dell, 1975), 40, 37.
37. Historians such as William Chafe and Joanne Meyerowitz have argued that, though most historical accounts of the immediate postwar era unquestioningly accept Freidan's proposition of an overarching ideology that pulled woman back into the home, in fact these conservative voices were countered somewhat by a more feminist perspective from social scientists and journalists such as Margaret Mead and Mirra Komarovsky, which called for new gender roles to meet modern conditions. William H. Chafe, "The Debate on Woman's Place," in *The American Woman: Her Changing Social, Economic, and Political Roles, 1920–1970* (London: Oxford University Press, 1972), 199–225. Similarly, through recourse to the same popular publications as analyzed by Freidan, Meyerowitz insists that the "feminine mystique" was only "one piece of the post-war cultural puzzle." She asserts that representation in short stories and debate in articles over "women's roles" provided a far more balanced picture than Freidan suggests. Joanne Meyerowitz, "Beyond the Feminine Mystique: The Reassessment of Postwar Mass Culture, 1946–1958," in *Not June Cleaver: Women and Gender in Postwar America, 1945–1960*, ed. Joanne Meyerowitz (Philadelphia: Temple University Press, 1994), 231.

38. See Polan, "Knowledge and Human Interests," 159–191.
39. Wanda Hale, "*Bewitched* Strange Film, at Criterion," *New York Daily News*, August 17, 1945.
40. John T. McManus, "Oboler Bothers and Bewilders," *PM*, August 17, 1945. The *New York Sun* concurred that "told as an out-and-out lurid thriller the plot might have served for a mild horror story. Here it is supposed to be drama." Eileen Creelman, "Bewitched, Psychological Thriller," *New York Sun*, August 17, 1945.
41. Bosley Crowther, "Bad Medicine," *New York Times*, March 9, 1946, p. 20.
42. John T. McManus, "A Film to Be Shocked About," *PM Exclusive*, March 10, 1946.
43. Bosley Crowther, "Hitting a Nerve: Shock Is a Painful Example of Distortions of Psycho-Pathology," *New York Times*, March 17, 1946, X1.
44. Franklin Fearing, "The Screen Discovers Psychiatry," *Hollywood Quarterly* 1, no. 2 (1946): 154.
45. Ibid., 155.
46. Crowther "Hitting a Nerve," X1.
47. Dr. Manfred Sakel quoted in A. H. Weiler, "By Way of Report," *New York Times*, March 24, 1946, 51. It might appear surprising that a respected scientist like Sakel would invest his time and energy into investigating such low-cultural artifacts as Shock and the Rialto. The following month Sakel's interest in the popular perception of his practices was demonstrated when the *New York Times* printed his urgent request for government funding to support a new institute for insulin therapy, and for greater numbers of trained physicians to administer it. He claimed that his methods offered the greatest promise for the recovery of America's psychologically damaged servicemen, who, claimed Sakel, represented 30 to 40 percent of America's war casualties ("Ill Veteran's Need for Insulin Noted," *New York Times*, April 18, 1946, 29). For more on Sakel and the history of the largely discredited psychiatric practice of insulin therapy, see D. Blythe Doroshow, "Performing a Cure for Schizophrenia: Insulin Coma Therapy on the Wards," *Journal of the History of Medicine and Allied Sciences* 62, no. 2 (2007): 213–243.
48. AFI, *The American Film Institute Catalog of Motion Pictures Produced in the United States* (Berkeley and Los Angeles: University of California Press, 1971), 2169.
49. "Psychiatric Study by Movies Is Urged," *New York Times*, April 24, 1946, 8.
50. Franklin Fearing, "Psychology and the Films," *Hollywood Quarterly* 2, no. 2 (1947): 118–121.
51. "Radio 'Plugs' Held Harm to Medicine; Misinformation Spread Also by 'Sensation Seekers,' Mental Hygiene Group Is Told," *New York Times*, October 31, 1946, 36.
52. "The New Pictures," *Time*, February 4, 1946.
53. *The Dark Mirror* Call Sheets, Duncan Cramer Papers, box 1-f.5, Margret Herrick Library, Beverly Hills, California.
54. Universal-International, "Check Story's Scientific Data," *The Dark Mirror* pressbook, 1946, BFI Library, London.
55. TMP, "*Dark Mirror* New Mystery at Criterion," *New York Times*, October 19, 1946.

56. Universal-International, "Lew Ayres Returns to Films; Chooses Role of Scientist," *The Dark Mirror* pressbook.
57. Edwin Schallert, "Dark Mirror Sinister Sister Tale," *Los Angeles Times*, November 7, 1946.
58. "The New Pictures," *Time*, October 21, 1946.
59. George Spires, "*The Dark Mirror*," *Motion Picture Herald*, October 5, 1946, 3237.
60. Herm, "*The Dark Mirror*," *Variety*, October 12, 1946, 8.
61. Universal-International, "Men Prefer Smart Women as Home-Makers," *The Dark Mirror* pressbook.
62. Mary Ann Doane, *The Desire to Desire: The Woman's Film of the 1940s* (Bloomington: Indiana University Press, 1987), 43.
63. Polan, "Knowledge and Human Interests," 186–187.
64. Lucy Fischer, "Two-Faced Women: The 'Double' in Women's Melodrama of the 1940s," *Cinema Journal* 23, no. 1 (1983): 33.
65. Victor Dallaire, "The American Woman? Not for This GI," *New York Times*, March 10, 1946, SM8. However, Dallaire's *New York Times* article "precipitated an angry flood of responses from readers—85% attacking it," titled "The Women Hotly Reply to That GI." Lillian Stabano, for example, responded, "It seems only the inferior male—or the type that Mr. Dallaire represents—fears competition from Woman." "The Women Hotly Reply," *New York Times*, March 24, 1946, 13, 46, 47.
66. Anne Leighton, "The American Matron and the Lilies," *Harper's*, December 1946, quoted in Marjorie Rosen, *Popcorn Venus: Women, Movies, and the American Dream* (London: Peter Owen, 1975), 204.
67. Edith Efron, "A Woman Worker Defends Her Kind," *New York Times*, March 31, 1946, 22, 42, 43.
68. Ferdinand Lundberg and Marynia Farnham, *Modern Woman: The Lost Sex* (New York: Universal Library, 1947), 203.
69. Universal-International, "Psychoanalysts Label Plot Basis 'Ambivalence,'" *The Dark Mirror* pressbook.
70. Polan, "Knowledge and Human Interests," 163.
71. Lutz Koepnick, "Doubling the Double: Robert Siodmak in Hollywood," *New German Critique* 89 (Spring–Summer 2003): 94–95.
72. Leighton quoted in Rosen, *Popcorn Venus*, 204.
73. Chafe, "The Debate on Woman's Place," 201. The pervasive discourse of "momism," initially coined by Philip Wylie in his provocative text *A Generation of Vipers* (1942), became a catchall philosophy that attributed many of society's "problems" to the current generation's emotional instability caused by "domineering mothers." This was infamously given by a psychiatric consultant to the Secretary of War as the reason for the nervous disorders that excluded three million men from military service. Chafe, "The Debate on Woman's Place," 202.
74. Thomas Brady, "Assorted Hollywood Tidbits," *New York Times*, December 8, 1946.
75. "American Woman's Dilemma," *Life*, June 16, 1947.
76. Schallert, "*Dark Mirror* Sinister Sister Tale."
77. "Reviews of New Films: *The Dark Mirror*," *Film Daily*, October 7, 1946.

78. See Diane Waldman, "'At Last I Can Tell It to Someone!': Female Point of View and Subjectivity in the Gothic Romance Film of the 1940s," *Cinema Journal* 23, no. 2 (1984): 29–40; Doane, *The Desire to Desire*.
79. Stressing the film's intertextual links to Bram Stoker's *Dracula* (1897) and Murnau's *Nosferatu* (1922), Darragh O'Donoghue suggests that Terry "rises like Max Schreck in her bed to terrorise her sleeping sister." Darragh O'Donoghue, "*The Dark Mirror*," *Senses of Cinema*, April 2004, http://www.sensesofcinema.com/2004/cteq/dark_mirror (accessed January 21, 2014).
80. Universal-International, "Crime Movie as Psychic Escape," *The Dark Mirror* pressbook. Subsequent psychiatric pictures, including *Possessed* (1947) and *The Snake Pit* (1948), were praised by critics for their responsible and authentic depictions of psychiatric conditions and treatments and their ability to allow audiences to experience them. Bosley Crowther, "*Possessed*, Psychological Film with Joan Crawford as the Star," *New York Times*, May 30, 1947, 25; Bosley Crowther, "*Snake Pit*, Study of Mental Ills Based on Mary Jane Ward's Novel, Opens at Rivoli," *New York Times*, November 5, 1947, 29. They also raised new critical concerns about the suitability of these realist psychological horror films for general consumption, however. Ten days after Crowther championed *The Snake Pit*, he would begin to ask whether such a hard-hitting picture should in fact be shown at an "indiscriminate 'entertainment' house" like Times Square's Rivoli. Crowther instead proposed that it was more appropriate to screen *The Snake Pit* on a bill of "better class pictures to which more discriminating patrons would be drawn." Once more, a clear politics of taste was in operation, as Crowther sought not only to position himself as a protector of the vulnerable masses but also to insulate sophisticated consumers from implications that they, by virtue of their consumption of films like *The Snake Pit*, were imbricated within this most lowly of audiences. Bosley Crowther, "*The Snake Pit*: Question of Exhibition Raised by New Film," *New York Times*, November 14, 1947, X1.

CONCLUSION: ONLY FOR THE DURATION

1. Peter Stanfield, "'Pix Biz Spurts with War Fever': Film and the Public Sphere—Cycles and Topicality," *Film History: An International Journal* 25, nos. 1–2 (2013): 224.
2. In his introduction to *Explorations in New Cinema History*, Richard Maltby makes a distinction between film history (a dominant history of films and their production) and the new cinema history (an emergent interdisciplinary field of study focusing on the history of cinemagoing across a range of national, regional, and historical contexts). Focusing upon film cycles allows the media historian to analyze the complex relationship between these two processes while neither sidelining nor overstating the significance of film and other media texts. Richard Maltby, "New Cinema Histories," in *Explorations in New Cinema History: Approaches and Case Studies*, ed. Richard Maltby, Daniel Biltereyst, and Philippe Meers (Malden, MA: Wiley-Blackwell, 2011), 3–31.

3. John Berks, "What Alice Does: Looking Otherwise at *The Cat People*," *Cinema Journal* 32, no. 1 (1992): 26–42; Colonel Howard Clark quoted in Emily Yellin, *Our Mothers' War: American Women at Home and at the Front during World War II* (New York: Free Press, 2004), 305.
4. Manhola Dargis, "A College Where the Exams Are Terrifying," *New York Times*, June 20, 2013, http://movies.nytimes.com/2013/06/21/movies/monsters-university-unfolds-before-monsters-inc.html?_r=0. The *USA Today* review also complained that "she-monsters are relegated mostly to cheerleading roles or in the background as moms." Claudia Puig, "It Won't Make Honor Roll, But 'Monsters U' Easily Passes," *USA Today*, June 20, 2013, http://www.usatoday.com/story/life/movies/2013/06/20/monsters-university-review/2367049/. See also Joyce Stanton, "Where Are the Girls in Monsters University?" *Baby Center* blog, June 25, 2013, http://blogs.babycenter.com/mom_stories/06252013where-are-the-girls-in-monsters-university/; Margot MacGowan, "Monster University Sidelines Females in Plot about Rival Fraternities," *Reel Girl*, June 21, 2013, http://reelgirl.com/2013/06/monster-university-sidelines-females-in-plot-about-rival-fraternities/.
5. Various, "Why Are There Never Famous Female Monsters," *Experience Project*, http://www.experienceproject.com/question-answer/Why-Are-There-Never-Famous-Female-Horror-Monsters/1221388/(accessed August 26, 2013); Didion, "Female Monsters: My Mother Made Me This Way," *Feminéma: Feminism, Movies, Pop Culture*, May 19, 2012, http://feminema.wordpress.com/category/movie-genres/cult-horror-movies-about-female-monsters/ (accessed August 14, 2013); Sophia McDougall, "I Hate Strong Female Characters," *New Statesman*, August 15, 2013, http://www.newstatesman.com/culture/2013/08/why-i-hate-strong-female-characters/ (accessed August 26, 2013).
6. McDougall, "I Hate Strong Female Characters."
7. It is perhaps not surprising that—outside of East Asia, where there is a cultural tradition of female ghosts and shape-shifters—the only other period of sustained film production focusing on female monsters was the British Hammer Horror of the mid-1960s to early 1970s, a moment marked by a comparable wholesale renegotiation of the meanings of women's bodies instigated by sexual revolution and second-wave feminism.

INDEX

ABOUT THE AUTHOR

TIM SNELSON is a lecturer in media history at the University of East Anglia in Norwich, England. His research addresses the relationship among media, cultural, and social history, focusing particularly on popular film and television cycles, trends, and genres; cultural histories of cinema-going; gender and popular media; youth culture and subcultures; critical reception; and the politics of taste. He has published articles on media and cultural history in *Media History*, *Cultural Studies*, *New Review of Film and Television Studies*, and *Refractory* and has contributed to a number of edited collections including *Explorations in New Cinema History: Approaches and Case Studies* (2011) and *Gendering the Recession: Media Culture in an Age of Austerity* (2014). Snelson is a member of and regular contributor to the international research network of the History of Movie-going, Exhibition, and Reception (HoMER) and the Repetition/Repetition research group based at the Centre for the Interdisciplinary Study of Film and the Moving Image, University of Kent.